Towards a Methodology for the Investigation of Norms in Audiovisual Translation

APPROACHES TO TRANSLATION STUDIES
Founded by James S Holmes

Edited by Raymond van den Broek
Ton Naaijkens

Volume 15

Towards a Methodology for the Investigation of Norms in Audiovisual Translation

The Choice between Subtitling and Revoicing in Greece

Fotios Karamitroglou

Rodopi

Amsterdam - Atlanta, GA 2000

∞ The paper on which this book is printed meets the requirements of "ISO 9706:1994, Information and documentation - Paper for documents - Requirements for permanence".

ISBN: 90-420-0619-6

Printed in The Netherlands

CONTENTS

LIST OF TABLES

ABBREVIATIONS

AV = Audiovisual
M&E = Music and Effects
SC = Source Culture
SL = Source Language
TAP = Think-Aloud Protocol
TC = Target Culture
TL = Target Language
TV = Television

ACKNOWLEDGEMENTS

There is a great number of people I would like to thank for assisting in the completion of the present thesis.

- Mona Baker as the supervisor of the research.
- The Greek State Scholarships Foundation (IKY) for their sponsorship.
- The staff at the Greek Institute for Audiovisual Media (IOM) for their co-operation in the approval of the questionnaires: especially Eleni, Dominique, Stavroula and the Chairperson Mrs Kliamaki.
- The staff at the various TV stations: especially Patty (ANT1), Dionyssis (MEGA), Mrs Dalla (ET1), Alexandra (STAR), Giola (SKY) and Grigoris (FILMNET).
- The staff at the various Cinema Distribution Agencies: especially Efi (PROOPTIKI), Stamatis (Spentzos Cinema).
- The staff at the various Video Distribution Agencies: especially Mr Siganos and Ms Dimopoulou (AUDIOVISUAL), Mr Papagrigorakis (VIDEOSONIC), Mr Piperas (Spentzos Video) and Ms Patinioti (HVH).
- The staff at AGB Hellas and especially Elena Thodou.
- The staff at the Greek National Statistics Bureau.

INTRODUCTION

Definitions of terms and concepts

"Talking through a translator is like shooting at a target and having someone else tell you whether you hit it or not" *Charlie Chaplin* (In Marks, 1983:18)

What is audiovisual translation?

'Audiovisual translation' is the term I use to refer to what has been also called 'screen translation' or 'film translation'. The term 'screen translation' emphasises the locative of the medium/carrier where the translation product appears, namely the TV, cinema, or video screen. In the same sense, the translation of websites seen on computer monitors could also be considered 'screen translation'. Nevertheless, translation for computer monitors is not regarded as 'screen translation', unless the text - written or spoken - accompanies moving images with built-in sound, i.e. it is a small clip. Of the two terms, I prefer 'audiovisual translation' because it emphasises the audio-visual dimensions of the communicative mode. Unlike communication through books, radio, telephone, or sign language, audio-visual communication implies that both the acoustic channel through air vibrations and the visual channel through light waves are simultaneously utilised[i] (Delabastita, 1989:196). The term

---

[i] At a first glance, the translation of silent movies could be regarded as an exception to the category above since communication through silent movies fails to satisfy the (verbal) acoustic parameter. In addition, both the demands and the procedures followed in the translation of silent movies differ significantly from the demands and the procedures followed in the translation of conventional audio-visual products. As a result, the translation of silent movies could be placed outside the scope of 'audiovisual translation' theory and inside the frame of written, literary translation theory. On the other hand, however, it has been claimed that the accompanying music and the visible features of the face of the actors when - hypothetically - uttering the words of the accompanying intertitles create an imaginative (paralinguistic) acoustic dimension which, for some scholars, contains features strong enough to place silent movies back in the general category of audio-visual

'audiovisual translation' then stresses the need to accommodate in the process of translation the requirements of both these channels. Similarly, one could incorporate within 'audiovisual translation' the on-stage translation of theatre plays and operas - mainly performed with the use of surtitles or supertitles (Hay, 1998:131-134; cf. Whitman-Linsen, 1992:103). Indeed some scholars do subsume the above two modes under 'audiovisual translation' studies (cf. Ivarsson, 1992:backcover). My own definition of 'audiovisual translation', however, does not include theatre and opera and adheres to the three basic media of TV, cinema and video that 'screen translation' represents, unless otherwise stated.

I also prefer the term 'audiovisual translation' to 'film translation' because certain scholars restrict the notion of 'films' to full-length feature films, i.e. to movies only, or sometimes even to cinema-movies only, leaving out series, sports programmes and documentaries (Delabastita, 1990:105). I use the term 'film' to refer to all kinds of recorded audiovisual material; for the restricted concept of full-length feature films I use the term 'movies'. In this sense, the terms 'audiovisual translation' and 'film translation' are synonymous, meaning *the translation of recorded audiovisual material*, and could therefore be interchangeable. Nevertheless, to avoid any possible confusion I will consistently use the term 'audiovisual translation' throughout.

The notion of 'recordedness' for film material comes to play an important role when distinguishing between the fields of 'audiovisual translation' and 'interpreting'. Some scholars treat the translation of material of live broadcast as a type of audiovisual translation, distinguishing it from the translation of recorded film products by adding the modifier 'simultaneous'[i] (e.g. simultaneous

---

products. In any case, however, the fact that silent movies are – and have always been - seen as 'film products', as well as the fact that their translation is – and has always been - carried out by the same people who (used to) translate all the other conventional full-sound audio-visual products too, suggests that the study of the translation of silent films can still be considered part of audiovisual translation theory.

[i] The term/modifier 'simultaneous' refers to the initial production of translation, and not to the cueing of pre-prepared subtitles or voice-tapes. When we talk about the cueing of pre-prepared subtitles or voice-tapes, the terms/modifiers 'live' or 'real-

subtitling and simultaneous revoicing vs. subtitling and revoicing proper) (Luyken et al., 1991:63). Others do not maintain this distinction and regard as audiovisual translation only the translation of recorded audiovisual material (Aaltonen, 1995a:284; Minchinton, 1993:1.1). I would side with the latter view, since I cannot accommodate the concept of 'simultaneous' subtitling or revoicing under the mode of audiovisual translation. To me, simultaneous revoicing does not differ from the conventional concept of interpreting: the only difference is that the original source message as well as the translated oral message are broadcast on TV. The same applies to simultaneous subtitling, though this time the translated message is presented in a written instead of an oral mode (simultaneously typed by a stenographer). There are people who stress the difference between interpreting for the media - namely TV - and interpreting for other purposes (e.g. conferences, court rooms etc.), claiming that since they need to incorporate their TL message within the framework of various audio-visual parameters their work can also be treated as 'audiovisual translation' (cf. Russo, 1995:343; cf. Kurz & Pöchhacker, 1995:350; cf. Reynoso & Cárdenas, 1998:240). Nevertheless, even they call themselves 'interpreters' rather than 'audiovisual translators'. In any case, I do not believe that it is possible in practice for the people who translate/interpret for the media to account for the audio-visual parameters involved in their task and that the text they eventually produce does not differ (because of audio-visual reasons) from the text they would produce anyway if they were to work in a non-audiovisual, non-broadcast environment. In this respect, my definition of 'audiovisual translation' does not encompass 'simultaneous audiovisual translation', unless otherwise stated[i].

---

time' are preferred (Luyken et al., 1991:63), although confusion still exists (cf. Baker et al., 1984:51; ITC (eds.), 1997:21).

[i] I acknowledge that the concepts of 'recordedness' and simultaneity' are fuzzy – like most theoretical concepts - and need further elaboration. How do we classify, for example, the translation of tapes of current affairs that were recorded from a satellite transmission and presented to the audiovisual translator only a few minutes before their second - translated - broadcast? Although the material is taped, there is no time for the audiovisual translator to prepare his/her text and try to accommodate all the audio-visual parameters involved. For such problematic cases I have to resort to a

Audiovisual-translation scholars seem to disagree even upon the rudimentary typology of the language transfer methods that constitute 'audiovisual translation'. Luyken et al. distinguish between subtitling and revoicing (1991:40). The category of 'subtitling' contains the sub-categories of a) 'traditional' subtitling, and b) simultaneous subtitling (ibid). The category of revoicing contains the sub-categories of a) lip-sync dubbing, b) voice-over/narration, and c) free-commentary (ibid). Gambier lists the following audiovisual language transfer methods: a) subtitling, b) simultaneous subtitling, c) dubbing, d) interpreting (pre-recorded and consecutive), e) voice-over, f) narration, g) commentary, h) multilingual broadcast, i) surtitles and supratitles/supertitles, and j) simultaneous translation (1994:277). Since simultaneity does not feature in the concept of audiovisual translation adopted here, I would exclude from my list of audiovisual language transfer methods Luyken et al.'s category of simultaneous subtitling, as well as Gambier's categories of simultaneous subtitling, interpreting and simultaneous translation. Since I do not incorporate the modes of theatre or opera in my concept of audiovisual translation either, I would also exclude Gambier's category of surtitles and supratitles/supertitles. As far as Gambier's category of multilingual broadcast is concerned, I do not regard it as an individual category of audiovisual language transfer method but a technological facility for the reception of multiple revoicing methods. My typology of audiovisual language transfer methods consists of what we are left with after all this editing. The remaining categories are: a) subtitling, b) (lip-sync) dubbing, c) narration (including voice-over) and d) free-commentary, with the last three categories constituting a broader category of revoicing. In the sections to follow the categories of subtitling and revoicing are discussed in more detail. 'Audiovisual translation', as defined here, *is* subtitling and revoicing.

---

definition of 'audiovisual translation' as everything which is presented or regarded as such within the target culture, on whatever grounds.

What is subtitling?

Subtitling can be defined as the translation of the spoken (or written) source text of an audiovisual product into a written target text which is added onto the images of the original product, usually at the bottom of the screen (Gottlieb, 1994a:104; Gottlieb, 1998:247; Luyken et al., 1991:31; Delabastita, 1989:200). Subtitling can be both 'intralingual' (or 'vertical'), when the target language is the same as the source language, and 'interlingual' (or 'diagonal'), when the target language is different form the source language (Gottlieb, 1994a:104; Gottlieb, 1998:247). 'Subtitling' in this thesis is used to refer to interlingual subtitling, unless otherwise stated.

Subtitling can be 'open', when the target text constitutes a physical part of the translated film and is transmitted together with the film sound and image, or 'closed', when the target text is stored in a digital/teletext format which is transmitted in - as well as accessed via - a separately coded channel at the discretion of the viewers (Luyken at al., 1991:63; Gottlieb, 1998:247). In this thesis, 'subtitling' refers to open subtitling, unless otherwise stated.

Subtitles are different from 'displays' or 'captions'. 'Displays' are "fragments of text recorded by the camera - letters, newspapers, headlines, banners etc." (Gottlieb, 1994a:107). 'Captions' (or 'toptitles') are pieces of "textual information usually inserted by the programme maker to identify names, places or dates relevant to the story line" (Luyken et al., 1991:31; cf. Gottlieb, 1994a:107). This distinction is maintained here and 'subtitles' do not include displays or captions, unless otherwise stated.

What is revoicing?

'Revoicing' is the term used to refer to the audiovisual language transfer methods of 'dubbing', 'narration' and 'free-commentary' collectively, and describes the attempt to cover (partly or entirely) the spoken source text of an original audiovisual production by a new spoken target text (Dries, 1995a:9).

'Dubbing' (or 'lip-sync dubbing') as a specific revoicing technique attempts to cover entirely the spoken source text with a target text adjusted to fit the - visible - lip movements of the original utterances (Fodor, 1976:9; Luyken et al., 1991:31; Dries, 1995a:9).

'Narration' as a specific revoicing technique does not emphasise the lip movements of the original utterances at all, nor does it attempt to cover the original spoken text entirely, but aspires at a more "faithful translation of the original text [in an] approximately synchronous delivery" (Luyken et al., 1991:80). Luyken et al., like other scholars, differentiate between 'narration' and 'voice-over' on the basis that a "narration is an extended voice-over", in a "more formal grammatical structure" which could also be carried out by more than one voice/speaker (ibid). I do not find the above argument sufficiently convincing to justify 'voice-over' constituting an independent category from 'narration' since a distinction based on the "extendedness" of the target text or the "formality" of its grammatical structures would be completely arbitrary, not to mention the fact that the number of voices involved do not interfere at all with the translation strategies to be followed in either method (cf. Mailhac, 1998:209). In this respect, I will subsume 'voice-over' under 'narration' here.

'Free-commentary' as a specific revoicing technique does not emphasise the lip movements of the original utterances, nor does it emphasise the faithfulness of the translated text or its synchronous delivery but, as the word itself indicates, it is a free and often scrambled delivery of the source message into the target language, quite frequently enriched with new journalistic elements and with the original spoken text entirely or partially covered (cf. Luyken et al., 1991:139-140).

The history of subtitling

Almost since the invention of films in the 'silent' era, efforts had been made to convey the actors' dialogue to the audience. The first attempt was in 1903 with what is nowadays conventionally called 'intertitles' or 'insert titles' (Ivarsson, 1995:294). At the time, these terms meant something totally different from what they mean today: an 'intertitle' or 'insert title' was a replacement shot for a part of a film that contained verbal information in the original language.

For example, if an American silent movie was shown in France and contained a scene where the contents of a handwritten letter were visible on the screen, this scene would be reshot in France with the equivalent handwritten letter in French (Minchinton, 1993, 1.1). This was an 'insert title' or an 'intertitle'. What we nowadays call 'intertitles' as parts of text, drawn or printed on paper and filmed and placed between parts of the film-action, were at the time called 'subtitles' (ibid). This is where the term 'subtitles' originates. At the beginning, 'intertitles' (in the current sense of the word) were independently projected through a magic lantern between the parts of the film, when the film was actually paused (cf. *The Picturegoer*, May 1921:21). It was only in 1909 that 'intertitles' became an indispensible part of the film, photographed and printed on the film-strip (Ivarsson, 1995:294).

In the same year, the first attempts were made in the US to produce 'subtitles' (in the current sense of the word), as optically inserted negative frames of text printed on blank frames (as black letters) and projected on the film negative; a positive print of the whole film containing the inserted subtitles would transform the colour of the letters from black to white (ibid:295). A similar attempt was made in Norway in 1930 by thermally pressing on the negative film-frames minute strips of typeset text (ibid:296). The chemical method of inserting subtitles by bleaching the emulsion of the film strips in the shape of the desired letter-sequence/text, frame by frame - invented in Hungary a couple of years later and immediately taken over by the French and the Swedes - was what boosted the implementation of subtitles since it was cheaper and quicker if multiple copies of subtitled films were to be made. All these methods (still applicable today) are used for the production of subtitles on cinema-films. The latest technology - since 1988 - for cinema subtitling involves the use of laser to bleach the emulsion of the film in the desired letter-sequence/text (ibid:297).

Things took a different course for TV subtitling[i]. At the beginning, the optical method for the insertion of subtitles was implemented as well, with the negative frames of black-text subtitles projected on the negative of the TV-film just as they were projected

[i] Video subtitling follows the same techniques used in TV subtitling.

on cinema-film (ibid:298-299). Soon, however, new technological developments changed the setting of TV subtitling dramatically. The invention of 'caption generators' for the electronic insertion of text as subtitles (ibid:299) was quickly followed by the advent of computers and the manufacturing of specific software which could process text and insert it on the television image/screen at automatically synchronised time-points (ibid:300). The first subtitled TV-film which was broadcast in Britain - and probably in the whole world - was the German full-feature film *Der Student von Prague* [The Student from Prague] broadcast by the BBC in 1938 (Minchinton, 1993:1.4; Giles, 1997:47).

The history of revoicing

The question of the choice between subtitling and revoicing emerged with the advent of sound-films, the 'talkies'. In 1927, the first sound-film *The Jazz Singer* (made in the US) signalled the death of intertitles (Barbe, 1996:256; Siefert, 1995:44); what it also brought along, however, was a set of linguistic barriers between the new film-products and the foreign audiences, which from that moment on would become obstacles to the sale of American films abroad. Nevertheless, this same opportunity to incorporate sound with image, which created the problem of linguistic barriers in the first place, seemed also to offer a solution to the problem. Between 1929 and 1933 the solution was found in the re-production of the same movie in multiple language versions by actors fluent in the desired languages. This alternative, however, had two major drawbacks: a) re-shooting the entire film proved too costly (Ascheid, 1997:32; Ballester, 1995:161), and b) the new actors did not have the impact of the already famous Hollywood stars (*FilmWeekly*, September 1938:14; Ballester, 1995:161).

'Revoicing' as an alternative solution to overcome the linguistic barriers raised by the imposition of sound on image was conceived alongside the imposition of sound itself, a process which was called 'dubbing' at the time. The presence of a number of unwanted sound-disturbances when actually shooting the original production led the film-directors to the decision to impose the sound at a post-shooting stage, with the actors in a studio re-rehearsing the same words they had uttered when the film was initially shot and trying to synchronise them with their own initial lip movements (Zucker, 1966:5; Whitman-Linsen, 1992:57). Thus, the term 'dubbing' was initially coined to refer to what we nowadays call 'intralingual dubbing'. Gradually, however, film-producers started thinking that in the same way they were applying the original-language spoken text to the already shot images, they could apply another, foreign-language spoken text to it as well. This is how 'revoicing' was born. Not surprisingly, then, the first revoicing method to be used was dubbing (in the interlingual sense of the word from now on), i.e. the method that aimed at lip synchronisation, since the existing technique of 'intralingual dubbing' emphasised lip-sync by definition. Narration and free-commentary which are not based on the lip-sync imperative were born later, almost at the same time as the appearance of TV.

Since 1931, film producers in Hollywood have been shooting films with future interlingual dubbing in mind, aiming at fewer close-ups and less culture-bound elements (Ballester, 1995:162). The first period was transitional and sometimes both the 'dubbing' and the 'multilingual shooting' alternatives were combined – shooting close-ups in multiple language versions and dubbing the rest of the film (ibid). The first fully dubbed movie was the US production *All Quiet on the Western Front*, dubbed into German in 1930.

The invention of magnetic recording tapes in the 1940's enhanced the quality of the sound films by allowing the separate recording of multiple sound tracks, e.g. one for the actors' voices, one for the noise and sound-effects, one for the accompanying music etc. (Siefert, 1995:53). Revoicing profited from this breakthrough by enhancing its own quality as well, since the new revoiced tracks could allow the replacement/transfer of voice only, with no need to erase or re-produce the rest of the sound-tracks.

General theoretical issues

Translation theory and audiovisual translation

A number of problematic issues in the field of audiovisual translation have quite frequently raised the question whether translation theory can actually incorporate audiovisual translation within its general scope. Research difficulties such as the atheoretical nature of most existing audiovisual translation studies and the lack of a consistent corpus of translated audiovisual material aggravate the problem (Fawcett, 1996:66). But it is a well-known fact that audiovisual translation has always been considered inferior to (written) literary translation, most probably because of the lack of cultural prestige in audiovisual mass-media, compared to canonised literature (Ballester, 1995:178). As Minchinton says about subtitling for example, even the term itself "sub-title is an old literary term for a subordinate or additional title of a literary work" (1993:1.1). Or as Ivarsson indicates, only a few years ago audiovisual translators "were not admitted to the translators' section of the Swedish Writers' Union on the ground that they had not published the two book translations that were a requirement for membership" (1992:9).

It is true that there are a number of constraints that derive mainly from the audio-visual nature of the original and target products and which distinguish audiovisual translation from (written) literary translation, the latter being the main inspiration for general translation theory: a) temporal constraints in revoicing, b) spatiotemporal constraints in subtitling, c) the accompanying visual source-culture elements in both revoicing and subtitling, d) the accompanying aural source-language elements in subtitling, e) the lip-sync imperative in dubbing, f) the cross-semiotic nature of subtitling, and g) the inability of backtracking (with the exception of video) in both subtitling and revoicing (O'Shea, 1996:240). All these parameters have made certain people even within the field of audiovisual translation regard their job as 'adaptation' rather than translation (Papadakis, 1997; Delabastita, 1989:213-214). But how can one define where translation stops and where adaptation begins? Is it the degree of alteration of the original piece of information (of the film as a whole or simply of the verbal message/text?) that will determine the transition from translation to adaptation? But "all types of translation involve loss of information, addition of information or skewing of information" (Nida, in O'Shea, 1996:241). And in any case, the problematic issue of translation vs. adaptation is not a property of audiovisual translation alone; a great number of – translated or adapted? – texts have raised the same issue within the field of literary translation (Delabastita, 1989:214). The heart of the matter lies in our conceptualisation and definition of translation. If we accept Toury's definition of translation as "any target-language utterance which is presented or regarded as such within the target culture, on whatever grounds" (1985:20) and we extend it to cover audiovisual translation as well, we can easily accommodate audiovisual translation within the broader realm of translation studies.

There are, however, a number of additional reasons that allow us to accept audiovisual translation as a sub-field of translation studies:

- First of all, audiovisual translation has more in common with written translation than one might initially assume (Whitman-Linsen, 1992:103). Most audiovisual translations nowadays are performed with a written form of the original source text in hand (cf. Remael, 1995:128), sometimes even without any further access to the film-product itself.
- Typological studies in audiovisual translation have already managed to present the various audiovisual language transfer methods within the general framework of translation studies and alongside the other 'traditional' language transfer methods, in a coherent and scientific way, on the basis of the multiplicity of the semiotic channels involved and the relative time of presentation of the source and target products (Gottlieb, 1994b:271; Gottlieb, 1998:246; cf. Delabastita, 1989:199). Other studies in audiovisual translation have identified links between certain audiovisual language transfer methods and established concepts from general translation theory, as for example with subtitling and 'overt translation', and dubbing and 'covert translation' (Ascheid, 1997:35).
- Audiovisual translation was born out of the same drive that guided literary translation: the need to overcome the

communication barriers imposed by linguistic fragmentation (Luyken et al., 1991:3).

- Just as "it is the discovery of the hierarchy of factors (constraints, parameters) which operate in translation processes, procedures and products which constitutes a major task for translation theory" (Even-Zohar & Toury, 1981:ix), the discovery of a similar hierarchy of the factors that operate within audiovisual translation is also the task of audiovisual translation theory.

The Polysystem approach to translation in the study of audiovisual norms

All the above indicate that audiovisual translation does not require a new theory of translation but can be based on findings which can be drawn from the field of general translation theory (Varela, 1997:316). We can see translation theory as providing a theoretical framework for the study of audiovisual translation.

Until some decades ago, translation studies tended to view translation through one-to-one verbal relationships or notions of textual equivalence (Gentzler, 1993:107). More recent approaches to translation, however, started to be increasingly concerned with issues related not only to verbal/linguistic or textual features but to issues of code-switching and systematic organisation, viewed from a descriptive rather than a prescriptive perspective (Even-Zohar & Toury, 1981:v). What was basically advocated was that

> "the idea that semiotic phenomena, i.e. sign-governed human patterns of communication (such as culture, language, literature, society), could more adequately be understood and studied if regarded as systems rather than conglomerates of disparate elements has become one of the leading ideas of our time in most sciences of man. Thus the positivistic collection of data, taken bona fide on empirical grounds and analysed on the basis of their material *substance*, has been replaced by a functional approach based on the analysis of *relations*" (Even-Zohar, 1990:9).

And moreover:

> "since the object-level of translation studies consists of actual facts of 'real life' – whether they be actual texts, intertextual relationships or models and norms of behaviour – rather than the merely speculative outcome of preconceived theoretical hypotheses and models, it is undoubtedly in

> essence an empirical science. [...But] no empirical science can make a claim for completeness and relative autonomy unless it has developed a descriptive branch" (Toury, 1985:16).

What emerged as a result of the above positions was an approach to translation which was both a) descriptive and b) able to cover translations as 'literary facts' in a systemic constellation of relations (Toury, 1995:170). Thus, the polysystem approach to translation was born. If we accept, however, that the polysystem approach to translation is capable of accounting for audiovisual translation, we have to accept that translations of audiovisual material are 'literary facts' in a systemic constellation of relations too. In this sense, the notion of 'literary facts' is considerably broadened. Nevertheless, the polysystem approach itself allows us to broaden the concept since, in contradistinction to traditional views, it regards 'literature' as "the totality of the activities involved with the literary system" (Even-Zohar, 1990:54) and defines 'literary system' as "the network of relations that is hypothesised to obtain between a number of activities called 'literary', and consequently these activities themselves observed via the network" (ibid:28). These notions of 'literature' and 'literary system' seem closer to the traditional notions of 'art' and 'art system'. From a polysystem point of view, therefore, the attempt to incorporate 'audiovisual facts' - as pieces of audiovisual material - within the scope of 'literary facts', as well as the attempt to consider audiovisual translation as an aspect of the broader 'literary system', are perfectly legitimate.

As polysystem theorists claim, "even when it is *texts* which are taken up and analysed, the focus of the study is not the texts as entities in themselves but rather what they can reveal with respect to the process which gave rise to them, i.e. the *choices* made by the translators and the *constraints* under which these choices were made" (Toury, 1993a:17). As a result, the attempt to investigate the choice between subtitling and revoicing could be legitimately undertaken within the scope of polysystem studies, since it focuses on a series of other choices and constraints that eventually gave rise to the production of a translated text, whatever the method of translation. Furthermore, what polysystem theorists also presume is that "social norms and literary conventions in the receiving culture ('target' system) govern the aesthetic presuppositions of the translator and thus influence ensuing translation decisions" (Gentzler, 1993:107). As a result again, the attempt to investigate the norms that govern (the choices and constraints within) audiovisual translation can be legitimately undertaken within the scope of the polysystem approach. Polysystem theorists consider translation studies as a 'normative science' per se. By the term normative, however, they do not imply 'prescriptive', as in 'normative guidelines for the purpose of teaching translation' (cf. Harris, 1990), but 'descriptive', as in 'a science that deals with the study of norms' (cf. Chesterman, 1993:11). I use the term 'normative' in this descriptive sense throughout, unless otherwise stated.

The term 'norms' was coined to describe not just linguistic or translational phenomena but a broader range of patterned social phenomena (Ross, 1968:78). Audiovisual translation, however, seems to be particularly dominated by a strong presence of norms, as a result of the impact of mass-media on the broader public and the fact that "viewers are creatures of habit" (Ivarsson, 1992:66). In audiovisual translation, choices at the lower text-level have already been seen to be based on existing norms in the target culture/system (Gottlieb, 1997:216). But even choices beyond the text-level appear to be conditioned by similar existing norms: the choice to subtitle or to revoice, which forms the topic/case-study of the present thesis, is thought to be related more to "what the audience is used to than rational arguments" (Ivarsson, 1992:20). In any case, it appears that audiovisual translation "constitutes a typical situation where one can expect norms to guide the selection of actual behaviour in each specific historical set of circumstances" (Delabastita, 1989:205). As a result, I believe that audiovisual translation both demands and deserves to be treated within the framework of the polysystem approach.

1. A THEORETICAL APPROACH TO NORMS

1.1 The notion of norms

1.1.1 The definition of norms

The concept of a 'norm' was not formulated to be initially and primarily associated with the field of translation studies. It was conceived within the social sciences and applied to a wide range of human behaviour of any kind. However, since translation is also a form of human behaviour, the term 'norm' was borrowed and refined to account for certain aspects of this particular type of human behaviour with all its peculiarities and constraints.

In its broader socio-cultural dimension, translation is inevitably and constantly subjected to various constraints of several types and degrees of intensity. These constraints often extend beyond the texts and the languages involved in the act of translation, and even beyond the possibilities and limitations of the cognitive apparatus of the translator as a mediator; cognition itself is modified by sociocultural factors (Toury, 1995:54). This means that conducting research into this area of translational constraints should be accompanied by a thorough investigation and analysis of socio-cultural factors. This is not an easy, perhaps not even a feasible task; such a study would be too broad, vague and unfocused and should be directed by someone who possesses specialised knowledge of both translation and sociology. What might seem more effective and appropriate, then, is to restrict such a study of socio-cultural factors to an investigation of the way they are reflected in translational constraints, i.e. their impact on translational behaviour. This, however, should not divorce the notion of 'translational constraints' from its wider sociological context.

In terms of their binding force, socio-cultural constraints have generally been described along a scale that fluctuates between two extremes: objective, stable, absolute *rules* or *laws* on the one hand,

and mere subjective *idiosyncrasies* on the other (Toury, 1978:83; 1995:54). The vast middle ground that lies between these two extremes is occupied by intersubjective factors that are commonly designated as **norms** (ibid). The sociologist Alf Ross describes norms as "social *state of affairs* - i.e. conditions which although changing, are of relative permanence and not merely a passing event" (1968:80). Toury describes norms as "the translation of general values or ideas shared by a certain community - as to what is right and wrong, adequate and inadequate - into specific performance instructions appropriate for and applicable to specific situations, providing they are not (yet) formulated as laws" (1978:83-84). From the point of view of norms, rules/laws are more objective and idiosyncrasies more subjective (or less intersubjective) normative formulations (ibid:85). Norms are acquired by individual members of the community during their interaction with society and can be perceived as tokens of "regularity of behaviour in recurrent situations of the same type" (ibid:84) and can serve as evaluative criteria against which actual instances of behaviour can be measured by a community as a whole or by any of its members. As psychological and social entities that regulate social function then, norms inevitably play a very important role in the interaction between (groups of) people: enabling people to generalise from past experience, they reduce contingency and unpredictability and allow for similar predictive speculations in the future (Hermans, 1996: 26).

Some sociologists believe that a norm is actually the meaning expressed by the linguistic formulation of the norm as it appears through the very use of this particular linguistic formulation (Ross, 1968:101). Others believe that it is the actual utterance of a command or prescription which brings a norm into existence by creating a certain relationship between the giver and the receiver of the command (ibid). However, discovering a norm and verbalising it would not have anything to offer as an end in itself. What emerges as an essential concern is the contextualisation of the verbalised norm. Even enumerating all the potential translational norms, assuming this were possible, would not be particularly productive; only a focused study of specific norms can shed some light on some unidentified aspects of their context of existence.

Ross claims that "norms must be intrinsically connected with *directives*" (1968:78), i.e. "the meaning content of a norm" (ibid), "or to be precise [with] impersonal directives, which alone can be norms (...) [since] impersonal directives have no author and no recipient as such" (ibid:106). Toury's views do not seem compatible with this idea. He discards the possibility of directives serving as laws or norms, even when they are distinguished as principles with general validity, because they are merely speculative, bearing no theoretical or empirical status. If a directive does not reflect any regularity of real-world behaviour and therefore does not reflect existing types of behaviour, its neglect would neither necessarily result in societal sanctions nor in new and innovative patterns of behaviour. Toury suggests that directives "represent little more than *recommendations*: while entailing a clear wish to promote certain modes of behaviour, the kind of behaviour they recommend can always be either accepted or rejected in actual practice; either followed or ignored" (1993b:22; 1995:261).

The definition which is usually given to the concept of 'norms' relates their existence to the existence of certain social facts. Ross, for example, believes that "a norm is a directive which stands in a relation of correspondence to social facts" (1968:82). Leaving aside the disputable attempt to associate norms with directives, we notice that the assumption that norms exist necessarily entails that certain social facts also exist. The formulisation of a descriptive comment on a norm would therefore directly count as a descriptive comment on society. The distinctive feature of this approach to norms is that it adopts an a priori descriptive rather than prescriptive viewpoint towards the whole spectrum of norms as aspects of behaviour.

To say that a pattern of behaviour is on the whole followed does not mean that every member of society would act in the same way in a given circumstance. As a matter of fact, there is a point in realising the existence of norms only in situations which in principle allow for variation in behaviour, eventually perceived as deviation from the norm either at random or in a systematic fashion. Hermans suggests that "in any case, non-compliance with a norm does not usually result in drastic sanctions for the individual concerned, just as non-compliance with a norm in particular instances does not invalidate the norm" (1996:31). The individual who breaks a norm and the norm to be broken depend on the nature, the strength and the particular situation in which both sides are seen to operate. As long as a norm is active and effective, however, one would be clearly able to pinpoint regularities of behaviour in recurrent situations of the same type, which would render these particular regularities the main source for any study of norms, always accompanied with a thorough analysis of the specific conditions that characterise the type of situation in which the norm in question is observed to operate.

1.1.2 Norms and conventions

The notion of 'conventions' was developed alongside the notion of 'norms'. Like norms, conventions denote generally accepted patterns of behaviour. Although explicit agreement among individuals this time is not a necessary condition for the appearance of conventions, they emerge once more as "arbitrary but effective solutions to recurrent problems of interpersonal coordination" (Hermans, 1996:29).

There seems to be some confusion as to whether conventions and norms are two terms that cover the same concept. Hermans prefers to differentiate between the two. On a scale similar to Toury's, he places conventions at the one end and decrees at the other, putting in the middle-space norms (closer to conventions) and rules (closer to decrees). 'Decrees' are "specific directives issued as commands by a particular authority and backed up by drastic sanctions" (Hermans, 1996:32). 'Rules' are "strong norms, usually institutionalised and posited by an identifiable authority, with or without the full assent of the individual subjected to them" (ibid). We already notice a fusion of the borders which were drawn to separate Toury's 'rules' and 'norms'. Conventions, however, cannot be taken to resemble Toury's 'idiosyncrasies' since they "arise out of precedent and rely on *shared habits and mutual expectations* which are common knowledge" (ibid) [my italics]. In this respect, conventions seem to be closer to Toury's view of 'norms' than to his view of 'idiosyncrasies'. Hermans however insists on a clear-cut separation between norms and conventions, claiming that norms differ from conventions in that the former "have a binding character, carry some form of sanction, and may either grow out of customs or be issued by an authorising instance" (ibid). From all this confusion with interrelated terms and notions it becomes apparent that what is needed is a simplified structure of terms and definitions that will not be based on minute details and nuances of meaning.

Hermans goes on to claim that conventions may become victims of their own success and grow beyond a mere preference, simultaneously acquiring the binding character of norms, if they have sufficiently contributed to the solution of a recurrent problem for a long time (ibid:30). Norms then can be conceived of as "prescriptive rules [since] they have a normative semantic load and are used to guide, control, or change the behaviour of agents with decision-making capacities" (ibid). We notice once more how relative all these notions become according to Hermans' terminological structure: idiosyncrasies intersect with conventions, conventions overlap with norms and norms resolve into rules.

Nord similarly suggests a separation between conventions and norms. She claims that conventions are neither explicit nor binding formulations but are simply based "on common knowledge and on the expectation of what others expect you to expect them (etc.) to do in a certain situation" (Nord, 1991a:96). Shifting Hermans' scale from horizontal to vertical, she establishes regulating principles between rules, norms and conventions, placing the former two on a higher rank than conventions (ibid:97). Even she, however, accepts that "conventions may be raised to the rank of (tacit or explicit) norms or even rules" (ibid:96).

Chesterman traces the difference between norms and customs or conventions (as he calls them) to the fact that "breaching a convention gives no cause for sanction if no norm is involved" (1993:6), and he criticises Nord's perception of conventions as opposed to norms saying that Nord's conventions are actually "norms precisely because their violation gives rise to some critical comment - her own" (ibid). Although he is a bit harsh in his criticism of Nord's views and ideas, since she has never claimed a clear-cut distinction between all these interrelated notions, he brings in some very interesting and productive dimensions concerning the functionality of norms and conventions, initially attributed to Renate Bartsch: "norms of language may be conventions from a phylogenetic point of view, with respect to their origins, but from the ontogenetic point of view, i.e. relative to the individual who has been born into a speech community, they are norms - that is they are experienced as binding by every new generation and every newcomer" (ibid:7).

I believe that the above perspective provides a balanced solution to the conflict between conventions and norms. It proves that both these terms/notions are actually two sides of the same coin. To avoid the confusion, however, I propose to follow the initial stratification of Toury (discussed in the previous section); after all, the new concepts proposed by various scholars were formulated in response to Toury's ideas. Since all these interrelated notions have become confusing enough after the introduction of the concept of 'conventions', I will take 'norms' and 'conventions' to be synonymous and treat them as such from now on. If we also accept that the difference between norms and conventions is a matter of chronological perspective and depends on a diachronic (phylogenetic) or synchronic (ontogenetic) approach to the subject, we can have an additional reason for taking 'norms' and 'conventions' as synonymous, since a study of norms/conventions is by definition synchronic (see also chapter 2).

1.1.3 The classification of translational norms

Translational norms can be classified under various categories according to the perspective we adopt towards them. Toury distinguishes primarily between two types of translational norms: preliminary and operational. *Preliminary* norms have to do with two main sets of considerations, "those regarding the existence and actual nature of a definitive translation policy, and those related to the directness of translation" (Toury, 1978:86; 1995:58). Considerations regarding 'translation policy' involve those factors which affect and determine the choice of the works to be translated, in terms of authors, schools, source literatures, etc. Considerations concerning 'directness of translation' involve the degree of tolerance for translating from intermediate languages, i.e. languages other than the initial SL (ibid).

Operational norms can be perceived as "directing the decisions made during the act of translation itself. They affect the matrix of the text - i.e. the modes of distributing linguistic material in it - as well as the textual make up and verbal formulation as such" (Toury, 1978:87; 1995:58-59). On a micro-structural level, 'matricial norms' govern the segmentation and distribution of the specific target linguistic items as well as the fullness of translation. On a macro-structural level, 'textual norms' govern the selection of the text-type and the mode of translation in which the TT as a whole is formulated (ibid).

From the above classification it becomes clear that preliminary norms have both a logical and a chronological precedence over operational norms (ibid, 90; 59). A methodology for the study of norms, however, should account for both categories. Although it might appear that the above broad distinction of norms suggests a direct relation to - and therefore essential analysis of - the source culture, text and language with their specific traits, preliminary and operational norms could actually be seen from a straightforward target perspective and examined simply as facts of the target culture. 'Translation policy' can be seen from a target culture point of view as the aggregate of target culture factors and conventions that will guide the final choice of the foreign literary material to be imported into the target system; 'directness of translation' can be regarded as the aggregate of target culture factors and conventions that will permit or dictate the use of pivot translations as an intermediate source for the translation of foreign material. On a lower level, finally, 'operational norms' can be viewed as the aggregate of target culture factors and conventions that will guide the final selection and realisation of the target language material, as a result of the functional equivalence which is established with the source material.

Nord expands Searle's sociological analysis of normative behaviour and distinguishes between 'regulative' and 'constitutive' translational conventions. *Regulative* translational norms (or conventions) refer to translational aspects and behaviour at the text level, whereas *constitutive* conventions refer to what can be regarded by a particular community as constituting 'translation' - as opposed to 'version' or 'adaptation' (Nord, 1991a:100).

Based on sociological research conducted by Jay Jackson in 1960, Toury classified norms along 'a return potential curve' describing the intensity of tolerated behaviour in a social group. At first, Toury's categorisation was tripartite (1978:95). *Basic (primary)* norms are more or less mandatory for all instances of a certain behaviour, indicating maximum intensity. *Secondary* norms or *tendencies* determine favourable behaviour, predominantly observable in special parts of the larger social group in question, indicating therefore a common but less intense and by no means mandatory kind of behaviour. *Other tolerated (permitted) behaviour* indicates minimal intensity of a behavioural pattern. Later on (1995:68), Toury attached another subcategory to the last one of permitted behaviour, which he called *symptomatic devices*, in order to account for behavioural occurrences that can be typically observed in smaller segments of the social groups under study. The more frequent a target text-phenomenon, the more it is likely to reflect a more permitted (tolerated) kind of translational activity, a stronger tendency, a more basic (obligatory) translational norm. The less frequent a behaviour, the smaller and the more specific the group it defines (Toury, 1995:68-69).

Chesterman distinguishes between 'professional' and 'expectancy' translational norms. *Expectancy* norms, which again govern professional norms, constitute the expectations of a certain target audience about what a translation (or a 'native' text) should be like in their target system (Chesterman, 1993:9). This type of norm appears to be of a particular interest since it clearly reflects the target system norms one might wish to study. As subclasses, we can talk of syntactic, semantic and pragmatic expectancy norms (ibid:10). In order to meet the expectancy norms as adequately as possible, a translator has to conform to the *professional* norms, which comprise the production norms that govern the accepted methods and strategies of the translation process (ibid:8). Taking a functional perspective on norms, Chesterman goes on to distinguish between three further types of professional norms, all of which emphasise the translator and another three key elements: the writer of the source text, the commissioner and the readership. The 'accountability' norms refer to the loyalty between the translator and the other three key elements mentioned above. The 'communication' norms deal with the communication that is established between the translator and the other three key elements above. The 'relation' norm focuses on the relation maintained between ST and TT on the basis of the translator's understanding of the intentions and expectations of the three key elements. Unfortunately, all three subcategories of professional norms can be regarded as given, i.e. as presupposed data for the study of target norms, since both loyalty and effective communication, as well as the translator's thorough understanding of the writer's, the readers' and the commissioner's intentions and expectations, are a prerequisite for any methodological study of target norms.

1.1.4 The function of norms

A norm is followed by a group of people in certain situations and has some binding force within a particular community. It is also logically connected with other norms, which ultimately constitute a coherent system. In an attempt to formulate laws, which he sees as the objective and absolute manifestation of norms, Toury (1993b:25, 1995:265) begins with a conditional form of the basic type:

if X, then the greater/the lesser the likelihood that Y

where Y is an observed behaviour and X is its conditioning factor. Laws of this type are meant to enhance the theory by building in a probabilistic element, thus making the theory more flexible and versatile and enabling it to elaborate eventually constructions of the multi-variable type:

> *if X1 and Z1, then the likelihood that Y is greater than if X1 and Z2, and even greater than if X1 and Z3.*

The idea is that interconnections can be established between conditioning factors that are observed to intervene in the realisation of a certain type of behaviour (Toury, 1993b:27; 1995:266).

What becomes apparent from the above conditional formulations is that "the process of scanning the list and selecting from among the options which comprise it can easily be given a *logical structure*" (Toury, 1995:260) as in a game where every move is influenced by the knowledge of and successively follows decisions which have already been made. Although such constructions are essentially theoretical, representing both the options and the logic of selection in a highly systematised form, they cannot yet constitute proper laws of behaviour, because the way they are formulated suggests that there is free variation in terms of either-or choices (ibid). And if we accept that it is difficult to pin down such free variations and describe them in terms of 'objective' and 'absolute' formulations or laws, then we should have to admit that in more complex situations where subjectivity plays an important role - as in the case of norms - it is even more difficult, if not impossible, to come up with a probabilistic approach which can account for every possible aspect of potential behaviour in a given situation.

An attempt to trace the individual parameters of a consistent pattern of behaviour in a systematic fashion which will be based on consistent similarities is still essential, because without a concept of sameness, we would not be able to determine whatever is new, different or mutant. This is the main contribution that can be derived from the conception of a systematised framework in the function of norms. A systematic approach to norms would enable us to distinguish between individual and collective norms and deal with a behavioural phenomenon accordingly (Lambert & van Gorp, 1985:51).

Toury believes that one should commence a piece of research by focusing on isolated individual norms or norm-units, which he calls 'normemes' (1978:94). Given that translation is a complicated and multi-dimensional phenomenon, however, "its manifold dimensions and levels are interwoven and reinforce each other, and therefore its full description can only be achieved by weighing the findings concerning its various levels" (ibid). The initiation of the notion of 'levels' in translation, therefore, appears to play an important role in the study of normative behaviour in this particular field. At this point, I would fully agree with Toury's position that:

> "coherence or integration of normemes active in different situations (dimensions, levels) is by no means self-evident or indispensable, and thus cannot serve as an assumption underlying research (...). In any event, an important task facing the student is to establish the relations obtaining between the normemes, and the thicker the network of relations he finds and describes, the more justified one is in speaking in terms of a normative *structure* or *system*" (ibid).

What becomes clear is that the integration of the notion of 'levels' as hierarchically organised strata on which translational activity is seen to operate might help to clarify any fuzziness of intersecting borders in the systematic function of norms, therefore creating a relatively clear and coherent grid.

In this respect, one of the basic problems primarily associated with the study of norms is the establishment of a hierarchical order. It is always necessary to determine whether a certain identified norm is a superordinate norm or simply a secondary one which follows from the implementation of the hierarchically superior norm (Toury, 1978:97). "It seems sometimes that the higher one goes, the more one finds that there is no end, as it were, to regulating principles" (Even-Zohar & Toury, 1981:x). This however does not mean that we can afford to work at lower levels only, since it might be a high-level norm that provides the key for interpreting a pattern of behaviour that we were able to detect but not completely explain. In order to allow translation studies to transcend traditional linguistic or even literary borders and to accommodate elements pertaining to the semiotics of culture, norm interference theory might need to account for constraints related to general sociological or at least linguistic-cultural phenomena (ibid:x-xi). Such a study, of course, runs the risk of getting out of hand. The complexity and multi-functionality of norms operating at the higher levels and influencing aspects of total - and not just translational - social behaviour necessitates an extremely wide spectrum of knowledge of both translational and sociological aspects at the same time, requiring in addition a number of time consuming and costly methodological techniques in order to ensure validity of results.

1.2 Elements of the translational polysystem

1.2.1 Norms and the translational polysystem

The notion of 'polysystems' was initially launched in the literary field by Tynjanov and the school of Russian formalists and was later developed by Even-Zohar. Tynjanov introduced the notion of systems in order to achieve a better understanding of the relationships between innovative elements and long established ones that constitute literary order. These new and old elements that do not exist in isolation but always in an interrelationship with other elements of other systems (Gentzler, 1993:112) constitute sub-systems in their own rights. The entire literary and extraliterary world could be divided into multiple structural systems which in turn comprise further smaller sub-systems. A piece of literary work itself constitutes a unique system that can be incorporated into the larger system of the literary genre to which this specific piece of work belongs, which in turn can be accommodated within the frames of the system of general literary traditions, and all these sub-systems together can be subsumed by the entire social order in which they operate (ibid). Interacting dialectically with each other and conditioning the function of each element, they constitute a major **polysystem** that has its own individual characteristics. Given the relation between central and peripheral functions in terms of strength and potency of their influence, we could organise these elements/systems according to a hypothetical notion of hierarchy of strata and distinguish between various levels within the broader polysystem.

Even-Zohar coined the term 'polysystem' to account for the aggregate of all possible kinds of literary systems, including canonised and non-canonised literary forms, as well as extraliterary systems within a certain society (Gentzler, 1993:105&114). As a global term, it is supposed to cover a very wide range of literary, semi-literary or extra-literary structures. Rejecting the possibility of a non-systemic origin of new elements and new structures, he argues that the constant bi-directional influence between literary and extraliterary systems determines the formulation of any literary work in such a way that it cannot escape its pre-destined eventual function as a literary fact itself. Even-Zohar's visualisation of hierarchical relations implies a similar distinction between primary and secondary literary systems and types according to their centrality or peripherality in the hosting, larger, superordinate system (Even-Zohar, in Gentzler, 1993:115). The translational system is thus seen to maintain a secondary position in societies where original literary works seem to prevail, or a primary position if it plays a more important role and dominates original literary creations. What should be brought in as another conditioning factor, therefore, is the relative prestige and power-relations of cultures and languages (Toury, 1993b:33), which clearly influence the position/status of local vs. imported/translated literature.

Literary works can no longer be regarded in isolation but always in a dialectal relationship with other systems. That which is innovative and new to the literary system/polysystem is dependent on that which is 'normal', i.e. product of the control and general application of norms, attracting value not through similarity with existing formulations but through a distancing differentiation from them (Gentzler, 1993:111). It would seem, then, that there is an inherent co-relation between the notions of 'systems' and 'norms'. Any type of system is actually the coherent grid, the network of norms that constitute it. A system therefore can be seen as a collection, a cumulative assemblance of all the norms that operate in it. On the other hand, a norm can be seen as a systematic constellation of a series of factors that lead to the emergence of a coherent behavioural pattern. The notion of 'system' and the notion of 'norm' then overlap and presuppose each other, in all aspects of human behaviour and not just in translation. A number of similarities between norms and systems support the above position. Firstly, the evolution of systems and the evolution of norms follow each other: a deviation from the norm will necessarily imply a deviation from the order of the system and vice versa. Secondly, both norms and systems operate in a consistent fashion, based on aspects of patterned behaviour. And finally, the notion of stratification and of established hierarchy between various operating levels (as discussed in the previous section) can apply to both norms and systems.

If we accept that there is no need for a norm to apply - to the same extent or at all - to all sectors within a society or, even less so, to apply across cultures (Toury, 1995:62), then we have to accept that there is no need for a norm to apply to all systems of a given polysystem. A norm gains significance through the system in which it is embedded and systems remain different even in occasional instances when they seem to show similar behaviour (ibid). A translation, therefore, can be regarded as a fact of whichever sub-system/target-sector is best equipped to account for and accommodate it as an actual fact (Toury, 1995:29). The study of the initial position of a translation in the hosting target system may have to pass through a process of continuous negotiation, starting with its historical contextualisation that can be considered a prerequisite not only for a diachronic but also for a synchronic kind of study (ibid:64). The mere enumeration of all the potential translation choices that could be allowed by the general normative structures of the target system outside the specific situational context, even if possible, would not lead to the discovery of the operation of any particular norms. Such a list would flatten out and neutralise all the constraints which affect decision-making in actual situations, "from the languages involved in the [translational] act and their genetic and/or historical relations, through the texts in which the problem-items are, and will be embedded, respectively, the models underlying these texts and the tradition to which each model (and text) pertains, through whatever is inherent to the 'bilingual brain' and/or acts of linguistic mediation, to the general concept of translation underlying the act, which is always norm-governed, and hence culture-specific" (Toury, 1993b:21-22). Lists of *options* instead of actual *choices* and *decisions* is not sufficient (ibid). The focus should be shifted from the notion of translatability to questions connected to actual translation situations (Even-Zohar & Toury, 1981:viii). A norm, therefore, is not an isolated "but a contextually connected concept, within a series which includes, among other things, *function*, *system* (and *polysystem*), *decision mechanism*" (ibid).

1.2.2 The elements of translational norms and sources for their investigation

From a sociological point of view, a norm consists of three main elements that specify and describe its function individually: a) a norm must contain an element which determines its *subject*, i.e. the agent that is expected to behave according to the norm, b) a norm must indicate the *situation* in which it is meant to be followed, and c) a norm must indicate how its subject is to act under the specific conditions, i.e. it must have a *theme* (Ross, 1968:107). The subject of a norm may be determined a) individually, b) universally or c) generically; a norm is considered 'particular' (or 'individual' or 'singular') when it is addressed to one person, 'universal' when it is addressed to everyone, and 'generic' when it is addressed to a group of people who satisfy a certain description (ibid:108). Similarly, the situation of a norm may be determined individually, generically or universally. A norm is considered 'occasional' when its situation is individually specified. When it is generically specified it is called 'hypothetical' and when it is universally specified it is called 'categorical', acquiring the status of a rule in both cases (ibid:111).

The scale of norms then, as determined by subjects and situations, is thought to range between 'occasional individual' norms and 'universal categorical' rules, quite resembling Toury's scale of pure subjective idiosyncrasies and absolute, objective laws. A methodology for the study of norms should be able to pinpoint the origin of the norm along this scale, a process identical to accurately tracing the level on which a norm is supposed to operate. The levels in the stratification of norms constitute and are determined by the nature of the two main parameters/elements involved in their eventual function, namely the subject and the situation. Still, the notion of 'situation' remains inadequately defined and requires further specification and analysis if we are to manage it methodologically. As Nord points out, it would be very useful to have a Magna Charta of translation and turn to it whenever we encounter any type of problem (1991a:92). She believes that such a project does not appear to be feasible exactly because the way in which a certain text will be translated depends on "culture-specific conventions" (ibid). I believe that these conventions are not simply culture-specific, but within the same culture can be situation-specific, in an even stricter and narrower sense.

Still, in the case of translational norms what might appear as a basic norm to a certain (school of) translators (or agents/subjects) with regard to a certain genre (literary system/situation), may only be a tendency compared to the entire period or literary polysystem in question (cf. Toury, 1978:96). Toury believes that there are two major sources for the study of translational norms: a) the translated texts themselves, as well as analytical critiques of these translations, and b) extra-textual, semi-theoretical or critical formulations such as prescriptive theories (or poetics of translation, statements made by the translators, editors, publishers and other persons involved in or connected with the activity of translation, critical appraisals of other translations or (schools of) translators etc., made in public as well in private (1978:91; 1995:65). The fundamental difference between these two elements is that whereas the texts, i.e. the translation products themselves, present us with the results of actual norm-governed activity, out of which the norms themselves can be discovered and reconstructed, direct normative pronouncements are simply formulations of the norms, i.e. by-products of their activity and verbalisations of the existence of norms as they directly and primarily appear through the translation products themselves (cf. Toury, 1978:91). As a result, these formulations should be treated with great caution not so much because they might be partial or accidental but mainly because they are likely to be influenced by biases and preoccupations, even if they claim to be objective (ibid). A mere quantitative analysis of such data is therefore not sufficient; it should be accompanied by a careful *qualitative analysis* as well. There may be wide gaps between the formulated arguments and demands on the one hand and their actual performance in translation on the other, yet all these reservations should not discourage us from studying them. On the contrary, if taken as pre-systematic and given an explication in a way that places them in a narrow, appropriately defined and precise framework, they might shed some light as to why they transmit this certain amount of subjectivity, possibly uncovering cultural correlations within which and for whose purposes they were produced, eventually enabling us to verify, refute or correct sets of norms (as revealed through translated texts) when finally confronted with them (Toury, 1978:92; 1995:66).

At this point, Toury is not proposing a coherent methodological framework to approach norms. His intention is rather to indicate potential sources for the extraction of norms without actually explaining how the norms themselves may be identified. As we will see in the following chapter, though, he inspired certain translation scholars (Christiane Nord for example) to attempt to construct such a methodological framework based on his assumptions. Irrespective of whether we try to approach norms through textual or extra-textual means and formulations, it is clear that no norm can be fully understood unless we specify the elements that constitute it and the conditions under which it operates. The discovery and the establishment of translational norms as regularities of translational activity therefore should be a result of a wide range of studies that will isolate all those factors which have a role to play in translation and determine their impact on both translational process and product (Toury, 1993b:25) (see also chapter 2).

1.2.3 The role of texts in the study of translational norms

There has long been a dispute about what is a translation and who has the right to designate it as such. Chesterman believes that a text can be considered 'a translation' if its producers and receivers say that it is (1993:2). Toury defines 'translation' as "any target language utterance which is presented as such within the target culture, on whatever grounds" (1985:20). These definitions might appear over-simplistic, circular or tautological; they do, however, help us avoid extensive arguments as to what should or should not be a translated text and, furthermore, whether it should or should not be incorporated in a study of translational norms.

There are two ways in which translated texts may be grouped to form a literary system within the major polysystem: a) in terms of the way their source texts are selected by the target literary system, and b) in terms of the way they adopt specific norms, behaviour and policies compared with other literary systems of the general target polysystem (Even-Zohar, 1978):108). Once this position is adopted, we can hardly go on talking simply about the analysis of individual translated texts and the study of the norms they exhibit; we have to shift our focus to translated literature in general (Lambert & van Gorp, 1985:51). A thorough study of translated texts on inter- and intra-systemic levels, however, should not just stop there. An analysis of the micro-structural elements of a translated text should be followed by an analysis of the relation of the translated text to the order of the translated literature, and moreover it should be followed by an analysis of the relation of the latter system/level to the higher general literary system. In order to follow a coherent methodology, such a study should be compartmentalised and disallow direct relations of individual translated works to the higher general literary system: for example, a normative aspect that appears to characterise at the lowest level a number of specific translation products of a specific type, genre and literary mode should not be directly associated with the norms that guide literature in general at the highest level, but should be primarily associated with the hierarchical structure of intermediate levels that account for broader types, additional genres and other literary modes. In other words, for an investigation into translational norms to be feasible and controlled, it should proceed on the basis of establishing relations between contiguous levels. For the same reasons, it should not attempt to establish relations between the higher literary system and extraliterary systems, although such relations might possibly exist (cf. Venuti, 1997).

We see that the text is always involved in a multitude of relationships with other elements of other systems. In every literary culture, the function of certain features, models and techniques creates a systemic constellation of relationships in the form of a coherent network of pre-existing phenomena into which the new phenomenon, the new literary text, will enter (Toury, 1993a:14). The surface realisations of such features, models and techniques are reflected in the specific text-types or literary genres. The importance of taking into account considerations of genres can be better seen in the case of studying bilingual corpora where a translated text may not belong to the same genre as its original and therefore there might be more than one genre involved in the translation process (Baker, 1995:230). Toury admits that "the sweeping generality of the correlation between socio-cultural circumstances and discourse interference in translation may well have to undergo further modifications still, along various additional axes; for instance, with respect to text-type" (Toury, 1993b:34). Within the same target system, one will find a wide range of different text-types. Moreover, "even for one and the same text, neither [normative] interference nor tolerance of it are necessarily the same with respect to all linguistic and textual levels" (Toury, 1995:279). Audiovisual translation involves a number of specific text-types, this time in the form of different film-genres. Toury, however, seems to confuse this notion and application of 'text-types' within audiovisual translation when he says that:

> "in cultures which resort to this [subtitling] practice, subtitles tend to be regarded as translated utterances. Very often they also function as such, so that they are sometimes even read differently from *texts* which are taken not to have been translated" (1995:76) [my italics].

In my view, we should not consider this fact as a different function of a different text-type, but as a different function of (an aspect of) a different translational **mode.** The special traits of audiovisual translation (picture-sound-text) which characterise and distinguish it from other translational modes such as written (literary or technical/specialised) translation of written texts or even from interpretation, are precisely those which prompt the audience to read subtitles from a different perspective. I will thus reserve the term 'text-types' or 'genres' to refer to text-types or genres as instances of (translational) literary activity *within the same translational mode*, the audiovisual one for example, and I will regard the level/system of genres or text-types as operating lower or within the level/system of the translational mode in question.

1.2.4 The role of human agents in the study of translational norms

Translation is increasingly being regarded as a complex transaction that takes place in a communicative, socio-cultural context where active human agents are constantly involved (Hermans, 1996:26). It is human agents who will initially decide which source texts will be selected and how they will finally be translated. Bringing all these human agents who participate in the translation process into the picture, either as individuals or as social groups with their own special traits, preoccupations and interests, becomes a necessary precondition for a broad and multi-dimensional study of translational norms.

The importance of the human agents in relation to the production of a translated text has received special attention in corpus-based studies, where both the number and the status of the translators represented in the corpus (professional/amateur, staff/freelance etc.) have to be specified (Baker, 1995:230). In the case of studying translational norms, where translated texts are often all that is available for investigation, sometimes there is no way of knowing how many different people were actually involved in the formulation of a translational product and what role they played. The common practice is to collapse them into one persona and have that conjoined entity regarded as 'the translator' (Toury, 1995:183). Although this might appear to be an easy solution, the actual process which led to the creation of a translated text may entail so many different types of activities dispersed in terms of space, time and agents that a careful analysis of the individual role played by any of the individual human agents involved might necessarily need to be specified (ibid). Vanderauwera uses the term 'translator' as a "convenient shorthand for the 'processor' who consists of the actual translator, the editor, the publisher, and all those who contributed to the production and presentation of the final target text" (1985:12). In audiovisual translation, a range of different activities is carried out by translators, adaptors, time-coders, (revoicing) actors, post-editors, film distributors and engineers, and quite often the final translational product cannot be examined without a prior investigation of the part that each side played in the formulation of the product, with their individual views, ideas and preoccupations to guide their (translational) behaviour. The study of translational norms might then benefit a great deal "from knowing whether the same attitudes were shared by all those involved in the production of a translation or whether a (direct or indirect) normative negotiation, maybe so much as a struggle took place, and if so - whose norms had the upper hand and on what grounds" (Toury, 1995:184).

Toury seems to share the views of neurophysiologists who maintain that "the mind is not only *trainable* in principle, but is actually *being trained* all the time, and that one of the factors which contributes to its training is *environmental feedback*" (1993b:32). The consideration of 'environmental feedback' leads us to the potential need for investigating the role of target audience/recipients and their reaction to translation products, as they are formulated by the human agents involved, although this topic seems to be neglected by Toury. What should be stressed about the role of human agents here is that qualitative studies of these agents' preconceptions and formulated beliefs of what constitutes a 'better' or 'worse' translational strategy will enable the researcher to get an overview of the norms that guide these agents' behaviour. A theory thus refined will therefore make possible the execution of yet more elaborate studies, on the basis of qualitative and not just quantitative data, "towards an increasingly better understanding of the way translation and translators as individuals and members of societal groups alike manoeuvre within the manifold constraints imposed on them and produce texts which look and function the way they do" (Toury, 1993b:26). It is not necessarily futile to study a single translated text or single translator in isolation; it would be a significant drawback, however, to disregard the fact that this translational product or this translator are (positively or negatively) connected with other translational products and translators in the general translational polysystem.

1.3 Target and source systems in the study of translational norms

1.3.1 The pivotal role of the target system

If we take the view that discourse transfer simply follows laws of cognition, then we should expect all translators in all cultures to behave similarly no matter what they translate. But it seems more reasonable to suggest that (patterned) translational behaviour has to do as much with the socio-cultural conditions in which translational activity is performed as it has to do with cognitive machinery (Toury, 1993b:29).

Toury's approach to translation attempts to effect a shift in emphasis in favour of the target system. The novelty of his approach has attracted criticism to the effect that according to his theory translational texts are regarded as facts of the target system only. This criticism has been expressed in reviews and comments which pointed out a variety of complex relations between source and target texts and cultures, therefore making it difficult to think of translated texts as belonging to the target pole exclusively (Hermans, 1995:28). What has attracted the most criticism is the idea that "translations are facts of target cultures; on occasion facts of a special status, sometimes even constituting identifiable (sub)systems of their own, but of the target culture in any event" (Toury, 1995:29). This, however, is only an isolated and de-contextualised statement of Toury's approach. Toury regards translated texts as outcomes of the observation that something is 'missing' in the target system but luckily already exists elsewhere, in another (source) system (ibid:27). In this respect, Toury's actual approach to the issue is best summarised in the following statement: "the position and function which go with a text being regarded as a translation, are determined *first and foremost* by considerations originating in the culture which hosts them" (1995:26) [my italics].

When a literary source text is translated, it does not just enter another linguistic system but also another literary system which may act in analogy to the source literary system but only as a secondary modelling system (cf. Toury, 1980:37). Due to the various individual socio-cultural peculiarities that characterise them, different systems rarely, if ever, concur; and since the functional identity of a phenomenon is governed first and foremost by the internal organisation of the system which hosts it, the functional identity of a translated text will be determined by the requirements of the target system (cf. Toury, 1993a:14). Thus, I would fully adopt Toury's idea that:

> "in fact, the extent to which features of a source text are retained in its translation (or even regarded as requiring retention, in the first place), which, at first sight, seems to suggest an operation in the interest of the source culture, or even of the source text as such, is also determined on the target side, and according to its own concerns: features are retained, and reconstructed in target-language material, not because they are 'important' in any *inherent* sense, but because they are *assigned* importance, from the recipient vantage point" (1995:12).

Borrowing some notions from the functional approach to support the above thesis, I also believe that for a methodological study of translational norms it is important to realise that a commission of a translation depends on the circumstances of the target culture (Vermeer, 1989:184). One might say that the commission of a translation depends on the relation between the demands of the target culture *and* the demands of the source text; "yet this would only be a special case of the general dependence on the target culture: a special case, that is, in so far as the commission is basically independent of the source text function" (ibid). Deviation from or conformity to translational norms is therefore a matter of what the *target system* is willing to accept, modify or even reject. "For to translate - means to produce a text in a target setting for a target purpose and target addresses in target circumstances" (Vermeer, 1987:29).

The act of translation as a teleological activity par excellence is conditioned by the goals it is designed to serve, as set by the target system. Inevitably, then, not just the translated texts but translators as well are expected to operate first and foremost in the interest of the system in which they work, and not in the interest of the source system (cf. Toury, 1985:19). Toury holds that "any research into translation, whether it is confined to the product itself or intends to proceed to the reconstruction of the process which yielded it (and on from there), should start from the hypothesis that *translations are facts of one system only*: the target system" (ibid). I would like to expand this view to the study of norms in audiovisual translation as well. Regardless of the extent of the retention of certain aspects of the source product, the translated product involves significant adjustments to the requirements of the target system, since it is basically designed to fulfil what is assumed to be the needs of the system which will eventually host it (cf. Toury, 1995:166).

Venuti defines translation as "the forcible replacement of the linguistic and cultural difference of the foreign text with a text that will be intelligible to the target language reader" (1995:18). The translated text again is seen to operate first and foremost in the interest of the target system that is hosting it and not in the source system that produced the original, since "whatever the difference the translation conveys is now imprinted by the target-language culture, assimilated to its positions of intelligibility, its canons and taboos, its codes and ideologies" (ibid). From this perspective, the whole range of linguistic and cultural transformations, reconstructions and alterations could be seen to result from the implementation of values, beliefs and ideas - i.e. of the norms - that exist in the TL community and are expressed in hierarchies of dominance and marginality (cf. ibid). Venuti distinguishes between the 'domesticating' method of translation, where the translated text is formulated in a way that adheres to the values of the target community, and the 'foreignising' method of translation, where the translated text is formulated in a way that does not adhere to the values of the target community but rather retains, emphasises and brings to the surface the values that are expressed in the source text (ibid:20). In the former method, the norms that dominate the target community take over and dictate the translation process; the translated text then clearly reflects and is a product of the target system norms. In the latter 'foreignising' method, it appears at first that the target system norms are neglected. However, it is (marginalised) ideas of the *target community* that will dictate the translation process and not ideas of the source community; the decision to retain, emphasise and bring to the surface the values that are expressed in the source text is a decision which is taken as a conscious response to target norms, for a number of possible reasons (e.g. to retain the flavour of the original, to expand the cultural awareness of the target community, to expose and preserve source values and ideas that might have been lost through the course of time, to create something different and enrich the literary repertoire of the target culture, etc.). It could still be seen, however, as a target culture-oriented decision.

Chesterman suggests a number of potential sources of investigation for the explanation of a particular aspect of a translator's behaviour, and consequently of the norms that have govern it (1993:16-18). First, the source text, since a translator might have performed an act because the source text required it; but all translators' decisions are motivated by and taken along the lines and on the basis of a given source text. We cannot consider therefore such an explanation adequate for the appearance of a certain kind of norm in the translator's behaviour, since the source text is always the piece of given data upon which certain normative formulations will later be applied. Second, target language norms, since a translator might have performed an act because of the expectations of his/her target language community. This, however, is adequate only to a certain extent, because it is not just the target *language* and its specific features that dictate a normative kind of behaviour, but a whole range of other features as well that constitute the general target (poly)system. Third, normative translation laws, since a translator might have performed an act simply following the translation laws of the target system. This view appears more adequate. What an analyst has to do, then, is expand the previous notion of TL norms to include norms of the target system as a whole, in order to account for these normative translation laws that are formulated (and operate) within it. Fourth, general communicative maxims, since a translator might have performed an act in order to conform to "overall communicative co-operative maxims, principles which are accepted as valid for any kind of communication, not just translation" (ibid). This, however, appears to decontextualise the translation product and disregard the particular situation in which this act of communication - with its normative characteristics - has been observed to take place, because it is constantly influenced by and filtered through the specific traits that delineate its situational context. And finally, there is the question of ethical values, since a translator might have performed an act in order to conform to general ethical principles. Venuti in particular advocates a 'call to action', inviting translators to resist rather than submit to dominant target culture ethical values that demand ethnocentric 'domesticating' translations and promote narcissism and imperialism (1995:308). He proposes instead the adoption of ethnodeviant 'foreignising' translation strategies that promote cultural diversity and open-mindedness (ibid). As previously, though, ethical values - just like norms and customs - are (target) culture-specific, since they are perceived, analysed and experienced through the specific constraints of the culture/system within and for the benefit of which they operate.

Where all the above positions seem to converge is in assuming that the value of a norm is clearly a matter related to the position this norm (and the products that manifest it) have managed to acquire within the target system. Once introduced into the target system "the fortune of an item in terms of success or failure becomes a domestic matter" (Even-Zohar, 1990:58).

1.3.2 The source system and its indifferent status

The presence of a translated text or a text that is regarded as such entails the assumption that there is another (source) text, existing as a fact of another system, which has both chronological and logical priority over the translated text in question, as long as the ST precedes the TT in time and serves as the basis for the creation of the latter (Toury, 1985:20). However, "it is the *assumption* of its existence, based on the observation that a target-language utterance is being presented or regarded as a translation, and not its existence in fact, which serves as a defining factor of a translation from the point of view of the target system" (ibid).

Toury does not seem to be very consistent with this view, despite the fact that his study is claimed to be undertaken from the perspective of the target system, since he resolves quite often into attaching importance not just to the *assumption* of the ST but to the very *existence* of the ST itself. By admitting that translational problems are always reconstructed "through *target-source comparison* rather than on the basis of the source text alone, or even of the source text and its relation to the overall possibilities of the target language to recode its (relevant) features" (Toury, 1985:28), he enhances the study of source texts and source systems and attributes significant status to them as crucial parts of investigation and analysis.

Toury disagrees with source-oriented studies because they "concern themselves mainly with *potential* translation, or even with *translatability*, rather than with *actual* translation, hence with the *act of translating*, which actually proceeds from ST, rather than with *translations* as actual textual-linguistic products (instances of performance), which belong first and foremost to the system of the texts written in TL" (1980:35). A source-oriented theory, he suggests, ignores the target system pole, i.e. the actual translation produced and the entire network of constraints within which it is produced (ibid:40). Nevertheless, being mainly preoccupied with the two notions of 'adequacy' and 'acceptability' (see also section 1.5) he has to direct the thrust of his investigation towards "**a combined operation** of TT-ST comparison on the one hand and the establishment of TT's position in the relevant target literary and/or linguistic systems in terms of its acceptability in them on the other" (ibid:49) [bold emphasis added].

Toury believes that there are three basic ways to examine a translated text and reconstruct its translational norms: a) the comparison of several translations of the same original text, carried out in different periods of time and/or by various translators, b) the comparison of literary phenomena as they appear both in translation and in original works composed in the target language, and c) "(above all) the comparison of a translation to the original text serving as its source, for without such a comparison one cannot even determine what type of initial norms underlies it" (1978:92). And he continues, "an indispensable prerequisite for the analysis of translated texts (and consequently also for a systematic study of translational norms) is therefore the development of a theoretically based and explicit method for the comparison of one translation and its original, taking into account general linguistic and literary theories (including some theory of the literary text) and involving complete and accurate systematic descriptions of SL, TL, and the two literary polysystems" (ibid). I cannot see the reason for studying the source text or system, or for determining the norms that characterise them. Whatever norms, constraints or elements characterise the source text and therefore signify deviation from or conformity to the existing source system norms, cannot affect - and consequently cannot tell us anything about - the translated text's performance in the target system, i.e. about its own deviation from or conformity to target system norms; the fact that source system and target system are separate systems means that the norms of the former can and might influence the gradual formation of norms in the latter, but still they cannot establish them nor guide the translated text's performance within their framework. This is the significance of accepting a translated text first and foremost as a fact of the target system; a translated text is formed and designed to operate in the target system. If the target system dictates the appearance in the translated text of the norms that characterise the source text and system, this is still a decision made on the part of the target system, and the source system has little to do with it. It reflects an attitude/tendency of the target system itself as to whether it will allow interference from the source system or not. Revealing such a systematic pattern of behaviour on the part of the target system we are actually discovering and establishing a norm of the target system. We do not have to study or analyse the source system for this reason though; we simply have to take all the linguistic and literary data/elements of the ST as they emerge through the source text, i.e. as given, and focus our study on how they are revealed or elaborated in the translated text, in the target system.

In an attempt to give an example of the usefulness of the study of source texts, Toury takes the case of subtitles. Pointing out that there can be many candidates for a source text (e.g. the original script before the spoken version, the final release of the script in the spoken version, a translation of the script in the TL or any other pivot language, or finally a combination of these alternatives) he criticises Delabastita for his neglect of "the need to establish the source text properly as a precondition for the extraction of translational relationships" (Toury, 1995:76, footnote) in his study. If what Toury wants to stress is the necessity to establish one and only one specific ST as a starting point for the creation and the eventual comparison of two independent translated texts (e.g. two subtitled film versions of the same movie, or even one set of bilingual subtitles on the same target-film version in certain bilingual countries), then this would seem to make sense. Both translated texts must have a common point of reference and should be regarded as results of the same initial source product, so that any possible variations of normative behaviour between them are accounted for on equal target premises and not on possibly different realisations of different source materials as the input for the translation, i.e. as the given data. Toury's supplementary comment that "the possible multiplicity of candidates for a source text has no bearing on the status of the subtitles themselves as assumed translations, which is established in the *target* cultural context alone - sometimes with a pre-systematic notion of the possible source text, and often with no regard for the very question" (ibid:75-76) complicates the issue even more since it contradicts his previous views.

The functional approach seems to have more absolute and clear-cut views concerning the role of source texts and systems. Vermeer claims that "the source text does not determine the variety of the target text, nor does the text variety determine ipso facto the form of the target text, (the text variety does not determine the skopos either); rather, it is the skopos of the translation that also determines the text variety" (1989:187). The functional approach regards the mechanism for the operation of the target system, and hence the norms it consists of, as autonomous and self-guiding. Siding with this view, I consider the role of the source text and the source system as bearing no relevance for the methodological study of translational norms as they appear in target texts and target systems.

One might see the target culture/system as a member of a greater (poly)culture/(poly)system (e.g. global, European, Mediterranean, Balkan etc.) which contains many potential source systems as well, interrelating with and influencing each other. It is true that a system as a 'unit' can never be clear-cut and that the borders that separate it from neighbouring systems are fuzzy and shift all the time (Even-Zohar, 1990:24). No matter how we define our system in terms of size and versatility, though, a norm which has been seen to operate within it is a fact of one and only one system, perhaps simply coinciding with the same norm in another (sub)system; and this happens because norms operate autonomously, since they are manifestations of an aspect of (e.g. textual-translational) behaviour which is encountered in and explained for a specific situation, i.e. a specific system. It is also true that a certain community cannot resist interference from the communities with which it comes in contact.

Similarly, a target system cannot possibly resist interference from the source systems with which it comes in contact, especially on its periphery, and it might take a long time before this influence actually appears on the surface (Even-Zohar, 1990:65); "but it surfaces or fails to surface subject to the conditions prevailing in the centre of the system, which may either encourage interference or neutralise resistance to it" (ibid). The status and the position of the source text and system may thus favour and activate resistance or submission to a dominant set of norms in the target system; overall, however, they do not participate in the battle that takes place within the target system as to which of these norms will eventually prevail. Toury, by contrast, emphasises the importance even of source micro-structures, suggesting that "an exhaustive contrastive description of the languages involved is a precondition for any systematic study of translations, and, on the discipline level, a developed CL [Contrastive Linguistics] is a necessary precondition for translation studies" (Toury, 1980:29-30). I would rather adopt Even-Zohar's view, namely that what actually counts is the position assumed by the target items in their target systems and "not their comparable items within whatever source" (Even-Zohar, 1990:71). And furthermore that:

> "the active role a target system plays in interference makes it clear that (a) the position and role of the source system itself are in principle irrelevant for the target system (source system-employable items may thus be transferred regardless of their perceived position in the source system); and (b) the function of the (directly or indirectly) transferred items in the source system is irrelevant for the target system, as long as they are employable for target system functions" (Even-Zohar, 1990:94).

Since a translator's command of the source norms and culture is, therefore, essential only in order to "enable him to reconstruct the possible reactions of an ST recipient (in case the TT skopos requires an 'imitation' of the ST functions by the target text)" (Nord, 1991b:11), there is no point in attempting an investigation of the source system or any of its elements. What one should rather do is turn to the parameters of the target pole and attempt to discover those target factors that contributed to the production of the translated text (Vanderauwera, 1985:12).

1.4 Function and equivalence in the study of translational norms

1.4.1 The function of translated texts

According to the functional approach, someone initiates the process of translation as intercultural communication because s/he wants the translated text for a specific purpose. It is inevitable then that the requirements which will (have to) be met by the translator depend on this purpose (Nord, 1991b:8). As a result, "it is not the source text as such, or its effect on the ST recipient, or the function assigned to it by the author, that operates the translation process, as is postulated by equivalence-based translation theory [...], but the prospective function or skopos [or 'scopos' elsewhere] of the target text as determined by the initiator's needs" (ibid:9). Since norms are supposed to operate during the translation process[i], the function or the skopos of the target text will determine the emergence of the respective norms from the target system. A text by itself, however, does not have a function; "a function can only be assigned to the text by the recipient in the act of reception" (ibid:16).

The importance of the function of translated texts from the point of view of Descriptive Translation Studies is recognised by Toury himself when he admits that the actual subject-matter for the development of such studies consists primarily of functional-relational concepts[ii], rather than textual-linguistic representations (1985:21). In a

---

[i] The translation process is here assumed to begin with the decision to translate and is not restricted to the act of translation itself.

[ii] It should be noted that Toury and the polysystem approach theorists use the term 'function' "in its semiotic sense, as the 'value' assigned to an item belonging in a certain system by virtue of the network of relations it enters into [...]. As such it is not tantamount to the mere 'use' of the end product, as seems to be the case with the *Skopostheorie*" (Toury, 1995:12 footnote). In this respect, there is a difference in the use of the term 'function' between Skopostheorie and the polysystem

schematic representation of the connection between function, process and translational products, he depicts the position and function of a translation in its hosting system as determining its surface realisations (i.e. the product), which in turn govern the strategies whereby a target text (or parts of it) has been derived from its original, (i.e. the product dictates the actual translational process) (1995:13). The initial impression of placing the translational product between the function and the process seems to be corrected with a later figure that presents a hierarchical course from function to process and then to product. In any case, functions are depicted as having logical priority over their surface realisations, noting that "since translating is a *teleological* activity by its very nature, its systemic position and that of its future products, should be taken as forming constraints of the highest order" (Toury, 1995:14).

It is Skopostheorie that mainly stresses the role of function in translation. Notwithstanding the fact that Vermeer seems to contradict himself when he says at one point that "we all translate by intuition" (1987:25) and at another that "what the skopos states is that one must translate, *consciously and consistently*, in accordance with some principle respecting the target text" (1989:182) [my italics], it is basically maintained that any translation is carried out according to an implicit or explicit specification. A translated text is primarily determined by its skopos or commission, i.e. by its presumed ability to carry out its aimed function; fidelity to the source text and hence textual equivalence, then, is just one possible and legitimate skopos or commission (cf. Vermeer, 1989:185). Nord notes that:

> "if the TT is intended to fulfil the same function as the source text (ST), there can be a relationship of 'intertextual coherence' or 'fidelity'

---

approach. However, both concepts seem to be compatible with the attempt to stress the role of the target text within the target system, emphasising the teleological dimension of the target text. This is the focus of the present section and it is from this perspective that I decided to use the term 'function' in a more general way. In any case, even Toury himself recognises the affinity between the two terms/concepts and admits that "the correlations between the two uses of 'function', which may well exist, still await scholarly processing" (ibid).

> between ST and TT; but the demand for fidelity will always be subordinate to the scopos rule. If the scopos demands a change of function, the required standard will no longer be intertextual coherence with the ST, but adequacy and appropriateness with regard to the translation scope (1991a:93).

What is accepted as a possible translation for a source text depends on norms and translational conventions of the target system alone (cf. Nord, 1991a:94). For the polysystem approach, all the hypothesised functional elements are interdependent and correlated (Even-Zohar, 1990:85). Even in the case of unilateral influence from the source to the target system, due to a constant contact that might result in the adoption of certain norms and items, however, "their function hardly ever remains the same as in the source [system]" (ibid:92). Therefore, since the TT skopos requires its conformity strictly to target system conventions, one is justified in neglecting the conventional textual properties of the ST in his/her investigation of translational (target) norms.

In discussing the notion of translated texts that either function as actual translations or pass as originals, Toury seems to suggest that what is introduced into the target system after translation is either just a new text that can be directly absorbed and adopted by the target system, or in more complex cases whole textual models and modes of language-use from the source system, as rules for the future generation of translated texts that will bear the cultural features of the source system (1995:166). In the mode of audiovisual translation, sometimes it is not just textual material which is changed but visual material as well, as for example in the case of reshooting new frames for a dubbed version of a film. This is done to achieve a desired function of the translated product, so that it can be regarded, and therefore function, as an original. This functional dilemma cannot be applied to the case of subtitled or voiced-over versions, where the presence of the original - not just visual but also acoustic – SL/SC elements poses as an ongoing obstacle for allowing these specific types of translation to be assumed, and function, as originals (Ascheid, 1997:33). We see, therefore, that the notion of translational function plays a particular crucial role in the case of the audiovisual mode. Toury notes that there can be no guarantee that translated texts will behave according to some preconceived source-oriented models of translation, based on strict bilingual and bitextual ST-TT equivalence, or represent - and function as - originals, in the target system (cf. 1980:41-42). As a matter of fact, these very deviations from target system or source system normality prove a deviation not just from the notion of textual but also from the notion of functional equivalence as well (cf. ibid). Measuring functional equivalence between ST and TT seems a utopian task. It is absurd to expect a text which is produced in and for a completely different environment to function in the same way as its original; not to mention the fact that the function of the same original shifts with its various recipients through time and space (Vanderauwera, 1985:147). The function of the translated text, then, can only be examined within the framework of its target system.

1.4.2 The notion of equivalence in translation

Toury uses the notion of 'equivalence' to elaborate his categories of 'adequate' and 'acceptable' translations. Translational equivalence is not considered simply as a target-source relationship established with different types of invariants but is regarded predominantly as a functional-relational concept that distinguishes between translation and non-translation in certain specific socio-cultural circumstances, "i.e. between adequate and inadequate instances of performance with respect to the governing model(s) and to the norms deriving from these models" (Toury, 1985:36). The question that still arises, though, is how one is able to discover, identify and establish these norms - and the extent to which they are seen to operate - in the first place, since the adequacy or non-adequacy of a given translated text can only be measured against a norm which has been established beforehand.

The way to approach and study translated texts, according to Toury (1985:21), involves an initial step of investigation of their acceptability in their respective home systems. The second step consists of mapping their constitutive elements as translational phenomena on their counterparts in the source text and system, therefore revealing the solutions that were given to the various translational problems. The final step is to identify and describe the irreversible relationships between the members of each pair/translational problem, and finally refer these relationships to the overall concept of translation, "by means of the mediating functional-relational notion of TRANSLATION EQUIVALENCE" (ibid). Toury believes that the comparison between a translated text and its original should be established on the basis of a stable invariant, without questioning the existence of equivalence that can or cannot be obtained between ST and TT, but rather exploring the type and degree of equivalence obtained at the end. At the same time, he claims that "a comparison of an actual translation to this 'invariant' (which is, of course, a hypothetical construct only) will reveal the shifts caused by factors other than rules, and a series of comparisons carried out along the lines of such a method will lead the student to generalisations and will enable him to form hypotheses as to the norms, among other things" (Toury, 1978:93). He therefore seems to view the entire network of possible TT-ST relationships as the system of potential equivalence, i.e. as translation 'competence', no longer as a 'material' but as a 'functional' concept of a theoretical and abstract nature (1980:47). The problem is that he himself stressed the need for focusing not on potential notions of competence that will lead us to possible translational options, but on actual translational facts as a pool of examples and data. Even if we accept, then, that "translational norms are the intermediating factor between the system of potential equivalence relationships and the actual performance, i.e. the reason for the functioning of certain relationships as translation equivalence" (ibid:50) we still cannot start our investigation into translational norms from the point of hypothetical 'potential equivalence' relations, but from the opposite point of the actual 'performance', i.e. the 'functioning' of the translated target product itself and its relations to the hosting target system.

The notion of 'equivalence' is one of the basic issues in translation theory. As a result, it has attracted the attention of various translation scholars. For Vermeer and the followers of the functional approach, there seem to be two major types of equivalence, now considered as instances of 'value equivalents': a) cross-cultural behaviour equivalents, and b) structural equivalents (cf. Vermeer, 1987:30), which however are not related to the study of translational norms. Lambert & van Gorp (1995:47-48) seem to side with Toury's view of the need to examine equivalence through TT-ST comparison in order to investigate translational norms, only if this comparison is carried out in specific areas and with specific elements in mind on the one hand, and with a wider perspective on the other, not just probing into the inter-textual links but into the links between source and target systems as well. Finally, Hermans (1995:217) criticises Toury's notion of 'equivalence' on the basis that it is regarded as nothing but the network of textual relations between translations and their originals. I believe that Hermans is right to the extent that Toury argues in his early works that "translation is a (linguistic) text in one language which is equivalent to another text in another language" (Toury, 1980:36). Toury claims that what his target-oriented approach to translation is geared to in fact "is the retrospective study of the production of translated texts, not their reception and consumption" (1993a:17). As a result, if we accept that a translated text's reception and consumption play a significant role in its particular function in the target system, we have to admit that Toury's preoccupation with equivalence restricts his vision and prevents him from developing a broader view of an individual target system with its own individual norms, irrespective of any kinds of relations in any forms of equivalence with other systems or texts/elements of those systems.

Toury defines 'equivalence' as "the existence (or the establishment) of a certain relationship between the two messages [ST-TT], irrespective of the relationships obtaining between the two codes" (1980:63). This relationship between the two messages is supposed to take place at a higher level that resembles the level of 'langue' or 'interlanguage'. The term 'interlanguage' was initially coined within the field of second-language learning to describe the intermediate, hypothetical, higher linguistic system which is created by a learner's conscious or subconscious attempt to reconstruct the norms of the second language under the influence of his/her mother tongue. Just as we do not have to investigate and analyse the 'interlanguage' in order to identify the second/target language norms, I do not believe it is necessary to investigate and analyse 'equivalence' in order to describe the norms that operate in a translated/target text.

At a certain point, Toury also claims that "it would be a flat contradiction to claim that a certain text is a translation, and at the same time also non-equivalent to its source" (1980:70). This suggests that equivalence is a notion that can be taken for granted, exactly because "only *parts* of TT (certain linguistic-textual units, or the like) can be said to be non-equivalent to their counterparts in ST, and that only on the assumption that the entire TT, by its very definition as a translation, is equivalent to its source, and on the basis of an inherently established concept of equivalence" (ibid). What he finds important, then, is " *in what manner* this equivalence manifests itself" (ibid:90). Since whether or not a translation is equivalent to its source product is already given by definition (and by the researcher's willingness to take them as such), whatever the manner in which this equivalence has been established should not be of any interest to us. And if by 'manner' he implies the norms that influence the translator's decisions during the translation process, we are not talking about 'equivalence' any more, but of *hypothetical visualisations of the function of the final TT within the target system.* Instead of considering equivalence as a phenomenon that is taken for granted, Toury focuses on what norms determine in relation to the source text and seems to neglect the orientation of these norms, i.e. the target system, or even their manifestation, i.e. the actual translations. He therefore sacrifices the immediate information that can be derived from the study of the products, for the sake of the study of the process, whose role is in fact intermediary, serving as a means to an end.

Vanderauwera totally discards the discussion of the notion of 'equivalence' simply because it represents an abstract problem "and like many abstract conceptual problems their chief characteristic is to remain problems to which there are no solutions" (1985:147). Toury on the other hand, instead of analysing the clear manifestations of actual translational behaviour, i.e. the target texts, and their functional position in the target system, proposes the study of the labyrinth of attempts for achieving this translational behaviour as a manifestation of the source elements/system. If we are studying the norms of the target system, though, and accept their individual status (as we have seen in 1.3.1 and 1.3.2), we have to take the source data/elements as they emerge through the source text, i.e. as given, therefore taking translational equivalence as given as well. Translational equivalence will be eventually achieved (and manifested) by the translator, at any level or extent; what will still be missing is the (information on) the reception and consumption of this manifestation of translational equivalence, i.e. the precise function of the target text in the target system.

The interference involved in cross-cultural contacts often leads to a movement of the individual systems towards each other. This is even more obvious in the case of audiovisual translation which deals with a popular mode, aimed at larger audiences and bringing together both visual and textual information about the source cultures/systems. The status of the target system can be, and very often is influenced and reformulated by the status of the source system, but the individuality of each cannot be erased, despite the translator's attempt to achieve some kind of equivalence. Their identity is unique and characterised by their own specific features/elements, against which the function of individual texts is going to be measured.

As Hermans points out, the process of establishing translational equivalence as a "process of decision-making, and hence the operation of norms in it, takes place in the translator's head and thus remains largely hidden from view" (Hermans, 1996:28), preventing direct access to this well-sealed 'black box'. Toury realises the difficulties inherent in the study of translational norms, for what is available for observation is not so much the norms themselves, but rather norm-governed instances of behaviour and, more often than not, the products of such behaviour (1995:66). He recognises that much more should be done to shed some light on the translation process and until this is achieved only conjectures can be formulated as to the exact steps and mechanisms of the translation process, simply on the basis of studies of translations vs. source texts (ibid:101). However, if we consider the basic mental processes involved in translation as constituting a universal mental apparatus for enabling us to switch, and therefore establish equivalence, between source and target code, we can accept equivalence as given data, thus avoiding potential constraints and pitfalls that an endless study of attempted equivalence as translation process might entail, and focus on the direct manifestation of translational norms as they appear through the function of translated texts in the target system.

1.5 Adequacy and acceptability in the study of translational norms

1.5.1 Adequacy and acceptability vs. conformity and deviation

Toury distinguishes between translated texts that constitute: a) an appropriate (literary) work in the target polysystem, or b) a faithful representation in the TL of a pre-existing text in another language, belonging to a different literary polysystem (1978:85). In terms of this distinction, he claims that "whereas adherence to source norms determines a translation's adequacy as compared to the source text, subscription to norms originating in the target culture determines its acceptability" (1995:56-57).

Even at first glance, this categorisation seems to be based on uncommon ground and is therefore somewhat unbalanced: 'adequacy' is determined by comparison to source *textual* elements, whereas 'acceptability' is delineated by comparison to target *cultural* elements. This mismatch ultimately results in an uneven characterisation of the translated texts themselves. From the perspective of a study that ventures to investigate translational norms as they appear in the target systems, I would suggest a modification of the above terms, calling **conformity** any kind of abiding by target system normative regulations, and **deviation** any lack of compromise in favour of the same target system normative regulations. In this framework, Toury's 'acceptability' necessarily coincides with 'conformity'. 'Adequacy' on the other hand does not necessarily imply 'deviation' from the target system norms. First of all, it is very probable, for a variety of reasons, that source and target norms may coincide. Copying source norms, therefore, does not ipso facto imply deviating from target norms. Even in cases where copying source norms may result in deviation from target norms, however, this deviation can be viewed from the angle of the target system as possibly signalling innovation, in the form of launching new ideas, which although pioneering – in terms of deviating from target norms - might still be accepted by the target system, further reshaping and reformulating the norms that have been violated or manipulated. Toury believes that if the TT is found to totally comply with ST norms, it is viewed as an artificial non-existent variety by the target system, not really trying to introduce but rather impose itself on the target system; if on the contrary it is found to comply to TT norms, it is perceived as introducing to the target system a version of the original work along the lines of a pre-existing target system model (Toury, 1995:60-61). This approach seems more source- than target-system-oriented. A clear target-oriented approach would rather consider the translated text as an independent product, which may or may not reflect the structures of the source text/system (or any other text/system) but which, in any case, introduces itself into the target system, bearing all its individual traits, irrespective of whether they are actually contradictory, non-conforming, revolutionary or norm-resisting elements that deviate from the target system regularities.

If we try to relate Toury's notions of adequacy and acceptability to his other key-concept, that of equivalence, we might find that what Toury actually suggests is that 'adequacy' implies equivalence of TT and ST norms, whereas 'acceptability' entails equivalence of TT and target system norms. Following his own line of thinking, then, that "any deviation from that which is established as translation equivalence according to a certain set of norms implies non-equivalence relative to these very norms, but relative to them only" (Toury, 1980:69), we could also say that non-adequacy or non-acceptability is a matter related to the same norms that also designate adequacy or acceptability in the first place. We have already argued that equivalence to ST norms (i.e. adequacy) is of no importance to a study of target system norms since by definition this equivalence is taken as given (see sections 1.3.2 and 1.4.2). What is then left to pursue is a study of a TT's acceptability, as an aspect of conformity or deviation (i.e. equivalence or non-equivalence) to target system translational norms. The corresponding question that emerges from such consideration is 'acceptability to whom?', since within a cultural milieu there can be various parties with contrasting opinions (Du-Nour, 1995:339-340). To avoid a lengthy discussion of this issue, I propose to regard as the judging party of a TT's acceptability the party that also determines its (target system) function, namely its recipients (cf. Nord, 1991b:16).

1.5.2. Adequacy and acceptability in (audiovisual) translation

Toury links norms with adequacy and acceptability by stating that "it is norms which determine the actual position of a translation, or a certain corpus of translations, between adequacy and acceptability and the entire concept of literary translation pertinent for the group (whether textual or social) under study" (1980:50). The importance assigned to the norm that determines adequacy or acceptability is considered sufficient enough for Toury to call this norm 'initial' norm, influencing decisions on the level of lower (operational) norms (1978:90).

Along these lines, he believes that the notion of 'literary translation' can either refer to: a) the translation of texts that are regarded as 'literary' in the source culture, or (most important) b) the translation of texts in a way that a product is acceptable as 'literary' in the target/recipient culture (Toury, 1993a:13-14). He uses 'literary' texts simply as an example, expanding this two-fold distinction to other types/fields of written translation as well. The notion of 'legal translation', for example, can refer to either: a) the translation of documents regarded as legal in the source culture, or b) translated documents that are regarded as legal in the target culture (ibid). I would hesitate to apply this distinction to the notion of 'audiovisual translation', however. The presence of the accompanying visual element obliges 'audiovisual translation' to be always considered a translation of something accepted as audiovisual in both the source and the target systems/cultures. For example, a transcript of a film into a novel, or the other way round, cannot be called audiovisual translation. On the other hand, we can apply this notion to the translation of film genres/types, i.e. within the audiovisual mode, and talk for example about what can be regarded as a translation of a documentary, a comedy, a TV advertisement etc. from the point of view of the source or the target culture. Still, however, neither an adequate representation of an ST nor a fully acceptable version of it can guarantee that the TT will be received and enjoyed in the target system in the same way that its original was received and enjoyed in the source system.

When translating - and before the final formulation of the target product - we can only make assumptions relating to the impact of the text we are creating, based on certain assumptions of what is acceptable at the target end (cf. Toury, 1993a:16). Reconstructing the network of relationships of an ST in an adequate fashion might raise no problems of acceptability at all, for instance when source and target systems have had constant contacts (and as a result, similar literary traditions) or when the target system is weaker and aspiring to imitate the source system (ibid:13). Along these lines, one might wrongly consider subtitling as an attempt to achieve adequate audiovisual translation (respecting and maintaining SL and showing a weaker literary system, as e.g. in Northern European countries, the Low Countries and Greece), and revoicing as an attempt to achieve acceptable audiovisual translation (respecting, maintaining and emphasising TL and showing a stronger literary system, as e.g. in France, Spain, Italy and Germany). The position of Great Britain as a predominantly subtitling country, despite the fact that it enjoys a powerful literary tradition/system, as well as the expression of strong feelings in favour of revoicing in other countries with weaker literary traditions (as e.g. in Slovakia or the Czech Republic), proves that we cannot actually apply these notions of adequacy and acceptability to audiovisual translation.

Adequacy in particular, as a term that signifies a TT's equivalence to ST norms, is very problematic in audiovisual translation, since the constraints inherent in this mode do intervene significantly in shaping the translator's decisions. In addition to the constant presence of SL and SC elements in the background, subtitling poses spatiotemporal constraints and demands that have to be taken into account by the translator and which might eventually dictate the rendering of a linguistic/textual item in a way that the translator would not have otherwise chosen in, say, written translation. Similarly in dubbing, an 'equivalent' rendering of an ST item might be dictated by lip-sync constraints (if it is a close-up scene), resulting in a solution that differs significantly from what the translator might produce in cases other than close-ups.

Toury's preoccupation with the 'initial norm' and his strict distinction between adequacy and acceptability attracted a considerable amount of criticism. He admits that, in practice, the decision made between the two extremes of faithful adequacy and complete acceptability will generally be a compromise, "such as an adequate translation with certain reservations, or under certain conditions, deriving from the target norms" (Toury, 1978:89). Despite the above moderate formulation however, Hermans still criticises Toury because even this notion of an intermediary 'adequate/acceptable' translation is established on the basis of purely textual material and leads only to contradictions, since "the separation of textual relations from linguistic means betrays a mechanistic conception, as if secondary modelling systems are simply superimposed on the primary system, language" (Hermans, 1995:219).

In any case, the importance which is assigned to the 'initial norm' as bearing at least logical and chronological priority over the choice between adequacy and acceptability can be disputed since what all the agents involved in the process of formulating the translation product need to have in the first place is an a priori pre-conception of the recipients' awareness and interpretation *of existing target system norms*, given that it is these norms which will eventually determine the function of the final translation product.

1.6 The evolution of norms and systems

Any scientific approach to social behaviour has to recognise the functional role of norms as factors ensuring the establishment and retention of social order (Toury, 1978:84). Synchronically, the borderlines between rules/laws, norms and idiosyncrasies are always diffuse; diachronically, each type of constraint shifts along this scale in phases of rise and decline, with idiosyncrasies occasionally becoming normative and norms sometimes showing rule-like strength and rigidity (ibid; Toury, 1995:54). It is exactly this constant fluctuation that makes it essential to pinpoint such constraints synchronically before investigating their diachronic dimension and evolution.

The notion of norm implies that in a certain situation an agent is prompted to act according to a specific, pre-established pattern, sometimes even when acting according to the norm might conflict with the agent's own needs and interests (Ross, 1968:85). This happens because the agent develops a particular kind of 'compulsion', not stemming from the threat of external sanctions as much as from an internal binding force that ties him/her to the patterned type of behaviour (ibid). This binding force is verbalised by 'deontic phraseology' (e.g. it is right, I ought, etc.) that reflects a prescriptive kind of psychological influence of the norm on its subjects/agents. A study of norms from the point of view of the subjects/agents might run the risk of empathising with the protagonists so much that our study is driven towards a prescriptive rather than descriptive viewpoint. A focused study of the manifestation of the norms as they appear through the specific behavioural patterns/products, however, will help us avoid this underlying danger. The statement that a norm/directive has some objective validity might then be justified. However, this is not the same as claiming that it is a 'true' norm/directive, because one may accept the truth of the statement but at the same time reject the validity of the directive by not feeling eventually obliged to act according to it (ibid:103-104). In this respect, then, a norm is a formulation that can be challenged. Since the truth value does not belong to the norm/directive itself but to its proposition or a statement of it, disregarding the truth value would imply doing something 'unacceptable', 'wrong' or 'incomprehensible' but by no means 'forbidden' or 'illegal'. Validity does not exist a priori but through experiences of the norm (ibid:104). Thus, a challenge to a norm is not an abstract challenge to its validity, but a challenge to the experience of its validity as patterned social behaviour. Such a challenge does not necessarily have to be considered an instance of illegal action per se but simply a *deviation* from the respective patterned behaviour.

Once a norm is formulated, it functions as a piece of knowledge that can be passed on to various agents as a suggested pattern of behaviour; an activity that contradicts this pattern, then, always constitutes a conscious deed, with the subject being aware of the fact that s/he is deviating (Toury, 1993b:35). Accordingly, a translated text does not ipso facto conform to target norms and expectations, but sometimes it is deliberately marked with the intention of expressing other (source culture) features (Vermeer, 1989:185). Not all translators/agents are passive consumers of their target system's norms; many help in shaping the process by intervening in the 'natural' course of events and diverting it according to their own preferences through their actual translation work and translation criticism, or translation ideology as expressed in translation-training institutions (Toury, 1995:62). The possible mismatch between existing norms and their scholarly verbal formulations underlines exactly this desire to control behaviour, i.e. to dictate norms rather than merely account for them (ibid:55).

Quite often, there will be a price to pay for any deviant instances of behaviour (ibid). These instances may result in significant changes in the target system; the question is who is allowed to introduce these changes and under what circumstances (ibid:64). The fact that some acknowledged translators may continue to produce texts in full accordance with the norms and models that dominate the core of the literary system but gradually fail to maintain their prestige proves that it is not through their texts that translators acquire their status (Even-Zohar, 1990:20). Systems are constant battlefields of relative power and control. If control can be achieved only by change and innovation, this will become the translators' guiding principle (ibid:22). On the other hand perpetuation ensures an agent's already acquired status. Somebody else's attempts at innovation, however, might manage to overthrow the agent's position. Once a takeover finally occurs the new controller might even reject the totality of his/her predecessor's repertoire and therefore dethrone not just the previous products/texts as potential textual norms/models but also the agent's persona as a (formerly) acknowledged translator.

Toury suggests that a translator can be seen as having "*gained* a position, which allows him to deviate from target norms and conventions and get away with it, sometimes even introducing changes into the target system itself" (1993a:13) [my italics]. But the problem that remains is: how do we know if the translator has gained this position beforehand? Or do we simply recognise and acknowledge this position after the system's reception and reaction to these deviations? In cases of deviation from the norm of subtitling in Greece we can list as possible influencing factors: a) the oligopoly-based structure of the local film translation industry which facilitates norm control, b) the financial independence of Greek National Television (ET1), as well as its pioneering research status, c) the recipients' inevitable contact with and influence by dubbing cultures through the (free) provision of satellite TV channels in various areas around Greece, d) the fascination with the initiation of something new and different, especially if it is accompanied with high quality performance, e) the gradual accustoming of the audience into using their hearing sense (instead of their vision) when attending other types of revoiced (instead of subtitled) TV programmes, i.e. voiced-over documentaries. This list shows that the range of factors involved are so complex and highly versatile that the reasons for instances of deviation cannot be simply credited to the persona of the translator.

What should be stressed as a conclusion is that it is quite likely that translations might deviate from the norms and the sanctioned patterns of the target system, for which they are designed to cater, and "it is not unusual for a certain amount of deviance to be regarded not only as *justifiable*, or even *acceptable*, but as actually *preferable* to complete *normality*" (Toury, 1995:28). Considering translated literature as simply a part of the larger home literary polysystem, Even-Zohar suggests that the peripherality of the former results in instances of translational conservatism, observing that "while the contemporary original literature might go on developing new norms and models, translated literature adheres itself to norms which have been either recently or long before rejected by the (newly) established centre" (1987:111); by contrast, if the position of translated literature is central to the larger polysystem, the emergence of new translational models is more frequent and expected (ibid:109). In either case, however:

> "new and innovative elements in the existing codified system is what causes a literary system to evolve. Throughout history, competing literary subsystems are constantly challenging and infiltrating higher orders and then resolving, so the entire system evolves in a systematically 'unsystematic' fashion" (Gentzler, 1993:116).

It is interesting to note that the evolution of something well-organised and established, as for example a system or a norm, is achieved by a deconstruction of its constituents. The progress of something systematic becomes the negation of its systematicity. As a result, the notion of system may indirectly imply conservatism and stability. Dynamic evolution in a system is characterised by a potential of self re-evaluation. It is very plausible to assume, then, that secondary polysystems where translated literature occupies a more central position will be more dynamic. The long-term survival of a polysystem can then be said to be a function of its ability to remain open to external influences and new ideas.

Even-Zohar uses the term 'transfer' to refer to this process of integration of new and imported goods and ideas into the home repertoire (1996a:4). In general, the inevitable transfer that results from constant contact with other norms and systems depends on the cultural promptness ('openness/readiness') of the target system (Even-Zohar, 1990:93). However, it is not just the target system's 'good intentions' or openness that will determine the adoption of non-canonical items: parameters such as "the nature of stratification (whether it is 'developed' or not), the age of the system (whether it is 'young' or 'old'/'established'), as well as the volume ('richness') of the repertoire available" (ibid:92) play a very significant role. Interference with another activity, then, within or outside the target system becomes the major source for supplying the means for change and innovation.

Once canonicity has been established, it runs the risk of stagnation and petrification, unless challenged by a non-canonised system/item (Even-Zohar, 1990:16). Although this constant battle might give the impression that it is in the interest of a system to be always unstable, one should not confuse the notions of 'instability' with 'change', just as one should not confuse 'stability' with 'petrification' (ibid:26). In this sense, 'instability of the norms of the system' does not mean 'instability of the system' but 'non-stagnation of the system'. The force of this dynamics is clearly explained by Even-Zohar when he claims that:

> "a system which is incapable of maintaining itself over a period of time and is often on the verge of collapse is, from the functional point of view, *un*stable; while a system undergoing permanent, steady, and well-controlled change may adequately be considered stable simply because it perseveres. It is not such stable systems which manage to *survive*, while others simply perish.(...) The system may be endangered only when the change becomes uncontrollable and hence unmanageable" (1990:26).

A set of normative formulations is actually a pre-condition for any system to be recognised as distinct and separate from other (neighbouring) systems. If we consider canonicity as a network of relations rather than a rigid development, we can also allow for normative oscillations within a system to be considered as perfectly 'systemic' rather than attempts for its demolition (ibid:88). The struggle between central and peripheral options and between high and low levels within the same system, then, becomes crucial for the system's own evolution and existence.

1.7 Summary

Norms are aspects of general human behaviour and not of translation alone. They represent values and ideas that are shared by a community as to what is right and what is wrong, what is accepted and what is rejected, what is customary and what is pioneering. They lie between absolute objective rules/laws and subjective idiosyncrasies. Conventions are normative formulations that have not yet acquired the social status of a norm; the fuzzy distinction between norms and conventions, however, suggests that we might reasonably treat them as synonymous.

In terms of strength, norms in general can be 'basic'/'primary' (i.e. mandatory), express 'secondary' tendencies, or other 'tolerated'/'permitted' behaviour. Translational norms can be classified above the level of texts into 'preliminary', 'constitutive' and 'expectancy' norms that deal with the broader framework of general translational attitudes; below the text-level they can be classified into 'operational', 'regulative' and 'professional' norms that deal with macro and micro-structural textual strategies.

What characterises norms is the underlying coherent and systematic pattern of behaviour. It is through this concept of sameness that we can determine what is different or mutant. A norm can be seen as the systematic constellation of a series of factors that lead to the emergence of a coherent behavioural pattern. On the other hand, a system can be seen as the cumulative assemblance of all the norms that operate in it. As a result, one could deduce that norms and systems presuppose and overlap with each other. A clear distinction between the various systems as hierarchically ordered and stratified levels is therefore essential for tracing the exact domain of a norm and the subsequent range of its influence.

The levels of the stratified norms constitute and are determined by the nature of two main parameters that are involved in their eventual function: the subject/agent and the situation. One can trace an existing translational norm through direct normative formulations of deontic phraseology, or indirectly, as it is manifested through translated texts. In both cases, quantitative analysis must be accompanied by qualitative analysis. Texts should be examined within their genre and translational mode, the role of the agents should not be minimised to the persona of translator and significant attention should be paid to the recipients' feedback.

When investigating translational norms it is not the hypothetical potential equivalence between the source and target text that is of importance; this will be eventually achieved (and expressed) by the translator, in some form and to some extent. The information required in a study of translational norms relates to the reception and consumption of the manifestation of this translational equivalence, i.e. the precise function of the target text in the target system. As a result, a study of translational norms should not occupy itself with questions of adequacy and acceptability or with the relationship of the TT to the source text or system; it should clearly deal with conformity to or deviation from target system normative regulations. The reproduction of certain ST features in the TT occurs because these features are assigned importance by the target system. Thus, deviation from or conformity to translational norms is a question of what the target system is willing to accept, modify or reject. The position and the value of a norm relate to the position this norm (and the products that express it) have managed to acquire within the target system. The constraints or elements that characterise the ST and signify deviation from or conformity to the norms of the source system cannot tell us anything about the translated text's performance in the target system, i.e. about its own deviation from or conformity to target norms. We simply have to take all the linguistic and literary data/elements of the ST as given and focus our study on how they are revealed in the translated text, in the target system. The status and the position of the source text and system may thus favour or even activate resistance or submission to a dominant set of norms in the target system; however, they remain indifferent to which of these norms will finally prevail.

If we think of a norm as a piece of knowledge that can be passed on to various agents as a suggested pattern of behaviour, an activity that contradicts or deviates from this pattern constitutes a conscious and deliberate deed. Although a certain amount of deviance can sometimes be justifiable, acceptable, or even preferable to complete normality, more often than not there is a price to pay for any deviant instances of behaviour. It is interesting to note, however, that it is new and innovative elements that cause systems - and therefore the norms that constitute them - to evolve; the progress of something systematic becomes the negation of its systematicity. Systems, by nature, tend to favour inertia, stability and conservatism; a static set of normative formulations actually constitutes a precondition for any system to be considered as such. When the static system starts becoming stagnant or petrified, however, it starts losing its power of re-evaluation and dynamic evolution. In order to account for oscillations within a system as perfectly systemic, therefore, we have to view canonicity as a flexible network of relationships rather than a rigid development.

2. TOWARDS A SYSTEMATIC INVESTIGATION OF NORMS IN AUDIOVISUAL TRANSLATION

2.1 The construction of a methodology

2.1.1 The communicative framework

Like any other use of language, translation can be considered an act of interpersonal communication. The translated text is the means by which the communication is made possible. If we accept the text as the totality of the semiotic signals employed for the formulation of some message, then we can think of a wide range of semiotic elements that might accompany the verbal/linguistic ones (cf. Nord, 1991b:14-15).

Audiovisual translation is an unusual type of communicative interaction. It employs target linguistic signals to accompany other source aural and visual semiotic elements. Quite often, these aural and visual elements are so characteristic of the source culture, or rather so un-characteristic of the target culture, that a translator finds it hard to adapt the target linguistic message to them. Although s/he might be able to manipulate and recreate the verbal part of the source message, s/he cannot normally interfere with the rest of the accompanying semiotic elements (Ascheid, 1997:32). Non-verbal elements like facial expressions, intonation and gestures can be crucial parameters that determine the choice of the linguistic signals the translator will implement. Written rendering (subtitling) will treat these non-verbal signals differently from oral rendering (revoicing); subtitling will have to respect them and build the linguistic message on them, whereas revoicing will erase the source aural elements and create a new set of target aural elements to constitute the oral/verbal message. In this sense of 'text' as only a partial carrier of the communicative message, the role of the audiovisual translator is considerably restricted. When investigating the norms that govern the rendering of the audiovisual source message in a target context one could regard non-verbal elements as belonging to the source system/culture only. Any distinction which disregards the presence of the accompanying audiovisual non-verbal parameters and focuses on the rendering of the verbal elements only - as *written or spoken* target texts – is clearly dubious (cf. Hatim & Mason, 1997:82).

Nord views translation as a process of intercultural communication which involves two distinct parts: that of ST production in a source communicative situation, and that of TT production in a target communicative situation (1991b:7). The integration of the accompanying source (verbal and non-verbal) semiotic elements in the new verbal target text, so that the final product is a mixture of directly adopted and freshly invented elements which nevertheless comprise a brand new individual target product, allows us to deal exclusively with the target communicative situation and the manipulation of the target message strictly within this target communicative framework, even when investigating the special mode of audiovisual translation (see also section 2.2.2).

Since a product-function is determined by the situation in which it serves as an instrument of communication, the translating instructions should contain as much information as possible about the situational factors of the prospective target-product reception as well as its production (ibid:9). Treating the target-product as an instance of communicative interaction, then, would inevitably require an analysis of the participants involved in the communication act and of their separate roles in their particular target-situational dimension (ibid:15). In this sense, translation constitutes communicative social behaviour that requires interaction and coordination between all the parameters involved (Hermans, 1996:29). Based on Jakobson's well-known scheme of communication and language, Even-Zohar (1990:31) produced a diagram with the factors and the agents involved in a literary polysystem, of which translation is thought to be an integral part (the terms in square brackets correspond to Jakobson's original communicative terms):

INSTITUTION [context]
REPERTOIRE [code]
PRODUCER [addresser]----------------------[addressee] CONSUMER
('writer') ('reader')
MARKET [contact/channel]
PRODUCT [message]

The above model constitutes a very efficient attempt to represent the situational parameters involved in the general translation process. Therefore, it could serve as the starting point for developing a model which might allow us to investigate the particular situational parameters of the norms which operate within audiovisual translation as well.

2.1.2 A model for the investigation of norms in audiovisual translation

The fact that interference and interaction play an important role in the evolution of systems suggests that the model for investigating norms in audiovisual translation should also allow for interference and interaction between the elements which constitute the system (which I call factors) and the levels at which these elements/factors operate (see also section 2.3.1). The relationship between the *factors* is one of mutual interdependency (cf. Even-Zohar, 1990:34). The relationship between the *levels* of the system, however, is one of hierarchical stratification, since a norm might derive from a higher level and reflect a more general phenomenon rather than be restricted to the situation where we first discovered it. In the model below, then, there is equality and free-flow between each of the factors that are listed in vertical columns, whereas there is hierarchy and dependence on the immediate superordinate between the horizontally stratified levels. A schematic representation of the model for the investigation of norms in audiovisual (AV) translation might look as follows:

Table 2.1.2.1 Audiovisual Translation as a Target Literary System

LEVELS	FACTORS			
	HUMAN AGENTS	**PRODUCTS**	**RECI-PIENTS**	**AUDIO-VISUAL MODE**
UPPER	Attitude of agents (commissioners, translators etc.) towards the translation of literary products in general	Realisation of all kinds of translation products in general	Attitude of recipients (the public) towards translation products in general	Relation between AV media and other types of literary media (as perceived within the target culture)
MIDDLE	Attitude of AV translation agents (commissioners, translators, spotters etc.) towards overall AV translation	Realisation of overall AV translation products (within all film types and genres)	Attitude of recipients (viewers) towards overall AV translation products	Relation between the 3 AV media: TV, video and cinema (as perceived within the target culture)
LOWER	Status and attitude of a particular AV translation-product's agents (commissioners, translators, spotters etc.) towards the particular AV translation product	Status and function of a particular AV translation product (within its own film type and genre)	Status and attitude of a particular AV translation-product's target audience	Status and function of a particular AV translation product's medium, film type and genre (as perceived within the target culture)

2.2. The factors of the model/system

2.2.1. Human agents

Even-Zohar uses the term 'producers' for what I call 'human agents'. A producer is "an actor, is an individual who produces, by actively operating a repertoire, either repetitively producible, or 'new' products" (Even-Zohar, 1990:18). In the case of audiovisual translation, a number of people are involved in the production of either subtitled or revoiced film-versions: spotters, time-coders, adapters, dubbing directors, dubbing actors, sound technicians, video experts, proof-reading post-editors, translation commissioners, film distributors and finally the translator him/herself (cf. Luyken et al., 1991:92&97; Dries, 1995a:12&27; Zabalbeascoa, 1996:249). The translator is the one who suggests the linguistic semiotic signals of the target product; a number of other individuals though intervene in a number of ways and contribute to the final shape of the translation product. In this respect, the term 'producers' is preferable to 'writers' (cf. Even-Zohar, 1990:34), but it still does not provide us with an accurate picture of the variety of people and the extent of the activities involved.

We might describe the role of human agents in an investigation of norms in audiovisual translation as follows: these are the people who will try to conform to (or deviate from) the norms. In some cases, they do not operate individually but rather as interrelated separately organised groups (Even-Zohar, 1990:35). The final product, which is the accumulation of their normative behaviour, will have to be promoted by the market, accepted by the consumers and finally adopted by the institution. In this sense, their contribution to any kind of change or evolution in the system is not immediately signalled by the launching of their product, i.e. by the instant performance of their translational normative behaviour. As creators of the translation products, however, they play a vital role, since it is their ideas that will eventually support the perpetuation or trigger the modification of the already existing normative patterns.

Unfortunately, it is not always possible to identify all human agents involved within a particular translation product. They may be dead, unknown or it may not be possible to trace or contact them. Nevertheless, the investigation of norms in audiovisual translation cannot afford to ignore the role of human agents. In some cases, the researcher will have to rely on 'guessing' the status and attitude of the particular human agents involved (Nord, 1991b:16); this will not invalidate the research but it will certainly restrict the conditions under which the results may be seen as valid.

2.2.2 Products

Even-Zohar uses the term 'products' to refer to "any performed (or performable) set of signs and/or materials, i.e. including a given 'behaviour" (1990:43; 1997:15). In this respect, "any outcome of any activity whatsoever can be considered 'a product', whatever its ontological manifestation may be" (Even-Zohar, 1990:43). Texts are the conspicuous outcomes of translational behaviour. Even-Zohar's definition, however, allows for many more 'products', in addition to texts; writers, for example, may also be considered 'products' within this framework (cf. Even-Zohar, 1997:17).

The notion of the translation 'product' in audiovisual translation is somewhat problematic. One could regard as translational product only the translated verbal content of the film, in the final form it has when it reaches the target system audience. On the other hand, one might include the whole film in the definition of translational audiovisual product despite the fact that the whole film is not the product of the translational act. When transferring the textual part of an AV product, the visual and aural background are constraints that have to be constantly taken into account and that shape the final verbal product. These were given by the source product/system, and the human agents involved in audiovisual translation can do nothing about them[i]. Aural and visual background are factors that could even determine the specificity of the mode, i.e. the choice between subtitling and revoicing. These aural and visual factors cannot be reshaped or manipulated to fit in the intended target text, but the target text has to be reshaped and manipulated in order to fit in with them. Even when the vocal tracks of the original aural element are erased, as in the case of dubbing, the text is still constrained by the visual element. And when the original vocal track of the aural element is turned down, as in the case of voice-over, the length of the target text and the choice of the first words of each target utterance are still constrained by what already existed in the source product. These are features that are intrinsic to audiovisual translation and the human agents involved in the translation process can do nothing about them. They are parameters of primary importance and have to be taken into serious consideration. One might argue that they do not constitute part of the 'translation product' and therefore cannot be called as such, simply because nobody involved in the translation process actually *produces* them; along these lines, the terms 'product' and (translated/target) 'text' could be used interchangeably. Such a distinction, however, does not seem to be recognised in the scholarly literature on audiovisual language transfer. The term 'translation product' has been established to account for the totality of the audiovisual aspects which accompany the text that has been transferred in the TL (Whitman-Linsen, 1992:125). This makes considerable sense since, although aural and visual parameters are borrowed from the source product and are simply carried over, they represent parameters that determine to a large extent the function of the whole film - including its textual side - as the final product that enters the target system. It is obvious that subtitles cannot exist on their own, outside the (audio)visual frame; similarly, a revoiced text cannot function as such outside its (audio)visual frame. I can see no alternative, then, but to consider as translation 'product' not simply the transferred text but the totality of

---

[i] In cases where whole film frames are reshot and added to the original film, we are no longer talking about translation but about film production, exiting the translation process and entering the film-making system.

the semiotic elements that are interwoven with this text, i.e. the whole audiovisual product as it is released in the target system.

From this perspective, "new modes of language use may be imported with groups of texts which embody recurring models and/or are translated in a similar fashion" (Toury, 1993a:10). The regularity of structural features, however, allows us to analyse and classify products not simply individually but also as parts of larger literary models (cf. ibid:11; Even-Zohar, 1990:44). Moreover, they have to be examined not just as TL-products in general, but as translations into this TL, and therefore as parts of the respective (translational) sub-system (cf. Toury, 1995:36). Thus, the making of canonised products will involve struggles within these sub-systems. Even-Zohar (1990:86) believes that these struggles are already conducted between possible 'options'/'models'; the launching of concrete products into the market is actually a result of the battle between potential options and the final product, whose eventual form may or may not conform to the already existing models that reflect the normative pattern. One however cannot possibly know or learn anything about this struggle between 'potential options' as such. We can only study the concrete products which manifest the choice of the one or the other (set of) norms or idiosyncrasies. The investigation of translational products can give us access only to this area of norms that reflects concrete existing choices and not possible intended options.

Even-Zohar believes that any product is part of the repertoire of its hosting system, and products cannot be created without a repertoire (1990:15). He analyses the structure of the repertoire as operating on two distinct levels: a) on the level of 'individual elements', which includes single disparate items, like e.g. morphemes or lexemes, and b) on the level of 'models', which are combinations of elements, rules and the syntagmatic relations that can be imposed on the product (1997:6-7)[i]. The importance he assigns to the second level of 'models' is twofold: from the point of view of the producer, it is the frame that

---

[i] In his earlier works (1990:41) he also refers to an intermediate level of 'syntagms' that includes any combinations of individual elements up to the level of the sentence.

guides the choices on the lower level of individual elements (ibid:6); from the point of the recipients, it comprises the presuppositions which aid the consumption and interpretation of a given text (1990:41). Although Even-Zohar claims that a classification according to the level of the 'model' would not be useful since there can be models for the whole text or just for segments of it (1990:41; 1997:8), a classification according to the various existing textual models, i.e. the text genres, is essential exactly for the reasons that he himself has recognised above, namely that these models guide both the production and the consumption of texts. In this respect, a genre may be identified as a constellation of features common to a number of products or it may be accepted as such simply because it is perceived as a 'genre' by the receiving community. The importance of studying a translation product as a member of a general genre is reflected in the number of normative studies that were conducted within this perspective (Du-Nour, 1995; Puurtinnen, 1989; Robyns, 1990). In any target system, translation products are the outcome of the process of normative canonisation; it is only through their function as members of a representative genre that we can perceive a deviation from or a conformity to this process of normative canonisation.

The notion of 'genres' in audiovisual translation as well as in film studies, however, is problematic since it is often confused with the notion of 'film types'. A distinction between the two terms/notions would place 'genres' within the category of 'film types'. In this respect, the term 'film types' is more generic whereas the term 'genres' is more specific. Science fiction, western, detective or thriller, for example, are all different 'genres' within the 'film type' of movies. Similarly soap operas, mystery or comedy can all be 'genres' within the 'film type' of series/serials, historic or geographic can be 'genres' within the 'film type' of documentaries, and games and guest-panel interviews can be 'genres' within the 'film type' of light entertainment (see also section 3.4.1). When I propose a study of audiovisual translation products within their own genres, then, I propose a study of the same products within the framework of their respective film types as well.

2.2.3. Recipients

The whole idea behind conventions relies on a set of mutual expectations: human agents act in certain ways because they expect that, in a given situation, other people expect them to do so (Chesterman, 1993:10; Hermans, 1996:30). The agents' and the recipients' expectations may not coincide, nor even be compatible (Nord, 1991b:16), which highlights the importance of investigating these expectations not just from the point of view of the human agents (see section 2.2.1) but from the point of view of the recipients too.

Willingly or unwillingly, we all become everyday recipients of a massive amount of literary material which nowadays, because of the impact of audiovisual media, is primarily of an audiovisual nature. Even-Zohar uses the term 'consumers' to refer to this notion of recipients. A 'consumer' is "an individual who handles a ready-made product by passively operating a repertoire" (Even-Zohar, 1997:20). Although each one of the consumers has individual characteristics, views and opinions, it is their collective profile that is of primary importance since "the aggregate of consumers is not an additive group of individuals, but a relative network of power which can determine the fate of a product" (ibid:21). The totality of the community as recipients is often designated as 'the public' (Even-Zohar, 1990:37). It is very rare, however, that a (translation) product is targeted at 'the public'; in the majority of cases, when the human agents are in the process of creating their product, they do not have in mind the expectations of 'the public' but the expectations of just, or primarily, a slice of it: that group of the consumers that their product is aimed at. In this respect, by 'recipients' I do not mean the totality of the people who just *happen* to have received the product, but that group of the general public that have consciously consumed the product and to which the target product is addressed, unless otherwise stated.

2.2.4 Audiovisual mode

Cattrysse's (1992) research into film (adaptation) as translation demonstrates the interrelation between film narrative and novel narrative[i] by proving the independent status of the film narrative in comparison to novel/prose narrative: film adaptations might give credit to the written text that inspired them but most of the time they are presented as autonomous works (Cattrysse, 1992:58). When the narrative conventions of the written text are not compatible with filmic conventions, it is the former that have to fit the standards of the latter and not the other way round (ibid:59). This survey shows that even on plain textual/narrative ground, the status of audiovisual texts is independent from what might constitute general literary material (e.g. prose, poetry, drama, even technical and specialised material); on the other hand it is still connected and constitutes part of it. As a result it is influenced by (and influences) all the other parts of general literary material through a kind of mutual interaction and transfer procedures. Even-Zohar suggests that:

> "in a target system *B*, either within the same polysystem or in a different polysystem - depending on whether it is stable or in crisis, and whether it is strong or weak, vis-à-vis a source system *A* - a target text *b* will be produced according to the transfer procedures plus the constraints imposed upon them by the intra-target-polysystem relations, both governing and governed by the target-polysystem repertoire of existing and non-existing functions" (1990:78).

The broad appeal of audiovisual media (TV, cinema, video) for the public implies that the translated versions of imported audiovisual products will be addressing a large percentage of the target community, compared to other modes of literary translation (e.g. written translation), especially in countries with no significant original audiovisual production. The fact that television has become a part of our everyday lives shows the impact that TV productions - at least - have on our personalities. Daily quotes or catchphrases often come from popular films and advertisements. Instead of staying in and

---

[i] His results come form a comparative research between the particular filmic genre of 'film noir' and the respective literary genre of detective novels.

reading a book, one is now more likely to go to the movies or watch a videotape. Therefore, it is not just the text (as a product) or its accompanying audiovisual medium (as the message carrier) that people have lately acquired but a whole new social ritual. As Even-Zohar claims, people "often consume the socio-cultural function of the acts involved with the activity in question (sometimes taking the overt shape of a 'happening') rather than what is meant to be 'the product'" (1990:36). From this perspective, the need to study the audiovisual mode not just separately from the other literary modes, but also according to the individual medium, film type and genre becomes essential.

The fluidity between the three major audiovisual media of a) cinema, b) television, and c) video makes a clear-cut distinction between respective productions rather difficult to maintain: cinema films can be transferred to video tape, video productions can be made into cinema films, and television can equally transmit live, filmed or video-taped material (Armes, 1988: 116). In addition, the presence and use of a pre- or post-production script as the basis for textual transfer for most cinema, television and video productions (ibid:117) might discourage an individual separation between the three media and encourage a holistic view of the audiovisual mode as a literary field. Since, however, our interpretation of and our involvement in the audiovisual material which is offered to us depends to a large extent on the viewing context, we can clearly distinguish between the cinema-goers, the television-spectators and the video-viewers (ibid:139). This classification of the recipients according to the medium that carries the product suggests that individual audiovisual productions are specifically conceived, shaped (and also translated) in order to serve the needs and the demands of the specific medium/carrier, with its own social viewing parameters (cf. Ivarsson, 1992:83).

Similarly, just as written translation products are conceived, shaped and received within the framework of their genre, so are audiovisual translation products within the framework of their particular film type and genre. The translation of the textual/linguistic part of an audiovisual product is determined by the function of the particular film-type, namely whether it is intended to entertain its recipients, inform its recipients or promote a commercial product. In addition, it is determined by the emphasis it puts on the visual-and-aural elements vs. the textual/linguistic ones, namely whether in the particular audiovisual production it is the people/action or the language/dialogues that are central (cf. Luyken et al., 1991:130-135; Nedergaard-Larsen, 1993:221). Last but not least, it is determined by the length of the film-product (short vs. long productions, self-contained vs. serialised productions). As a result, every audiovisual translation product has to be examined and classified along the lines of all these parameters which, in turn, will have to be independently studied and carefully understood as specific determinants of the audiovisual mode of the product.

Hermans points out the need to study the norms of particular 'domains of translation' individually rather than collectively (1996:39). Audiovisual translation constitutes one of these domains. Even-Zohar uses the term 'repertoire' to refer to "the aggregate of rules and materials which govern both the making and handling, or production and consumption, of any given product" (1990:39; 1997:3). Instead of applying this broad notion of rules and materials to the whole range of factors that intervene in the construction of a target product, however, Even-Zohar seems to restrict it to a linguistic level and by 'repertoire' actually imply the combination of 'grammar' and 'lexicon' (1990:39). He accepts that "the nature, volume and amplitude of a repertoire certainly determines the ease and freedom with which a producer and/or consumer may move around in the sociocultural environment" (1990:40; 1997:4), but he refuses to identify 'repertoire' with 'culture'. I agree that such an identification would be over-generalising. In a stricter sense, however, we could identify the audiovisual mode with (a type of) 'repertoire'. The audiovisual mode as a kind of repertoire can be seen as the framework into which all the intervening and interacting factors are seen to operate. This framework provides the features that distinguish audiovisual translation from other types/modes of translation. The audiovisual mode as a kind of repertoire, then, is not a passive, static pool of already formulated norms but rather a dynamic system which actively engages in the formulation of norms and provides the background against which we can measure and compare them. The audiovisual mode/repertoire is the aggregate of rules, items and interrelations with which a specific audiovisual text is produced and understood (cf. Even-Zohar, 1990:40), therefore comprising not just linguistic but also sociocultural elements.

Greece is one of those countries which do not resist borrowing from the outside and quite often try to copy foreign elements and attitudes in areas in which they think they lag behind (cf. Even-Zohar, 1990:64). In the international film industry, on the other hand, only a few large companies control the majority of (original) audiovisual productions and, because of the impact of audiovisual media on our everyday lives, these companies actually shape with their products fundamental aspects of human life (cf. Even-Zohar, 1996a:7). Especially in the case of Greece, then, where cultural invasion through foreign audiovisual products is inevitable, the separate study of the audiovisual mode, as an individual framework for the translation of these foreign products, seems to be particularly important.

2.2.5 Institution and the market

In his schematic representation of the factors involved in the act of translation, Even-Zohar incorporates another two aspects: the 'institution' and the 'market'. By 'institution' he means "the aggregate of factors involved with the maintenance of literature as a socio-cultural activity" (1990:37); it consists of critics, publishing houses, mass-media people, government bodies, academics etc. (ibid). The 'institution' controls a system's literary culture by controlling the norms that operate in it (1997:21). Normally, then, it is engaged in the perpetuation of a pattern of behaviour, only occasionally supporting agents who promote changes in the existing repertoire (ibid:22).

By 'market' he means "the aggregate of factors involved with the selling and buying of literary products and with the promotion of types of consumption" (1990:38; 1997:23); it consists of merchandising institutions like bookshops, libraries etc. What actually constitutes the 'market' is the whole network of consumers (1997:21).

Both the 'institution' and the 'market' stand outside the actual production of translation as they are not the agents who actually produce the target text. They influence, however, both the agents/text-producers and the recipients/text-consumers by formulating their mutual expectations and presuppositions. Both the 'institution' and the 'market' mediate the production of translated texts by intervening at different stages: the 'institution' intervenes at the pre-production stage by reflecting previous post-consumption established opinions; the 'market', on the other hand, intervenes at the post-production stage by placing a pre-consumption filter. The translation agents will have to hypothetically visualise both these roles before creating the actual text. The norms that will finally be chosen will be manifested through the texts/products.

In any case, those who constitute the 'institution' and the 'market' can be at a certain stage both (real or imaginary) recipients of the translated products or (real or imaginary) agents. As Even-Zohar points out, on the one hand "although any person-in-the-culture is normally both a producer and a consumer, the knowledge and skills required for production are not identical to those required for consumption" (1997:20); on the other hand, however, "in the socio-cultural reality, factors of the cultural institution and those of the market may naturally intersect in the same space" (1994:23; 1997:24). In this respect, I do not believe it would be useful to attempt a clear-cut identification of the 'institution' and the 'market' with either of the sectors of 'agents' or 'recipients'. Since members of both sides could function in a variety of ways according to the situation they are in and our point of view towards it, it is less confusing and more feasible to treat members of the 'institution' or the 'market' according to their occasional role/status as either agents or recipients.

2.3. The function of the model/system

2.3.1. The system as an aggregate of heterogeneous factors

Even-Zohar uses the term 'system' to refer to the:

> "network of *relations* which can be hypothesised for an aggregate of *factors* assumed to be involved with a socio-cultural activity, and consequently that activity itself observed via the network. Or, alternatively, the complex of activities, or any *section* thereof, for which systemic relations can be hypothesised" (1990:85) [my italics].

The above definition is quite satisfactory for the system/model I propose as well, provided that the 'factors', the 'sections' and the 'relations' that operate in the system are adequately specified. One has to define the system he is working on, in order to pinpoint the set of norms that operate in it and the factors that are involved in their production. I propose to investigate audiovisual translation as a target literary system. Intra-systemic interference involves relations between the general literary and the audiovisual mode as well as relations between translations and original productions within the target framework. In order to maintain a coherent structure in my system, then, I propose to call the vertical columns of the system 'factors' and its horizontal rows 'levels' (for Even-Zohar's general notion of 'sections', since 'levels' is both a more widely applied term in model structures and presupposes hierarchical order).

I believe Vanderauwera is right to claim that "literature does not work as a mechanism whose actions can be predicted on the basis of given constraints and coordinates" (1985:9). Within a socio-cultural context, however, all actions can be considered: a) part of a respective system, and b) governed by the norms that operate in this system. In other words, the launching of a translated film-product will be both governed by the norms of the target system and constitute/reflect part of it. Norms as patterned activities are by definition systemic. Systems (or systemic relations), therefore, can be thought of not simply as a prerequisite to norms but as actually constituting (sets of) norms. Systems shape their norms and norms shape their systems. It is not unreasonable to argue, then, that (poly)systems *are* actually the (sets of) norms that constitute them and that norms in turn reflect the (poly)system that hosts them (see also section 1.2.1).

Considering that the totality of norms constitutes the polysystem, one could think of one norm constituting a micro-system or a sub-system. Equally, the relations and the functions of this micro/sub-system can be thought of as constituting one norm. As a result, the emergence of a new norm implies the emergence of a new system as a newly established set of relationships. The size and the superordinacy of a norm is associated with the size and the superordinacy of the system. My definition of a 'system', then, is rather closer to that of a 'polysystem', and my definition of a 'micro/sub-system' is closer to that of a 'system'. Since "there is no property relatable to the 'polysystem' which could not, as such, be related to the 'system'" (Even-Zohar, 1990:12, footnote) the term 'system' can be equally interchangeable with the term 'polysystem' "if by 'system' one is prepared to understand both the idea of a closed set-of-relations, in which the members receive their values through their respective oppositions, *and* the idea of an open structure consisting of several such concurrent nets-of-relations" (ibid). I will then apply the term 'system' to refer to what Even-Zohar might also call a 'polysystem' and the term 'micro-system' to refer to something smaller and more concrete that constitutes part of the broader 'system'.

2.3.2. The system as a compilation of stratified levels

If we consider a system as an aggregate of heterogeneous subsystems and therefore as an aggregate of (sets of) norms that operate in it, it is necessary to start searching for the type of relationship that exists between these subsystems. Every subsystem has its own centre and its own periphery. By means of constant interference, the centre of a subsystem can dominate the centre of a neighbouring subsystem. The choice of the items to be transferred through the borders of the various subsystems is made according to the prestige and the relative dominance of (the centre) of one subsystem over the other (cf. Even-Zohar, 1990:66-68). The fact that interference is regulated according to relative prestige and dominance reveals that the relation between the various subsystems is not one of equality but rather of hierarchy. The relationship between the various factors within a subsystem might be based on free and unimpeded interaction; the relationship between the various levels (or subsystems), though, is established on the basis of stratified hierarchical order. The interference of certain items from a dominating subsystem perpetuates its domination over the subsystem that borrowed the items on the one hand, and on the other proves the existing hierarchical structure of the larger hosting system.

Even-Zohar believes that "there is no symmetry in literary interference" (1990:62), since it is lower subsystems that are interfered with by higher subsystems. If we discover that some of the (sets of) norms that constitute a lower subsystem constitute part of a higher subsystem as well, we will be able to measure the breadth and the applicability of these norms. The meaning of this hypothesis is that parts of a subsystem may have contact and interfere with only parts of a higher subsystem (cf. Even-Zohar, 1990:63). This, on the one hand, means that although lower systems are influenced by higher subsystems, they do not lose their independent/individual status. On the other, it means that interference is a result of friction with the immediately superior subsystem and only with that; it cannot skip the hierarchical order and interact directly with a system that lies on an even higher level. Even if we discover that a given (set of) norms constitutes not just part of the 'lower' subsystem and of the 'higher' subsystem, but also part of an even more 'superordinate' subsystem - therefore having an even greater breadth and applicability - the interference between the 'superordinate' subsystem and the 'lower' one is still not direct but filtered through the mediating 'higher' system.

Along the lines described above, I have split my model/system into three levels/subsystems: the lower, the middle, and the upper. Each of these levels constitutes an individual subsystem. The lower level is the particular, case-specific level; in this subsystem I will examine the particular audiovisual products under study, within their specific situational context of production. The middle level is the overall audiovisual level; here I will attempt to investigate the relationships between the specific situational contexts and the overall context of audiovisual translation. The upper level is the general literary level; in this subsystem I will attempt to investigate the audiovisual translation context within the framework of the general literary context. Within the general literary context, one could also distinguish between various other middle levels/systems, e.g. the level of translated drama. To discover that a norm which applies in audiovisual translation applies in another mode of literary translation as well, in our example in translated drama, would neither reveal the full breadth and applicability of the norm, nor prove anything relevant to our specific (audiovisual translation) study; this discovery would have to be directed at the upper general literary level and if it had a broader application it might be claimed as a superordinate literary norm that influences audiovisual translation too. Similarly, one could draw a parallel lower-level distinction between the translation of products from each of the three audiovisual media, i.e. between the translation of cinema, TV or video products. Again, the breadth and the applicability of a norm discovered to apply in the translation of products from one of these media will have to be tested at the middle level against the overall view of audiovisual translation throughout the media, and if it has a broader application it can be claimed as a superordinate audiovisual norm. In this respect, I believe that the above three levels (lower, middle, upper) are sufficient for an investigation into the norms of audiovisual translation.

2.3.3. The system in a broader polysystemic context

Since literary activities are aspects of general cultural activities, a target literary system can always be viewed as part of the broader TC-system. In this respect, a norm that is found to account for the totality of the literary system can derive from an even higher level of constraints: the socio-cultural system/level. "Conceiving of literature as a separate semi-independent socio-cultural institution is therefore tenable only if the literary polysystem, like any other socio-cultural system, is conceived of as simultaneously autonomous and heteronomous with all other co-systems" (Even-Zohar, 1990:23). Audiovisual translation as a literary activity can thus be regarded as part of the broader socio-cultural system as well (cf. Delabastita, 1989:210). Socio-cultural systems are extremely complex and constantly evolving (Hermans, 1996:39). Investigating the origins of a literary norm within its broader socio-cultural polysystem is, therefore, not an easy task.

Venuti criticises Toury's work because, although it is supposed to identify target norms, it does not "turn to cultural theory in order to assess the significance of the data, to analyse the norms" (Venuti, 1997:362). Venuti correctly stresses that:

> "norms may be in the first instance linguistic or literary, but they will also include a diverse range of domestic values, beliefs, and social representations which carry ideological force in serving the interests of specific groups. And they are always housed in social institutions" (ibid).

It would certainly be very valuable to expand the target literary levels upwards, to the direction of the higher socio-cultural level. A *methodological* investigation into this level, however, would require an enormous amount of sociological background-knowledge, in order to appropriately specify those aspects of cultural life that initiate a norm which can also be found at the lower literary level. My proposed model/system has already been defined to investigate audiovisual translation strictly within the target *literary* system. Further investigation at the higher levels cannot reasonably be carried out within the scope of this study. It is certain that a number of the norms which will be examined will have their origins in the socio-cultural constraints of the broad target (poly)system (cf. Delabastita, 1989:211); but it would be an unmanageable task for this thesis to try and systematically connect purely socio-cultural features/norms with their literary counterparts or realisations. Venuti's comment that Toury's - and Even-Zohar's - work "perpetuate the marginality of translation studies by discouraging an engagement with the trends and debates that fuel the most consequential thinking about culture" (1997:363) because they ignore "the varieties of psychoanalysis, feminism, Marxism, and poststructuralism" (ibid) is rather unwarranted. On the contrary, I believe that Toury's and Even-Zohar's work provide the necessary insights for expanding the study of translation from the literary to the broader socio-cultural level. Neither scholar ever denied or discouraged such a connection. They might seem reluctant to establish this connection themselves. There are many reasons for this hesitation, though, since such a project would require much time and a very broad base of knowledge.

2.3.4. Synchrony vs. diachrony

Whenever researchers investigate the past they are bound to project their own contemporary ideas onto the data they are dealing with and filter them accordingly (cf. Hermans, 1996:46). It is inevitable that they will interpret their input through the contemporary socio-cultural perspective in which they belong and from which they can never escape. In this respect, total objectivity when probing into the past is never feasible; this of course applies also to any scholar wishing to investigate the translation norms of previous periods.

Even-Zohar does not agree with Saussure's concept of a system being 'synchronic'(or rather 'synchronistic'), in the sense of being static, and rejects the deliberate elimination of the factor of time-succession from the concept of 'system' (Even-Zohar, 1990:10). As a network of relations a system can never be static; it is rather a result of constant dynamic heterogeneous interactions. "Synchrony cannot and should not be equated with statics, since at any given moment, more than one diachronic set is operating on the synchronic axis" (ibid:11). Synchrony is a slice of diachrony. It carries all the elements that operate in diachrony; it is the dynamic interaction of these elements which is deprived of time-succession. In this respect, we cannot call a system 'synchronic' and mean that it is static.

Since the dynamic interaction between the elements that constitute a system operates irrespective of the time-dimension, diachrony can similarly be conceived of as an infinite series of synchronic slices. My proposed model/system attempts to capture one of these slices. Norms that operate and constitute a system evolve along the time-scale. Regarding a system from a synchronic rather than a diachronic point of view enables us to pinpoint the norms through their process of evolution and place them in their time-context. Toury suggests that the comparison of several translations of the same text at various diachronic moments (and therefore in different literary and socio-cultural contexts) will enable us to discover the similarities and differences between the norms that characterise the two eras, and therefore draw conclusions about their diachronic evolution (Toury, 1980:140). A text reflects and is a product of a specific situational context. To compare two texts, then, means to compare the situational contexts that produced them. What Toury actually proposes is a parallel comparison of two synchronic systems; conclusions on diachrony are established through comparisons of various synchronies. In theory, this methodology cannot be refuted. In practice, however, it is very difficult to collect data for all the elements/sectors involved in the production of a text that belongs to the past; and such a collection is a pre-requisite for our results, because an insufficient description of the system that hosted the text *at the time of its production* will restrict the validity and the reliability of the whole survey.

2.4 Procedures and techniques for data analysis in Audiovisual Translation

2.4.1 Discovery and justification procedures

In his proposed methodology for the investigation of translation Toury suggests a series of discovery and justification procedures. Preoccupied with his ST-TT comparison, however, he implements these procedures only at the textual level and mostly as a tool for contrastive analysis, trying to establish micro-structural norms of linguistic formulations (cf. Toury, 1980:108; 1995:38). I believe that the same discovery and justification procedures, from a different perspective, could be expanded in order to apply to a broader investigation of norms in (audiovisual) translation too.

The hypothetical existence of a norm constitutes a speculation; the discovery of the actual operation of the norm gives the answer to this speculation. On this basis, all possibilities between hypothetical norms and actually existing ones constitute a coupled pair of translational-speculation-and-translational-answer (cf. Toury, 1985:25). This coupling will enable us to distinguish between what we think might be happening and what actually happens. This is the bottom-line of the discovery procedures. A specific case/behaviour is studied to see if the hypothesis applies to it (Silverman, 1993:161). If not, the hypothesis is reformulated; if yes, a number of other cases are also examined to see if the initially verified hypothesis applies to them as well. Examination of multiple cases and reformulation of the initial hypothesis are repeated until we can claim that we have reached a sufficiently reliable result that shows a consistent pattern of behaviour, i.e. a norm (cf. ibid). Deviant cases are scrutinised until we can modify our hypothesis no more and until we realise that we cannot include them in what appears to be the norm (cf. ibid). Silverman calls this process 'Analytic Induction' (ibid) but it certainly coincides with Toury's discovery procedures.

At this point, we have established the existence of a norm amongst a sufficient number of similar cases, therefore we may claim that we have established the existence of a norm in a micro/sub-system. The next step is to discover if the same norm applies to a higher/superordinate subsystem too. From the existing, empirical descriptive data available to us, then, we resolve again into possible, theoretical speculations (cf. Toury's schematic representation of Translation Studies, 1980:65). The already formulated normative patterns we have identified will help us to direct our research accordingly (cf. Chesterman, 1993:15). The predictions will be probabilistic and tested until they are proved or disproved (ibid). Chesterman calls this process 'prediction and explanation' (ibid) but it still coincides with Toury's discovery procedures. Once more, data are collected, cases examined, and the hypothesis that was established as a norm at the lower subsystem is reformulated until it can account for the new broader input. If yes, the breadth and applicability of the norm are expanded; if not, the norm remains as it was initially formulated and its applicability remains restricted.

The new and broader norm will undergo similar discovery procedures until it is established as a norm of a subsystem at the highest level possible. At the same time, however, another procedure starts: the broader norm will be investigated back at the lower level again by incorporating more cases that perhaps were left out or discarded as exceptions. This attempt to augment the data back at the lower level according to the findings of the higher level corresponds to the justification procedures. As a mirror of the discovery procedures, but guided in the opposite direction, a new hypothesis is formulated and new cases are put to the test, only this time the hypothesis is not reformulated; it acts as the fundamental basis for the expansion of our quantitative input (cf. Toury, 1995:37). Justification procedures therefore always follow a series of discovery procedures. This, however, does not stop them from operating in parallel with discovery procedures: at the same time that discovery procedures will attempt to expand the norm at a higher level, the justification procedures will attempt to strengthen the norm at the lower level.

By investigating the lower level again, the justification procedures will trigger new hypotheses and therefore new discovery procedures that, again, will have to be verified, and again justified, and so forth. This constant to-and-fro that resembles the movement of a 'pendulum swing' constitutes one of the two basic principles for the operation of the discovery-and-justification procedures (Toury, 1980:110). The other principle is the decisive role of the majority: (translational) behaviour patterns are established on the basis of representing the majority of the examined cases (ibid).

Our discovery-and-justification procedures will be guided by the nature of the translational problem and the conclusions of previous research into the same area (cf. Toury, 1980:109). They will always account, however, for the sectors of the subsystem we are working on. The versatility of the cases that will be picked and examined will be determined by the variety of the sectors involved; a large corpus of data will attempt to include cases from the widest possible range of sectors. Such qualitative analysis will help us maintain the size of the corpus at a manageable level. It is easy to assume that a corpus for study can include an enormous amount of cases as data. In order to avoid this pointless and time-consuming exercise, we can direct our discovery-and-justification procedures in such a way that as many combinations between the sectors as possible, and therefore as many situational scenarios as possible are covered; otherwise, our study will still lack validity and reliability, irrespective of the size of the corpus.

2.4.2 Quantitative and qualitative data

No research can proceed without a sufficient amount of data on which it can be based. Shlesinger protests that she cannot go on with an adequate research into the norms of interpretation without a sufficient amount of data (1989:112). Toury provides extensive quantitative data in all his studies of norms providing statistical analyses and figures to support his views, even counting syllables when investigating the norms of metrical texts (1985:34). The use of figures, either as part of statistics or as absolute numbers of examined cases, reinforces the validity of most types of research. 'Triangulation' (i.e. comparing quantitative and qualitative data), generalising results on a larger sample-basis and the use of simple counting procedures are just a few methods for enhancing the validity and the reliability of research results, and they are all based on the use of quantitative data (Silverman, 1993:156&166).

Pure quantitative data, however, is not revealing on its own and should always be accompanied with the use of qualitative analysis, according to our specific aims and the nature of the problem in question. Norms in audiovisual translation, for example, can be investigated from a variety of angles since they involve a wide range of variants which are subject to everyday challenge, modification and flow. If we are to establish a norm correctly, we need to specify its situational context, identify the role of the elements/factors involved and investigate their interrelationship at a specific point in time. As a result, a mere quantitative analysis will de-contextualise the norm, possibly leading to exaggerated over-generalisations, faulty conclusions and half-truths. What is essential, then, alongside the quantitative analysis, is the establishment of a qualitative framework that can cover the various parameters and intervening factors in the realisation of a norm.

2.4.3 Observation

A study into the norms of audiovisual translation should start, like any other study, with the observables (cf. Toury, 1995:36). Those facts that lend themselves to scrutinisation are the ones that will initiate the hypothesis for the existence of a norm.

The observational method has always been recommended for understanding the situational context of a particular aspect of behaviour; as a result, it has always been considered fundamental to qualitative research (Silverman, 1993:9). Conducting observational analysis will help us realise what is going on in a particular system/setting, who are the participants and what is their general role. Starting a research which is based on observational analysis will include: a) looking at - as well as listening to - the elements of the situational context, b) writing fieldnotes about the inspected items in a systematic and organised fashion, c) formulating hypotheses, and d) testing them by comparing them to conclusions reached by other researchers (cf. Silverman, 1993:36). In the case of norms in audiovisual translation, observation might prove a very useful technique for the adequate understanding of the particular mode, as the general framework of investigation.

2.4.4 Product analysis

An investigation into the norms of audiovisual translation will primarily deal with the products of the translation process, i.e. with the film-products themselves. From a quantitative perspective, 'content analysis' will provide reliable data about a large sample by establishing hypotheses and counting the number of instances/items that are compatible with these hypotheses (Silverman, 1993:9-10). Toury suggests a series of comparisons for the extraction of quantitative data, depending on what we are looking for: a) different translations into the same TL, performed by different translators, b) different phases in the establishment of the same translation, and c) different translations of the same ST into different TLs (1985:24). His third method opens an extremely wide range of investigation into a number of target systems and therefore it is not easily applicable. His second method is applicable to one specific target system, but it is rather difficult to accomplish, because we can hardly ever have direct access to the agents who perform the translation at the time they are performing it, and therefore we cannot monitor their process; most of the time, we simply receive and try to analyse their final product. The first method he suggests, however, can yield useful conclusions after a process of thorough content analysis.

Content analysis can hardly be conducted on the general level of the target film-product; most of the time the attempted mapping involves textual micro-structural items/segments, not even the whole texts themselves (cf. Toury, 1995:37). For a valid and reliable content analysis, however, we need a well defined set of products to compare, i.e. a well designed corpus. Corpus analysis can be useful in audiovisual translation – if an investigation of textual norms is pursued – in the same way it is useful in written translation. Advanced software packages of corpus analysis can trace Key Words In Context (KWIC), as they appear in the corpus, and even count their frequency automatically, providing useful statistical information (Baker, 1995:226-228). Especially for the modes of TV and video subtitling, it would not be difficult to compile a desired corpus, since the subtitled data (text and cueing time) are stored on computer disks anyway. For cinema subtitling, one would need to word-process the subtitled text from the screen on a computer and store it on a disk. For the revoiced products, the compilation of a corpus presents more difficulties, since the oral text is stored on magnetic tapes and a full written transcription of all the accompanying semiotic elements (e.g. pitch and tone of voice) is largely unfeasible. An audiovisual-translation corpus can be designed with the same criteria used for a written-translation corpus: subtitled vs. revoiced versions, genre/mode/agents/recipients specific, synchronic vs. diachronic productions, general language vs. dialects etc. (cf. Baker, 1995:229). Unfortunately, though, I am not aware of any kind of ready-made corpus of audiovisual translations. Still, the basic concept of compiling a large corpus of coherent samples can guide our attempt to identify patterning in audiovisual translation as well, as much as possible. At the upper level, though, we might make use of comparable corpora of written originals and written translations (into the same target language/system) to discover if a norm that might have been established at the middle level of overall audiovisual translation actually derives from the upper general literary level (cf. Baker, 1995:234-235; 1996:185).

Product analysis should not be restricted to quantitative content analysis of the target-product. A parallel qualitative analysis should shed considerable light on the way these individual products come to be released, who is actually involved in their production, and who they are aimed at.

2.4.5 Interviews, questionnaires, polls and cloze tests

One of the most common ways of examining the personal attitude of a human agent is through the technique of interviewing. An interview of a human agent involved in the production of audiovisual translations can help extract data about: a) translational facts and the decisions that led into them, b) the agent's personal beliefs, feelings and motives for the decisions s/he made, c) the standards s/he followed in the course of production, and d) the conscious reasons that explain his/her specific decisions (cf. Silverman, 1993:92). What is particularly valuable about the use of interviews is that one can have some access to aspects of translational behaviour that might have been performed in the past and not just in the present. Silverman suggests two types of interviews: a) based on 'positivism' and being useful for collecting facts about behaviour and attitudes through standard questions, random samples and tabulations, and b) based on 'interactionism' and being useful for recording authentic experiences through unstructured open-ended interviews (ibid:91). Both methods can prove helpful for interviewing agents involved in the process of audiovisual translation. The former will yield more straightforward results but could be criticised for leading the interviewee's answers. The latter will provide natural answers which will, however, require further analysis from the interviewer in order to extract useful data.

The former method is more widely applied (ibid:10) and I have found it less problematic for the current study.

The need for an objective interviewer who will not take sides or force answers is essential for the reliability of the interview. Of course it is absurd to presume that an interviewer can be completely unbiased. As members of a social community interviewers have their own experiences and pre-occupations; nevertheless, they should try to put them aside as much as possible. In order to acquire the most reliable results from an interview, then, we have to secure that: a) the interviewer is well trained and aware of the subject-matter, b) the interview has been appropriately prepared and pre-scheduled, c) most of the expected answers are based on a fixed repertoire of possible answers, and d) open-ended questions can and should be subjected to further analysis (Silverman, 1993:148).

In order to avoid any possible pitfalls produced by the interpersonal interviewer-interviewee contact, and in order to allow ample time for the interviewee to think about his/her answers in a relaxed environment, questionnaires are preferred to interviews. Toury suggests that "by and large, the most common way of studying aspects of translated texts (or rather addressees' responses to them) in an empirical way consists in devising questionnaires, and having groups of subjects - hopefully big enough as well as controlled for their background variables - react to the texts by answering the questions" (1995:228). Both interviews and questionnaires are techniques basically implemented for the extraction of qualitative data about the translational product and the situation in which it is produced and received by humans. Since both are most often based on a relatively large sample of individuals and carried out over a long period of time, one has to find a means of ensuring that the interviewer maintains the same degree of interest throughout the series of interviews/questionnaires (cf. Silverman, 1993:93). Fortunately, for the reception of television programmes, viewing rates are calculated practically every second. In most of the European countries, this task is undertaken by professional companies and institutions who specialise in the business (e.g. 'AGB' in Greece). In the same countries, these quantitative viewing rates are accompanied by qualitative poll results into the specific social, educational and age groups and their specific film-type preferences. The fact that the amount of capital allocated to advertising depends on these viewing rates makes these figures highly relevant and reliable as research data.

Cloze tests can be used as a technique for establishing the readability of a text (Toury, 1995:223). Especially in the case of subtitling, where a lot of original dialogue is inevitably condensed, cloze tests are both useful and feasible. If conducted in parallel with eye-movement tests (cf. Gottlieb, 1994b:266), one might be able to measure the success of a subtitled film-product, since a high level of readability reduces the number of times the eye has to 'visit' the subtitles, thus allowing more time for audio-visual satisfaction, and for following the plot (d'Ydewalle et al., 1991:652).

2.4.6 Transcripts, recordings and Think-Aloud Protocols (TAPs)

Transcripts and recordings obtained in experimental research provide vivid data of human behaviour. Compared to observational data, they are in some respects more reliable because the variables can be controlled (cf. Silverman, 1993:11). Compiled in a systematic fashion by using standardised transcription symbols, transcripts provide raw material that can be used for multiple investigations and the (re)formulation of multiple hypotheses at a present or a following stage of research. Based on conversation analysis, transcripts and recordings can help us detect decisions taken in a team situation by a number of agents. Transcripts and recordings of group-work will help us interpret and assess the role and the status of each of the participants involved in the conversation.

Think-Aloud Protocols (TAPs) are used for monitoring human agents' translation performance and providing self-corrective feedback. TAPs aim to reveal the nature of the cognitive processes of the translator. The translator verbalises the thoughts, the hesitations and the decisions s/he makes during the actual translation process, therefore revealing the reasons that led him/her into the particular choice of a specific translational behaviour. The advantage of TAPs is that they can (sometimes) also help us access other potential translational behaviour - as thoughts and possible alternative choices that cross the agent's/translator's mind. Of course it is impossible to expect everything that goes on in the agent's mind to be verbalised in the TAP. Decisions that are based on an automatic choice of an established normative pattern are not marked as 'problematic' in the translator's mind and, as a result, they are made subconsciously without being verbalised (cf. Toury, 1995:185). For an investigation into the norms of (audiovisual) translation, then, TAPs are not that helpful. Concurrent TAPs usually reveal instances of non-conformity, rather than conformity to a norm, as problems that cannot be automatically solved by the application of the norm on the spot. Retrospective TAPs, as self-observation methods, might prove more useful to a normative investigation, since they are not restrained by an immediate necessity for an application of a norm but allow for an overall consideration of the translation process-and-product, as after-thoughts in the translator's mind (cf. Lörscher, 1991:267).

2.5 Previous methodological approaches to (audiovisual) norms

2.5.1. Toury's approach

Toury's contribution to the systematic investigation of translation consists of a set of rough methodological guidelines, discussed in various publications, which mainly attempt to develop the branch of Descriptive Translation Studies. When investigating translation in general, Toury suggests that the first step should be to regard the text as a product of the target system (1980:83). After investigating the target system, he suggests an analysis of the target text (ibid). Such an analysis is bi-directional: it is an independent analysis of the translated text as a fact of the target system, and a comparative analysis of the target vis-à-vis the source text (ibid:84). Finally, depending on the goal of our investigation, another series of comparisons can be conducted between: a) different translations of the same ST into one TL, b) different translations of the same ST into different TLs, c) different translations of the same ST into the same TL, performed by different translators at various points in time, and d) different phases in the preparation of the same translation (ibid) (see also chapter 1.3.2).

Toury views the investigation of translational norms as a cultural task of Descriptive Translation Studies. He deals largely with micro-structural operational norms and, as a result, his TT analysis concentrates in the main on linguistic details (see the investigation of the translation of Japanese poems into English, in Toury, 1993a:19). His most systematic attempt to investigate norms has been in the area of literary translation into Hebrew. The parameters he took into account consist of the genre of the TTs, the specific time-period in which they were produced, the translators and the publishers who produced them and their source languages/systems (1980:122-126). His approach seems rather patchy because his methodology lacks a consistent framework and resembles a series of investigations based on intuition. He takes a lot of preliminary norms for granted and bases his later hypotheses about operational norms on these preliminary norms. The parameters/factors he investigates are not part of a general project or strategy, he neglects the vital role of the recipients and puts a lot of unnecessary emphasis on the source languages/systems. But even when investigating these parameters, Toury does not look for links with major/superordinate norms and levels - to follow his own acclaimed discovery and justification procedures - and simply sticks to the level of the genre he has chosen. Furthermore, his diachronic investigation is not conducted on synchronic slices of various situational contexts, but rather on an abstract time-scale, directly comparing various translations from different periods and situational contexts. At any rate, Toury's proposed methodology cannot be applied without modification to the investigation of audiovisual translation, since he neglects the parameter of the audiovisual mode.

2.5.2 Lambert & van Gorp's approach

Perhaps the most coherent theoretical attempt to describe translations is that of Lambert & van Gorp (1985). At the outset of the presentation of their model they give credit to Toury and Even-Zohar, on whose theories they claim to base their model (Lambert & van Gorp, 1985:43). In a schematic representation they depict the basic parameters that have to be taken into account when investigating translations; these consist of: a) the source literary system and b) the target literary system. Both systems consist of the author, the text, the reader (source and target respectively), viewed within broader groups of authors, texts and readers (ibid). They suggest that all the possible relations between these parameters have to be studied, namely the ones within the same system as well as cross-systemic relations (ibid:44).

Their methodology, although hypothetically constructed and bearing "no ontological status" (ibid:45), provides a series of steps that can be followed for the extraction of actual data. Firstly, inter-systemic links have to be established between the source and target systems, links which will be later used as a background for the ST-TT comparison (ibid:47). Secondly, intra-systemic links have to be established between the various elements that constitute the particular systems (ibid). Information has to be collected about the macro-structural and the micro-structural features of the TT (ibid:49), as well as about the translator and the recipients (ibid:50).

Lambert and van Gorp acknowledge the limitations of their approach – limitations which apply to all research – in terms of the impossibility of summarising and collecting data about all the relationships involved in the translation process (ibid:47), but they also defend their approach for its systematicity as well as its ability to avoid the source-oriented bias of other models (ibid:45). I would agree with the former but do not fully side with the latter. Their systematicity is based on a series of open-ended questions as potential topics of investigation, none of which however, is actually put to test. If put to practice, they would perhaps realise the need to specify the techniques they should follow precisely in order to extract the information they want from the reader, the text or the translator.

Within a broad theoretical framework, they sensibly try to establish hierarchical relationships between macro- and micro-structures, as well as relationships between other larger groups/genres of texts at a superordinate level (ibid:53). Their proposed levels, however, are still very shallow for a broad investigation into normative structures, since they mostly emphasise micro-structural analysis. But most of all, Lambert & van Gorp still adhere to the idea of the source system being an essential parameter for investigation, without even specifying, in the end, precisely how the data about the source system might prove useful to their field of research. At any rate, audiovisual translation does not feature in this model.

2.5.3. Nord's approach

Nord (1991a) proposes a series of precise methodological steps for investigating translational conventions. The first is the analysis of TTs, since they reflect conformity to or deviation from existing norms; the need for a large number of samples is emphasised (Nord, 1991a:103). The second is the study of available critical reviews of the TTs, which will indirectly reflect the normative expectations of the reviewers (ibid). Theoretical statements, either by scholars or practitioners, will also reflect the dominant concept of translation in the society in question (ibid:104). Feedback from users of the translation also needs to be sought, with due regard to the validity of the method for collecting such responses (ibid:105). Finally, multilingual comparisons of translations will help us draw conclusions about the realisation of particular conventions in various target cultures (ibid).

Nord's approach is fairly well defined. Its main advantage is that it does not involve unproductive investigations of the source texts and systems, and focuses solely on the elements of the target system. It nevertheless fails to address the role of the human agents/translators themselves. It also makes no suggestions on how to conduct qualitative analysis of either the translators' or the recipients' status. In addition, reviews and theoretical statements might be available for written translation; in audiovisual translation, however, few reviews of subtitled or revoiced texts are published, and no consistent theoretical formulations have been elaborated for audiovisual translation yet. Especially when investigating a target system which is not so well-developed, then, we cannot rely on this type of data. Finally, the multilingual comparison of translations is not an easy task and involves a further investigation of the target systems involved.

2.5.4. Puurtinen's approach

Puurtinen's research (1989) investigates the acceptability of translated children's books. In order to establish the acceptability of the TTs under study, she has to compare her results with the expectations and the existing norms of the hosting target system (Finnish children's fiction) (Puurtinen, 1989:211). She believes that complex non-finite constructions reduce the readability of a text, and this can be considered one criterion for the acceptability of children's books in their hosting system (ibid:203). To prove this, she takes two translations of the same text, produced by two different translators, around the same time, with the same function and aimed at the same target group (ibid:202). She analyses their micro-structure thoroughly and concludes that whereas one uses complex constructions, the other does not (ibid:205-206). Based on a number of experiments that have already been carried out, she believes that these complex constructions hamper the reading speed and the comprehension process (ibid:206). Puurtinen uses cloze tests, reading comprehension and read-aloud tests, all performed by children (ibid:207-211) in order to ascertain the effect of complex structures in readability. Finally, a stylistic criticism of the translations was also sought from adults (ibid:210).

Puurtinen's study is methodologically adequate. By using precise techniques, she hopes to reach a conclusion that will verify or refute the existence of specific norms. She begins by taking certain norms for granted: "the requirements of a high degree of readability (i.e. the text being easy enough for children to read and understand) and natural, unaffected style can be regarded as prevalent norms of children's literature in Finland" (ibid:203). Thus, her methodology might not be useful for the recognition and *discovery* of norms, but it could be helpful for the *justification* and verification of the norms in question. Her primary concern is with the target text/system and her only interest in the source system is to ensure that the comparison of the TTs is made on equal basis, namely as products of the same ST. The factors she covers involve the texts that are thoroughly analysed and the recipients who are adequately specified; the factor of the translator, however, might require further qualitative analysis. All her tests are based on large samples, although her cloze test could be made more rigorous by not deleting random words (every sixth one in the passage) (ibid:208&210), but e.g. by deleting the verbs or the objects of the sentences. She attempts to further substantiate her findings by soliciting the views of adults; this attempt, however, should be elaborated more explicitly and tests should be carried out in other sectors as well, in order to establish such a broader applicability of the norm. Obviously, this is not her real intention; her scope is very precisely defined and remains restricted to the justification of a particular norm in a particular situational context/system. As such, she sets an example for avoiding fuzzy and vague philology, and reaching methodologically sound and concrete conclusions. Her methodology, nevertheless, has to be supplemented with discovery procedures in order to enable a full investigation into the norms of (audiovisual) translation.

2.5.5 Du-Nour's approach

Miryam Du-Nour (1995) sets out to investigate norms in the translation of children's books into Hebrew over a period of 70 years. In order to achieve this, she collected a corpus of 25 translations, some of which were re-translations of the same original STs (Du-Nour, 1995:331). After a micro-structural linguistic/stylistic analysis of the TTs she manages to identify certain translational patterns that appear to characterise specific eras; these patterns represent the dominant norms (ibid:337). By comparing the various norms prevalent at different points in time, she is able to reach conclusions about their diachronic evolution (ibid:342).

Du-Nour's approach is coherent and methodological. Again, she focuses solely on a specific target subsystem: that of Hebrew children's fiction. The TTs are examined in their hosting genres. Some links are attempted with other systems/levels, e.g. of adult fiction, poetry and drama (ibid:336&342), which, however, require further investigation and elaboration. Interviews were held with language-policy makers, who can be thought to determine both the production and the reception of the TTs; the results were interesting, since what they said seems to contradict the quantitative normative patterns, as actually revealed through the investigation of TTs (ibid:339&342). However, further qualitative analysis of either the agents/producers or the recipients does not seem to have been conducted. Still, the major drawback of Du-Nour's work is failure to compartmentalise the various experiments she undertakes; the various factors she investigates are not neatly and separately presented and, as a consequence, the whole project gives an initial impression of a messy collection of (otherwise very well-chosen) experiments. A more systematically organised presentation of her research would make it more convincing and more readable.

2.5.6 Delabastita's approach

Delabastita (1990) is the only scholar to propose a methodology for the specific investigation of norms in audiovisual translation. Assuming that a corpus of audiovisual translation products is available, he suggests a series of questions whose answers would lead to the identification of translational norms in this corpus as a whole (Delabastita, 1989:206). Some general questions concern: a) the target language and the geographical variants involved, b) the language transfer method - subtitling or revoicing - that dominates (parts of) the translated product, c) the number of language transfer versions in which the film is finally released in the market, d) the verbal or non-verbal elements that have been added to or deleted from the original, e) the possible use of a pivot language, and finally f) the treatment of source products that contain dialogues in more than one language (ibid: 206-207). Some dubbing-specific questions concern the translator's attempt at synchrony and the dubbing actors' attempt at 'acting' the dialogues (ibid:207), whereas some subtitling-specific questions concern: a) the type of source material that is left out, b) the subtitles' resemblance to oral vs. written language, c) the average number of characters per line, and d) whether the subtitles are presented in two languages simultaneously (ibid:208). On the general level again, attention has to be paid to issues such as potential resemblance of the TT grammar, lexicon and style to the same features in ST, the treatment of foreign culture elements, the treatment of taboo elements, and finally the treatment of target-culture-related elements that might be present in the ST (ibid).

This series of questions suggests that Delabastita's approach, though pioneering, lacks coherence and strategic planning. His questions seem to reflect problems that spring out of concrete examples; but the number of possible audiovisual translation problems is endless and a list that would account for each one of them can never be finite. In addition, he seems to neglect certain audiovisual translation methods such as voice-over, narration and free-commentary, and his questions tend to fluctuate from general to specific and then again to general. As a result, his study seems unfocused and disoriented.

In case the above series of questions fails to produce a homogenous set of data, Delabastita suggests a second, follow-up series of further questions that "will enable the scholar to detect the *mechanisms* that have governed the production of the translation in his corpus" (ibid). These questions deal with: a) the source language and culture, b) the target language and culture, c) the relations between the two cultures, d) the frequency and status of these intercultural contacts, e) the 'text-type' of the source film (i.e. whether it was meant to communicate information or entertainment), f) the 'genre' of the source film (i.e. whether it is a documentary, an interview, a reportage, a western, a cartoon, a video-clip, etc.), g) whether it is a cinema or a TV product, h) whether the vocal source performance is part of an artistic sign (e.g. operas and musicals), i) whether the target product is aimed at a specific audience, j) the status of the source film, k) the status of the target genre, and finally l) whether the genre of the original film exists in the target culture (ibid:209-210). The answers to the above questions would shed some light on issues such as film-genre conceptions in the target culture, general textual/translational conceptions in the target culture, the structure of the whole target literary polysystem, the linguistic organisation of the target culture, and the openness of the target culture (ibid:210).

Again, this second - and more ambitious - set of questions seems to fluctuate between aspects of the source system and others of the target system. My view is that an investigation into the source text and system cannot reveal anything relevant to the operation of target norms in the target culture (see also section 1.3.2). That aside, however, it further indicates that Delabastita's approach lacks strategic organisation and is not adequately compartmentalised. It jumps from one problem to another without logical sequence. It restricts the versatile role of the human agents in audiovisual translation to the persona of the translator. It does not place proper emphasis on the catalytic role of the audience/recipients. Although it seems to be focused around the film-product, it still does not clearly distinguish between different film-types and different film-genres. It does not openly emphasise the distinction between cinema and TV productions. Finally, it seems to neglect completely the mode of video. The basic problem, however, remains that a series of questions cannot possibly treat *all* aspects of normative audiovisual translation. For example, in the case study that follows and in which I will attempt to investigate the initial choice between subtitling and revoicing children's TV programmes in Greece, Delabastita's questions concerning the necessity of quality lip-sync in dubbing have to be taken for granted, others do not appear relevant at all and are consequently left out, and others still will have to be added to account for aspects specifically related to the topic under study. Despite all these drawbacks, however, one has to acknowledge that Delabastita was - to my knowledge - the first translation scholar to attempt to investigate this particular field, therefore "mapping out the contours of a still virgin area of research" (ibid:206).

3. CASE STUDY: THE CHOICE BETWEEN SUBTITLING AND REVOICING CHILDREN'S TV PROGRAMMES IN GREECE (IN 1995 AND 1996)

3.1 Methods of data collection

3.1.1 Collection of data related to products

A hypothesis is generally triggered by observable phenomena. For the present research, the issue of the choice between subtitling and revoicing children's TV programmes was inspired by the versatility of the actual broadcasts on Greek television: some of them were observed to be broadcast subtitled, others dubbed. As a result, the first move towards discovering the extent of the norm-related hypothesis was to collect data on the exact number of products broadcast subtitled or dubbed during the specific period under study.

A visit to the top five TV stations in Greece ensured the collection of a valid sample. Although there is a large number of TV stations operating on the Greek territory (over 50), not all of them transmit a signal across the whole country. The top five TV stations are accessible by almost all the Greek residents; in addition, they attract almost 80% of national TV viewing (AGB Hellas eds., 1995:40; AGB Hellas eds., 1996:42). Therefore, a norm - and the motivations behind it - established for these five TV stations could be considered fairly valid and representative of Greek TV stations in general. In order to enlarge the sample it was decided to collect data from a cable TV station as well. The top five open-broadcast TV stations are the privately owned ANT1, MEGA, STAR, SKY, and the state owned ET1. The cable channel is the privately owned FILMNET. All these stations are based in Athens.

The survey was designed to cover the period 1994-1996. A list of all the products broadcast during this two-year period would be unmanageable as data. Following discussions with personnel from the relevant TV-stations and those responsible for collecting viewing rates, it was decided that one representative month for each of the years could provide both a sufficient and manageable amount of data. The month chosen was March because it comes right after the winter peak of viewing, when the TV-stations staff have a clear picture of their audience needs and formulate their programme flow accordingly, without further experimenting. All the above stations provided me with daily programme flows for March 1995 and March 1996. Restricting the data to one month per year, however, did generate certain problems in the case of film-types that are rarely shown on Greek television, whatever the time of year (like children's puppet movies and series for example). In such cases, the weakness of the sample has been recognised and unwarranted conclusions are avoided.

Alongside the daily programme flows that were made available to me, I also received advice on how the various programmes are classified into types and genres. First of all, Greek and foreign programmes TV programmes form two different categories. Foreign TV programmes are divided into children-targeted or adult-targeted[i]. Foreign children's TV programmes are classified as a) cartoon, b) live-action, c) puppet or d) a combination of the above. Then, they are further sub-classified as a) full-feature movies or b) series/serials of successive episodes. Foreign adult TV programmes are classified into a) full feature movies, b) series/serials of successive episodes, c) light entertainment shows, d) documentaries, e) sports programmes, f) news/information programmes, and g) music/opera/ballet programmes. The source language of the audiovisual product is specified and the presence of a pivot language in the post-script[ii] is

[i] For a more detailed analysis of how children-targeted products were distinguished from adult-targeted products and the way 'adult' and 'children' audiences were specified see also section 3.1.3.

[ii] 'Post-script' in the filmic jargon is the amended transcript of dialogues, as they are actually uttered and heard on screen. It often contains other essential non-verbal information of visual or aural elements (eg. 'laughter', 'throttle', 'hum', 'eyes wide open' etc.) (cf. Ivarsson, 1992:84). Most often it is also time-coded, indicating the exact moment (starting form the first frame of the film) that a certain part of the dialogue is uttered. Audiovisual translators nowadays work almost consistently with

pointed out where applicable. In addition to these parameters I was also provided with information on whether a particular programme was broadcast a) subtitled, b) dubbed, c) in narration, d) in free-commentary, or e) in a combination of any of the above language transfer methods.

The same procedure was followed for video releases. This time, it was video distribution agencies that were providing the data. Instead of daily programme flows for two months, data were collected for the entire two years 1994-1996[i] in terms of video sell-through releases[ii], since the number of samples, this time, was more manageable. Following a discussion with the Greek Institute for Audiovisual Media, the top four video distribution agencies were thought sufficient to provide me with the necessary data, since - as I was informed - they cover approximately 85% of the market. These four video distribution agencies are AUDIOVISUAL, VIDEOSONIC, Spentzos Video, and HVH. They are all privately owned and based in Athens.

The situation with cinema products was easier since no distinction into various film-types was necessary: all cinema products are movies. The manageable size of the number of samples allowed the collection of data related to the full cinema-years 1994-1995 and 1995-1996. The Greek Institute for Audiovisual Media informed me of the cinema distribution agencies that would provide me with the essential data. The top six cinema distribution agencies were thought

---

a post-script and they do not have to decipher the dialogues auditorily, from the source film itself. Sometimes they are even asked to provide a translation just from the post-script, without watching the film.

[i] 'Video-years' are estimated similar to calendar years, from January to December. 'TV-' and 'cinema-years' are estimated similar to academic years, from September to June (winter period) and from June to September (summer period). In order for data on video products to coincide with those on TV and cinema products, video-years had to be overlooked. As a result data was eventually collected for the full 1995 video-year, plus the period from September 1994 to December 1994 and from January 1996 to June 1996. This unavoidable confusion is the major reason for avoiding a separation into two independent years and opting for a presentation of a unified two-year period when presenting tables related to video-data.

[ii] 'Sell-through releases' refer to the launching of the video product into the market not just to video-clubs for renting but to individuals as well for full direct purchase and ownership of the videotape.

sufficient. These agencies are Prooptiki, Spentzos, ELKE, Nea Kinissi, OVO and Rosebud. They represent approximately 85% of the market; they are all privately owned and based in Athens.

Just as for TV programmes, the parameters involving Greek vs. foreign, as well as adult vs. children'sproducts were specified for cinema and video products too. So were the parameters related to the language of the original product, the possible presence of a pivot language postscript and - of course - the language transfer method.

3.1.2 Collection of data related to audiovisual mode

In terms of audiovisual mode, I again used observation as the main method of collecting data. This time, my personal experience of Greek audiovisual reality was enhanced by the perusal of various writings. Topics included mode-specific language-transfer constraints, the social role of cinema, TV and video, and the relationship of each of the audiovisual modes with children'sviewership. Furthermore, in order to establish a connection with general literary norms at the upper level, I had to collect data related to written literary products as well.

From the National Statistics Bureau I obtained data related to local written literary production and foreign literary imports. Although data on foreign literary imports was available for the calendar year 1995 (the main calendar year of the present study), the latest available data on local literary products was for 1993. This obviously restricts the validity of the research and any conclusions should be cautiously treated. In order to define 'written literary products' I followed the classification that was established by the National Statistics Bureau in terms of a) books, and b) newspapers and magazines. Books were further classified into a) fiction and scientific, b) dictionaries and encyclopaedias and c) other. This distinction makes clear that 'written literary products' do not simply cover 'fiction products' but basically all kinds of written material regarded and defined as literary. This perception/definition is also consistent with Toury's non-prescriptive definition of 'translation' as everything that is regarded and defined as 'translation'.

My interaction with people in the audiovisual media also provided me with insights on the relative position of the various audiovisual modes in Greece. Informal chats and unofficial face-to-face or telephone interviews proved particularly enlightening, because they gave me access to anecdotal material that written scholarly writings hardly ever cover, especially since the bibliography on the Greek audiovisual industry and practices is considerably restricted.

3.1.3 Collection of data related to recipients

The company responsible for assessing TV viewing rates in Greece is AGB Hellas. AGB is a multinational company that conducts public surveys in various countries around the world. The branch in Greece, founded in 1988, has an independent management committee; nevertheless, it is directly linked to the Southeastern European headquarters in Italy (AGB Hellas eds.,1995:8). All data related to TV viewing was provided courtesy of this specific company.

TV audience research is conducted by AGB Hellas in a very scientific way, based on international standards and supervised by the local Special Committee for the Control of Viewership Research. It covers the greater Athens and Salonica areas (i.e. large urban areas), as well as Patras, Heraklion, Larissa, Kavala and Ioaninna (smaller cities and towns) (ibid). The sample size is 700 households - 2,100 individuals representative of the average Greek family - and is controlled with respect to geographical distribution, age, gender and socioeconomic class (ibid). Viewing is registered via modem on a daily basis and for the time between 05:00AM and 02:00AM with the help of a specifically designed electronic system - the 'People Meter 4900' - that measures viewership for each of the TV sets owned by the household (ibid:9-10). The system consists of: a) the TV detector installed inside the set and collecting information about the TV channel to which the set is tuned every minute, and b) the remote control through which every member of the household indicates his/her TV watching by pressing his/her own individual button (ibid:10). All this information is directed to a Central Data Storage Unit and transmitted through a telephone line to the central AGB computers (ibid). Nevertheless, certain inherent difficulties in measuring exact viewing rates with this electronic method impact on the validity of the results. For example, it is impossible to know how many people forgot to push the button on their remote control each time they entered or left the room, or even when they were in the room, how much of their attention was directed at the screen (Gunter & McAleer 1990:2). Still, this electronically controlled method has been proven to be the most reliable so far.

According to AGB, a 'children' audience is the group of viewers aged between six and fourteen (daily audience research does not cover children up to six years old). Members of the audience who are over fourteen years of age belong to the 'adult' audience (AGB Hellas eds., 1996:100). This is the specification followed by TV, cinema and video companies in order to classify their products into children-targeted and adult-targeted.

AGB provided TV viewing data on children's programmes, documentaries and news/information programmes, i.e. on programmes that presented a variation in the choice of the language transfer method. Viewership was indicated through 'TV Viewing Rates' and 'Average TV Market Shares'[i]. I was handed two pairs of sheets, one for every month of study, i.e. March 1995 and March 1996. Each pair of sheets consisted of a) a number of sheets with collective data, and b) a number of sheets with analytic data. The analytic sheets consisted of the daily programme flow in one column with the change of viewership along the time scale for every quarter hour in an adjacent column. The collective sheets - only for children's programmes – contained comparative viewing data for children viewers in one column and overall viewers (i.e. including adults) in an adjacent column.

---

[i] 'Viewing Rates' (or 'TV Rating') is defined as the percentage of viewers of a specific programme relative to the total potential viewership, i.e. to the number of people who own a TV set (AGB Hellas eds., 1995:106). The 'Average Market Share' is defined as the percentage of viewers of a specific programme relative to the number of people watching TV at a specific time point (AGB Hellas eds., 1995:107).

Collecting analytic attendance figures for cinema products and sale figures for video products was not feasible, since the policy of cinema and video distribution agencies is to conceal exact figures for the viewership of their products. In any case, absolute viewing data on cinema and video is unlikely to prove useful. For the study of middle level recipients, what was essential was a set of data with contrastive, relative percentages of viewership for all the double cinema and video releases[i], so that the audience's appreciation of the one or the other language transfer method could be comparably measured. Even these relative percentages however - still on numbers of tickets for cinema and number of sell-through copies sold for video – could not be made available to me in an official written form but only as unofficial oral quotations. The absolute figures published in the Greek *Cinema* magazine in order to compile the monthly cinema or video top ten are provided by cinema-auditorium holders and video-club owners, and not by the cinema and video distribution agencies. This made me reluctant to use and apply such data. I decided to include only one instance of such absolute figures in a case where the exact numbers were printed in a foreign periodical with international status (*The Hollywood Reporter*) and the gap between the compared elements was so high as to render any minor mistake or miscalculation trivial in terms of its effects on final results.

3.1.4 Collection of data related to human agents

In order to collect data related to human agents involved in the audiovisual language transfer process I conducted informal, unofficial interviews and submitted formal, official questionnaires. Informal, unofficial, off-the-record interviews based on 'interactionism' (see chapter 2.4.3) provided me with a number of essential details and shed considerable light on the motivations behind the choice to subtitle or

[i] A 'double release' is the release of the same original audiovisual product in two different language transfer methods, e.g. one copy subtitled and another copy of the same product dubbed.

revoice. The structure of the audiovisual translation industry in Greece is very fragile, cliquey and based on personal networking. Through such informal chats - rather than interviews – I managed to collect information that would not be otherwise stated, since it might conflict with other peoples' interests.

Nevertheless, a set of formal questionnaires was needed as a solid basis on which I would found my conclusions, something that can be scrutinised by other researchers. The questionnaires were compiled by me, checked by professionals with thorough knowledge of statistics and popular surveys in the particular field of the audiovisual media, and officially approved by the Greek Institute for Audiovisual Media. A different questionnaire was designed for a) people in the television industry, b) people in the cinema industry, and c) people in the video industry. All three, however, were designed on a similar basis so that the various answers from all the audiovisual modes could be compared. The questionnaires start off with general questions on how the particular commissioners organise the team of people who decide on the choice of the language transfer method and finish with questions related to attitudes and motivations behind the actual choice of the method. Ample space for elaborate answers was provided - especially in the second part of the questionnaire when more analytic data on the agents' motivations was expected - and ample time to deal with these issues was allowed (some commissioners replied about two months after they were actually handed the questionnaire due to the presence of work which, naturally, had priority over the questionnaire). No one who answered the questionnaire asked for explanatory comments but all wanted to know if their answers were satisfactory enough. All five TV stations, six cinema distribution agencies and four video distribution agencies who had already provided me with the data related to audiovisual products completed the questionnaire. No one refused to fill a questionnaire or avoided answering any questions.

3.2 Methods of data analysis: some observations

Most of the TV-audience research carried out by various viewing-rating companies is primarily concerned with helping programme flow planners and aimed at guiding TV advertisers (Kovacic, 1995:378). This, however, does not necessarily mean that its findings are irrelevant or non-applicable to a study generally interested in recipients'/viewers' attitudes. Still, this data has to be handled with care and viewing rates as well as market shares have to be carefully examined and evaluated, since "the analysis of audience reactions is full of imponderables" (Hood, 1967:44).

The exact time of a programme's broadcast is a very important parameter when examining viewing behaviour. Viewing rates for programmes broadcast very early in the morning, for example, cannot be directly compared to viewing rates for programmes broadcast during peak viewing times. The sequence of programmes on TV is another very important parameter. If a specific programme is squeezed between two successful programmes, it will attract equally high viewing rates irrespective of its own quality, due to the phenomenon of audience duplication[i]. The actual TV station that broadcasts the programme is a third important parameter. Programmes broadcast by a channel which is not so popular cannot possibly reach the levels that programmes from the viewers' favourite channels achieve, irrespective of the individual qualities of the programmes, because the degree of bias that surrounds the not-so-popular stations and the lack of interest on the part of the viewers discourages regular checking of what is shown/broadcast on any of them. For all these reasons, the tables that contain the viewing rates of the various programmes had to be structured in such a way that TV programmes are presented per TV station and along the time scale.

As far as data on cinema and video viewing is concerned, it was relative percentages rather than absolute figures that were available (see also section 3.1.3). The percentages themselves, referring to

[i] 'Audience duplication' is the phenomenon of consecutive viewing of programmes along the time scale, i.e. of programmes that follow what we had already been watching simply because we left the television on.

different language transfer versions of the same audiovisual products, naturally ensure the validity of the comparable results. In order to account for the reception of phenomena related to the peculiarities of an individual cinema or video agency's code of practice rather than a general norm, data on the reception of cinema and video products are presented per agency before they are compiled in a summary table.

Techniques of data analysis in themselves cannot be good or bad, but rather more or less fruitful (Silverman, 1993:2). A qualitative analysis of the data on human agents - as collected through unofficial interviews and questionnaires - would render the findings more relevant by enhancing their validity. A retrospective reconstruction of the human agents' choices and motivations that led to the emergence of a specific norm has to be placed within a framework of other sciences/disciplines like psychology, sociology and psycholinguistics (cf. Toury, 1985:18).

After establishing the social context within which the human agents expressed their views, I decided to establish a communication pattern based on feedback from the human agents on my reactions to their initial views. They expressed their attitudes, I collected them, but I did not restrict the interaction: after an initial evaluation and analysis of their views I returned my interpretation of their comments - in conjunction with the views of some of their fellow colleagues - and they, in reply, confirmed whether my original conclusions/assumptions were well formulated and whether their views had been well understood. This was achieved by either face-to-face meetings or telephone conversations, again in the form of unofficial mini-interviews. In this way, human agents had the chance to reformulate, elaborate and clarify points they had expressed when filling the questionnaires but were not so clear after all, especially since the questionnaires were structured in open-ending question-forms that can sometimes allow multiple interpretations.

3.3 Norms and motivations at the Lower Level

3.3.1 Findings related to lower level products

The audiovisual map of Europe divides its member states into predominantly 'subtitling' or predominantly 'dubbing'. On this map, Greece has been traditionally charted as a predominantly subtitling country (Papadakis, 1998:65; Luyken et al, 1991:181). A survey conducted in 1989 showed that 90% of TV programmes broadcast in Greece were subtitled, only 5% dubbed, and another 5% voiced-over (Luyken et al, 1991:33; *Screen Digest*, 1992:157). Nevertheless, when it comes to children's TV programmes in particular the situation seems to be modified since "cartoons are invariably revoiced even in subtitling countries [...] because of the age-range of their expected audience and because of the need to preserve their visual integrity" (Luyken et al. 1991:134). What the present case study will set out to investigate is the question: do these absolute statements reflect the Greek audiovisual reality as well or is there variation in the language transfer method chosen not just for cartoons but for all children's TV programmes? And if we hypothesise that there is variation in the choice of the language transfer method, what are the motivations behind it? What we need to do, thus, is firstly establish whether the language transfer method chosen for children's TV programmes in Greece does actually deviate from the general subtitling norm, and then move on to investigate what might motivate such a deviation.

The need for statistical data in order to establish the presence of a norm as a consistent pattern of behaviour is obvious (cf. Delabastita, 1989:212). In order to provide statistical data one has to classify his/her raw data into categories. Turner says that "genre is the product of at least three groups of forces: the industry and its production practices; the audience and their expectations and competencies; and the text in its contribution to the genre as a whole" (1988:86). But how can one classify children's TV programmes into categories of genres when there is no existing typology and the 'groups of forces' - as described above - seem to be far from reaching a consensus? Some people say that the aim of children's programming is "to provide a microcosm of adult television for the children's audience" (Anna Home, Head of the Children's Department at the BBC, in Davies, 1989:35). If this is the case, a typology of children's TV programmes should not differ from the one established for adults. At the same time, others claim that children "tend to organise pictures of television characters into discrete groups of human, animated and puppet characters" (Gunter & McAleer, 1990:45). Since this different perception of the world appears to influence the way the 'second group of forces', namely children, perceive TV programmes targeted at them, these parameters of varying perception should not be neglected from the construction of a potential typology either. It is also worth pointing out that children tend to watch a "heavily verbally loaded cartoon" exactly as adults do, but they do not read the subtitles in an "action-oriented cartoon" as much as older subjects do (d'Ydewale et al. 1991:653). Thus, a study that is specifically interested in the choice of language transfer method might further have to distinguish between those products where action is important and those where dialogues are important.

Taking all the above views into consideration, I have tried to come up with a typology for children's TV programmes that does not set out to offer guidelines for the classification of such audiovisual products for all kinds of purposes and in all kinds of studies, but rather help clarify and shed some fresh light onto the motivations behind the choice of the language transfer method in particular. As far as the traditional classification in terms of length and serialisation of products is concerned, I maintain a classification into 'movies' and 'series'[i], especially since these two different film-types seem to be broadcast on different blocks of airtime/show-time (cf. Davies, 1989:35). With respect to children's psychological perception of events and characters, I distinguish between a) cartoon, b) live-action, c) cartoon/live-action, and d) puppet character-containing genres. Finally, in order to investigate the influence of the verbal load on the

---

[i] Some scholars establish a further distinction between 'series' and 'serials'. The former have self-contained plots whereas the latter have a continuing story-line (Goodhart & Ehrenberg, 1975:4). My use of the term 'series' covers both these notions.

choice of language transfer method, I examine the possible correlation between the choice of method and the balance of action vs. dialogues in each individual case where a specific product shows diversity from the norm which is established for its broader category of film type and genre.

The picture of the language transfer method, then, as chosen by the top 5 TV stations in Greece (ANT1, MEGA, STAR, SKY, ET1) and 1 cable TV station (FILMNET) for children's broadcasts in March 1995 and March 1996 expressed in terms of number of products and minutes of screen-show, looks as follows[i]:

[i] All programmes translated from English unless otherwise indicated.

Table 3.3.1.1 Children's programmes on ANT1 (private channel)

TV STATION: ANT1	**MARCH 1995**				**MARCH 1996**			
PROGRAMME TYPE	**SUBTITLED**		**DUBBED**		**SUBTITLED**		**DUBBED**	
	Prod/s	Min/s	Prod/s	Min/s	Prod/s	Min/s	Prod/s	Min/s
Children's movies (cartoons)								
Children's movies (l/action)								
Children's movies (cart + l/a)								
Children's movies (puppets)								
Children's series (cartoons)	2[i]	90	7	210	1[ii]	60	7	180
Children's series (l/action)			1[iii]	30			2[iv]	60
Children's series (cart + l/a)								
Children's series (puppets)								
TOTAL	**2**	**90**	**8**	**240**	**1**	**60**	**9**	**240**

Show times: Weekends 07:00 - 12:00/12:30

[i] *Garfield, Bugs Bunny and Friends*

[ii] *Bugs Bunny and Friends*

[iii] *Power Rangers*

[iv] *Power Rangers, VR Troopers*

Table 3.3.1.2 Children's programmes on MEGA (private channel)

TV STATION: MEGA	**MARCH 1995**				**MARCH 1996**			
PROGRAMME TYPE	**SUBTITLED**		**DUBBED**		**SUBTITLED**		**DUBBED**	
	Prod/s	Min/s	Prod/s	Min/s	Prod/s	Min/s	Prod/s	Min/s
Children's movies (cartoons)								
Children's movies (l/action)	2	195			2	210		
Children's movies (cart + l/a)					1	105		
Children's movies (puppets)								
Children's series (cartoons)	8[i]	240	8[ii]	315	2[iii]	60	8[iv]	300
Children's series (l/action)								
Children's series (cart + l/a)	1[v]	60						
Children's series (puppets)								
TOTAL	**11**	**495**	**8**	**315**	**5**	**375**	**8**	**300**

1995 Series show times: Weekends 06:00 - 11:15/12:15
1995 Movies show times: Saturday 11:15 - 13:00, Monday 08:00 - 09:30
1996 Series show times: Weekends 07:30 - 11:00
1996 Movies show times: Saturdays 11:00/11:30 - 13:15

---

[i] *Laser Patrol, Kidd Video, Space Cats, The Simpsons, Taz-Mania, Yo Yogi, Adam's Family, Yogi's Space Race*

[ii] *Smurfs* (French), *Scooby's All Star, Flintstone Frolics, Mighty Max, Young Robin Hood, Captain Planet, Saban's Adventures, Disney Club*

[iii] *Two Stupid Dogs, Droopy Master Detective*

[iv] *Smurfs* (French), *Tin Tin* (French), *Tale Spin, Flintstones, Mighty Max, Darkwing Duck, My Little Pony Tale, Disney Club*

[v] *Walt Disney Hourly Programme*

Table 3.3.1.3 Children's programmes on STAR (private channel)

TV STATION: STAR	MARCH 1995				MARCH 1996			
PROGRAMME TYPE	SUBTITLED		DUBBED		SUBTITLED		DUBBED	
	Prod/s	Min/s	Prod/s	Min/s	Prod/s	Min/s	Prod/s	Min/s
Children's movies (cartoons)								
Children's movies (l/action)								
Children's movies (cart + l/a)								
Children's movies (puppets)								
Children's series (cartoons)					2[i]	40	9[ii]	250
Children's series (l/action)	2	140			3	120		
Children's series (cart + l/a)								
Children's series (puppets)								
TOTAL	**2**	**140**			**5**	**160**	**9**	**250**

1995 Show times: Weekends 10:00 - 11:30
1996 Show times: Saturdays 07:00 - 09:30 & 12:00 - 12:30 / Sundays 06:00 - 09:30 /Weekdays 14:20 - 15:00

---

[i] *Woody Woodpecker, Popeye*

[ii] *Maya the Bee, Dennis the Menace, Police Academy, Spiderman, Fantom 2040, Lucky Luke, Rupert, Botsmaster, Iznogood*

3.3.1.4 Children's programmes on SKY (private channel)

TV STATION: SKY	**MARCH 1995**				**MARCH 1996**			
PROGRAMME TYPE	**SUBTITLED**		**DUBBED**		**SUBTITLED**		**DUBBED**	
	Prod/s	Min/s	Prod/s	Min/s	Prod/s	Min/s	Prod/s	Min/s
Children's movies (cartoons)								
Children's movies (l/action)								
Children's movies (cart + l/a)								
Children's movies (puppets)								
Children's series (cartoons)	3[i]	120	8	390				
Children's series (l/action)	1[ii]	30						
Children's series (cart + l/a)								
Children's series (puppets)								
TOTAL	**4**	**150**	**8**	**390**				

Show times: Weekends 07:30 - 11:30
(except for *Key West*, shown on Saturdays at 14:00)

[i] *Les Miserables* (French), *Cartoon Festival, Key West*

[ii] *The Little Gladiators*

Table 3.3.1.5 Children's programmes on ET1 (state-owned channel)

TV STATION: ET1	**MARCH 1995**				**MARCH 1996**			
PROGRAMME TYPE	**SUBTITLED**		**DUBBED**		**SUBTITLED**		**DUBBED**	
	Prod/s	Min/s	Prod/s	Min/s	Prod/s	Min/s	Prod/s	Min/s
Children's movies (cartoons)	2	180						
Children's movies (l/action)	1	90						
Children's movies (cart + l/a)								
Children's movies (puppets)								
Children's series (cartoons)	4[i]	90	4[ii]	110	3[iii]	90	8[iv]	230
Children's series (l/action)	3	70			3	120	1[v]	10
Children's series (cart + l/a)								
Children's series (puppets)								
TOTAL	**10**	**430**	**4**	**110**	**6**	**210**	**9**	**240**

1995 Show times: Weekdays 10:00 - 12:00 and 16:00 - 18:00 / Saturdays 08:30 - 10:30 and 12:30 - 14:00
1996 Show times: Weekdays 13:00 - 15:00 / Saturdays 08:00 - 14:00

---

[i] *Captain Hawk, Treasure Island, The Incredible Melops, Walt Disney Originals*

[ii] *Orson and Olivia* (French), *Jenny and Jenny, The Little Ones, Smogeys*

[iii] *Star Trekkers, Escape from Jupiter, Become an Artist*

[iv] *Annette: The Alpes Girl, Spirou and Fantazio* (French), *Pifs and Hercules* (French), *Let's Go Higher, Casper and Friends, Taking off, The Little Ones, Buzzy Bee*

[v] *This is How the Chinese Call It*

Table 3.3.1.6 Children's programmes on FILMNET (private cable channel)

TV STATION: FILMNET	**MARCH 1995**				**MARCH 1996**			
PROGRAMME TYPE	**SUBTITLED**		**DUBBED**		**SUBTITLED**		**DUBBED**	
	Prod/s	Min/s	Prod/s	Min/s	Prod/s	Min/s	Prod/s	Min/s
Children's movies (cartoons)								
Children's movies (l/action)	4	480			4	420		
Children's movies (cart + l/a)								
Children's movies (puppets)								
Children's series (cartoons)								
Children's series (l/action)								
Children's series (cart + l/a)								
Children's series (puppets)								
TOTAL	**4**	**480**			**4**	**420**		

1995 Show times: Weekdays 10:00 - 12:00
1996 Show times: Weekdays 08:00 - 10:00, Weekends 09:00 - 11:00

Table 3.3.1.7 Overall children's TV programmes

OVERALL	MARCH 1995				MARCH 1996			
PROGRAMME TYPE	SUBTITLED		DUBBED		SUBTITLED		DUBBED	
	Prod/s	Min/s	Prod/s	Min/s	Prod/s	Min/s	Prod/s	Min/s
Children's movies (cartoons)	2	180						
Children's movies (l/action)	7	765			6	630		
Children's movies (cart + l/a)					1	105		
Children's movies (puppets)								
Children's series (cartoons)	17[i]	540	27	1025	8[ii]	250	32	960
Children's series (l/action)	6	240	1	30	6	240	3	70
Children's series (cart + l/a)	1	60						
Children's series (puppets)								
TOTAL	**33[iii]**	**1785**	**28**	**1055**	**21[iv]**	**1225**	**35**	**1030**

The first conclusions that one can draw from the individual tables for every TV station and the table of overall children's TV programmes (Table 3.3.1.7) can be summarised as follows:

- Greek TV stations do not broadcast many children's movies (only 9 in March 1995 and just 7 in March 1996). Although the number of children's cartoon movies (2) is not statistically sufficient for drawing reliable conclusions, we see that in 1995 they are both subtitled[v]. In addition, both were broadcast by the national/state-owned TV station (ET1), a TV station that: a) did not show a

[i] **39%** of the total children's cartoon series for March 1995

[ii] **20%** of the total children's cartoon series for March 1996

[iii] **54%** of the total children's TV programmes for March 1995

[iv] **37%** of the total children's TV programmes for March 1996

[v] Unfortunately there were no cartoon movies broadcast, and therefore no data for 1996.

special tendency towards subtitling or revoicing the rest of its cartoon programmes that month (4 subtitled vs. 4 revoiced), and b) most importantly, has the financial resources (state money), the technical resources (fully-equipped own revoicing department), as well as the support of the government to disregard existing norms (if it wished) and broadcast dubbed programmes, arguably promoting the Greek language. One might cautiously suggest, then, that children's cartoon TV movies in Greece tend to be broadcast subtitled.

- The case for live-action children's TV movies is much more straightforward. All 7 for March 1995 and all 6 for March 1996 were subtitled, indicating a clear pattern of choice. It is true that the data come from only 3 TV stations (MEGA, ET1, FILMNET) but their different statuses (the first private wireless, the second state-owned wireless, the third private cable) strengthen the validity of the result. Children's live-action TV movies in Greece, then, seem to be invariably subtitled.
- The size of the sample (1) for the category of TV movies that contain both cartoon and live-action images/characters does not allow us to draw any conclusions at all. What can be observed, however, is that even this category does not deviate from the overall norm that requires children's TV movies to be subtitled (all 9 for March 1995 and all 7 for March 1996).
- There are no puppet programmes at all (movies or series) broadcast in March 1995 or 1996. Unlike the United Kingdom, where puppet series like *Wallace and Gromit* and *Pingu* are quite popular and attract high viewing rates, TV in Greece never had a big puppet hit (except for a local production, *Frutopia,* around 1990). One would expect the language transfer method that will be chosen for new puppet movies or series to follow - rather than dictate - the norm that has already been established for/by the rest of the products that belong to the respective film-type of movies or series.
- Children's cartoon series are the most interesting case. What we notice immediately here is that the percentage of subtitled children's cartoon series dropped from 39% of the overall genre in

March 1995 to 20% in March 1996 (see table 3.1.1.7 footnote), i.e. it was reduced by almost 50%. The number of products in this category/genre (44 for March 1995 and 40 for March 1996) allows us to draw reliable conclusions even about potential diachronic tendencies; and the tendency for the language transfer method of children's cartoon series seems to point towards dubbing. It is actually two TV stations (MEGA and ET1) that seem to change their approach between 1995 and 1996 leading to that increase in the percentage of dubbed children's cartoon series. MEGA had only 50% of those programmes dubbed in March 1995 (8 out of 16), but the percentage rose to 80% in March 1996 (8 out of 10). Similarly, ET1 had 50% of this genre of programmes dubbed in March 1995 (4 out of 8), rising to 73% in March 1996 (8 out of 11). Again, the former is a private station whereas the latter is a state-owned station, therefore indicating the breadth and applicability of the normative trend. Of the rest, ANT1 seems to be the most consistently committed to dubbing children's cartoon series (78% in March 1995, 87.5% in March 1996), STAR comes second (82% in March 1996) and SKY third (73% in March 1995).

- The source language of the postscript (the text on which the translation is based) could be seen to play some role in the choice of the language transfer method for children's cartoon series. The only source language other than English is French, and this is only subtitled once, on SKY(*Les miserables*, see table 3.3.1.4), for a product rather targeted at older children and shown early on Sundays (07:30, opening the station's daily session). The rest of the products transferred from a French postscript, like *The Smurfs* and *Tin Tin* on MEGA (see table 3.3.1.2) or *Orson and Olivia, Spirou and Fantazio* and *Pifs and Hercules* on ET1 (see table 3.3.1.5), were dubbed like most children's cartoon series. As expected, it is the state-owned ET1 that broadcasts most of the non-English productions (4 in 1995, 2 in 1996), in compliance with the EBU (European Broadcasting Union) regulations to promote European rather than American productions.

- Of particular interest in this context is the motivation behind subtitling the rest of the children's cartoon series. A large number of these seem to draw on more adult themes/humour (*Garfield* on ANT1; *The Simpsons, Adam's Family, Two Stupid Dogs* on MEGA; *Key West* on SKY; *Captain Hawk, Treasure Island, Star Trekkers, Escape from Jupiter, Become an Artist* on ET1), so that they can be seen as targeted at older children. Some are re-releases or new episodes of previous series that were initially broadcast subtitled years ago (like *Woody Woodpecker* and *Popeye* on STAR), so that the special, existing audience of these programmes would find a change in the language transfer method quite disturbing and alienating from what they might expect from the programme. Another possible reason, closely connected with the expectations of an existing audience, is the respect for a source product's original status and nature. Delabastita raises exactly this question of the importance of the status that a source product might have acquired within the target system (1989:209), Zabalbeascoa stresses the target audience's preference for original voices on such products (1994:92), Fodor stresses the immense constraints imposed by what he calls 'character synchrony' if the individual character's timbre, pitch, intensity and speech tempo are so well-known that they can be easily recognisable by the audience (1976:72), and Zabalbeascoa again gives the example of certain cartoons (like *Tom and Jerry)* where the pace of action is conditioned by a famous piece of classical music (1997:339). All these constraints apply in the case of all-time classic cartoon series like *Bugs Bunny and Friends* on ANT1, *Taz-Mania* and *Droopy Master Detective* on MEGA, *Cartoon Festival* on SKY, and *Walt Disney Originals* on ET1. Such constraints ultimately encourage a children's TV programmes commissioner to think twice before s/he interferes with the original soundtrack without taking into consideration aspects such as: high quality status, accustoming of the audience in terms of the characters' voices, unique phonetic qualities of the characters, and visual action strongly dictated by music. This combination of source-product related aspects, I suggest, motivates the choice of subtitling the only cartoon + live-action series as well (*Walt Disney Hourly Programme* on MEGA). I cannot seem to be able to find any consistent - set of - special reasons, however, for the choice to subtitle other cartoon series like *Laser Patrol, Kidd Video, Space Cats, Yo Yogi, Yo Yogi's Space Race* on MEGA, or like *The Incredible Melops* on ET1. The existing broader subtitling norm of these specific channels in particular (as described above) as well as of the whole country in general, the possible late arrival of the episodes, and - most of all - the cost factor, in combination with the expected low viewing rates for the specific programmes, might have led their commissioners to choose subtitling as the preferred language transfer method. All these possible motivations will have to be investigated further.

- Unlike children's cartoon series, children's live-action series tend to be subtitled (6 out of 7 in March 1995, 6 out of 9 in March 1996). The only station that does broadcast its children's live-action series dubbed is ANT1 (1 out of 1 in March 1995, 2 out of 2 in March 1996), which in any case, as mentioned above, has the highest ratio of dubbed cartoon series as well. STAR, SKY and ET1 have all their children's live-action series subtitled[i]. The children's live-action series that ANT1 dubs (*Power Rangers, VR Troopers*) do not differ at all from those broadcast by the rest of the stations: they are all action-loaded series aimed at 'average' children and not at one age sub-group in particular. One can assume then that the norm to subtitle children's live-action series might be influenced by a broader norm to subtitle live-action programmes in general; the potential existence of such a broader norm, therefore, should be further investigated. ANT1 is clearly deviating from this norm, experimenting with the audience's preferences and trying to establish a new audiovisual reality in the country. What should be also investigated, then, is the reception by the audience of this pioneering attempt, i.e. the viewing rates of these ANT1 programmes.

---

[i] Except for *This is How the Chinese Call It* on ET1, a special case of children's programme, more like a documentary, using not only dubbing but sometimes voice-over too.

- The relative airtime figures had to be added to the tables in order to see if products from any fuzzy categories were transferred one or the other way because of their time-length (longer products require more time - and money - in order to be properly dubbed). The only fuzzy category proved to be children's cartoon series. Not surprisingly, the airtime percentage of the overall subtitled children's cartoon series matches the actual statistical percentage of the numbers of the products themselves (39% subtitled products with 35% airtime in March 1995, 20% subtitled products with 20% airtime in March 1996). As a result, one can safely say that the relative length of this type of product does not play any role in the choice of either language transfer method. Nevertheless, it should be mentioned that although the total number of subtitled children's TV programmes in general drops from 54% in March 1995 to 37% in March 1996, the overall airtime devoted to subtitled children's TV programmes remains quite high (63% in March 1995, 54% in March 1996), due to the continued appeal of subtitled lengthy children's movies and live-action series. This implies that although there were relatively more dubbed cartoon series in 1996, viewers of children's TV programmes in general did not become significantly more accustomed to dubbing as a language transfer method, since the airtime devoted to the dubbed productions remained below that occupied by subtitled productions.

3.3.2 Findings related to lower level audiovisual mode

Part of television's success over printed mass media lies in the fact that TV does not necessarily require reading abilities. In this respect, revoicing as a language transfer method for foreign TV programmes should have an automatic advantage over the method of subtitling. For languages like Arabic, for example, which many can understand but relatively few can read, revoicing offers the opportunity to the masses to enjoy TV without effort (Volmar, 1950:540). Young children are similar in many respects to Arabic speakers, since many of the former, although able to understand what they hear in their native language, have not yet developed the ability to read at speed. However, just as several governments of countries with large Arabic-speaking populations see in subtitling a means for encouraging the masses to learn to read and write (ibid), educational authorities worldwide might similarly envisage in the method of subtitling a way to promote reading and writing abilities in their children population at quite an early age (Panourgia, 1998:5; cf. ITC (eds.), 1996:12).

Children nowadays grow up with television as a feature of their daily lives. Whereas TV was a novelty and a luxury to their parents, for contemporary children it forms part of their daily routine, a simple piece of furniture (Davies, 1989:179). Their own drawings of themselves in front of the TV set depict them smiling, enjoying themselves, having fun (Palmer, 1988:143). Even their physical posture in front of the TV, curled on the floor close to the set, reflects their sense of ease, cosiness and intimacy with the habit of TV-watching, although they seem to be aware that their parents do not appreciate so much the fact that they like TV (ibid). For adults who have not grown up with TV, it is very hard to overcome this bias against the medium and enter the children's psychology of TV viewing. Still, many adults who belong to this TV-deprived generation might have to make decisions related to children's TV programmes, including the choice of the language transfer method. Many of those who have a say in the audiovisual media have repeatedly lamented the decline of 'quality' in children's TV programmes, linking 'quality' with 'educational didactic intentions', and persistently "trying to 'improve' children through 'educational' activities, overlooking (and surely forgetting) that, for a child, the best toy, the best game, the best story and the best programme, is one that is fun" (Davies, 1989:135). These children's TV programme commissioners who are motivated in their choice of subtitling by the attempt to promote reading abilities and other educational skills seem to neglect the attitudes of the main recipients themselves, judging children's intentions and expectations through their own perspective.

Some audiovisual experts, like Thomas Herbst, claim that "there can hardly be any doubt that, from a foreign language teaching perspective, subtitling is much to be preferred to dubbing" (1995:258). Scientific research, however, has proven that even this aspect is a myth. Sandra Blane who investigated the influence of interlingual subtitling on improving foreign language skills shares the findings of previous reports which claim that "subjects' efficiency in processing messages presented in this form [Standard Subtitling], when post-editing was conducted in L2 was relatively poor, suggesting to us that the Standard Subtitling procedure is an unpromising method of strengthening or improving skills in L2" (1996:188). This is because the attention needed to grasp the meaning of the foreign dialogues is thwarted by the automatic tendency to process the corresponding native language subtitles (ibid:189). It is Reversed Subtitling (native language dialogues with foreign language subtitles) that has proved to be particularly fruitful. Children's TV agents who base their choice of language transfer method on educational considerations are, then, out of touch with educational reality.

In a traditionally subtitling country like Greece, TV stations do not revoice all their children's programmes, for a variety of reasons, some of which have already been explained in the previous section and more will be investigated later. One reason that does not apply to any of the Greek TV stations but led the European Children's Channel to decide to subtitle their programmes has to do with the currently available technological developments in TV broadcasting and the linguistic heterogeneity of the targeted audience. Children's Channel is a satellite TV channel that broadcasts in the Netherlands, Norway, Denmark, Sweden and Finland. The only way to allow multiple translations of the same transmitted product's dialogues to reach the various audiences simultaneously is via Teletext subtitling (cf. Kilborn, 1993:656). For Children's Channel then, and since Stereo Sound Broadcast does not allow a simultaneous transmission of more than two Sound Waves, the choice of subtitling as the eventually favourite language transfer method is a one-way choice, dictated purely by technical considerations.

This observation does not concern Greek reality since the implementation of Teletext is still in its infancy in Greece. One issue that has gained extensive attention in Greece, however, is the effects of television on children's eye-sight. I still remember my mother shouting to me to switch the TV off because I will become blind! A number of paediatricians in the country have conducted various surveys on the topic. Interestingly enough, however, they do not seem to come up with the same results. A report quoted by Papageorgiou suggests that "the focusing of the eyes on the rapid changes of spinning or quivering light images, dark, subtly lit or blindingly bright at times, wears the eyes out" (1981:7) [my translation]. Subtitles aggravate this effect by burdening the eyes with both additional flashing images at the bottom of the screen and the need for careful cognitive processing of the verbal message. Given that subtitling, then, is not 'healthy' for the eyes, commissioners of children's TV programmes should be particularly careful not to choose a method that might prove more harmful to those members of the audience whose health and vision are an extremely sensitive issue, especially since children do tend to sit very close to TV sets. On the other hand, the results of another survey published by the Medical School of Athens are less worrying. According to this research "the weariness of the eyes as reported by many viewers after prolonged TV watching is due to the weariness that was produced as a result of their usual labour and which was simply emphasised by television" (Kanavakis, 1977:24) [my translation]. It would be interesting, then, to investigate whether any Greek TV commissioners claim that they choose to revoice children's TV programmes in order to protect viewers' eyes.

3.3.3 Findings related to lower level recipients

The role of the audience in the media has always been critical. For television, as well as for the rest of the audiovisual media, the audience is the entity that directly affects the economics of the business, participating actively in the formulation of the constantly evolving marketplace by nominating the favourites - programmes and

TV stations - on a daily, if not an hourly, basis (cf. Drummond & Paterson , 1988: 1). Audiences have to be predicted by the human agents involved in the commissioning and promotion of TV programmes, and be constantly borne in mind before, during and even after the programmes' broadcast, when some kind of feedback is often sought. However, the audiences that are constructed in the human agents' minds are not the people who actually watch the programmes themselves but idealised representations of people *expected* to watch the relevant programmes (Hartley, 1989:227). At any rate, it is exactly these speculative constructions, however, that the human agents will have to predict and measure in advance, in order to achieve the highest possible viewing rates for their broadcasts.

As a potential audience, children have their own individual opinions, preferences, idiosyncrasies and sensitivities which are distinct from those of adults. Certain ethical considerations will also have to be catered for (e.g. exposure to brutality, obscene language etc.). Nevertheless, in the commercialised era of the television industry, the way they are perceived as potential market/buyers/consumers does not ultimately differ from the way adult audiences are perceived (Palmer, 1988:152). What could one define the audience of 'children' to be, then, in order to distinguish it from that of 'adults'? Once again, there is no fixed rule one could follow or a straight line between the two groups that one could draw. Paediatricians and child psychologists tend to regard the general group of 'children' as consisting of three age sub-groups: a) 0-3-year-olds (toddlers), b) 3-7-year-olds (young children), and c) 7-11- or 7-14-year-olds (youngsters) (Papageorgiou, 1981:2). In the field of television, it is mostly companies that measure viewing rates who have to sort recipients into 'children' and 'adult' groups, in order to carry out their statistics accordingly. TV programme commissioners normally comply with the established convention. Even amongst the various viewing-rate companies, however, there has been no consensus in terms of group definitions. In England for example, BARB/AGB treats as 'children' audience the aggregate of viewers belonging to the age group of 4-15 years (Davies, 1989:40). In Greece, the same company (AGB, associated with the Italian headquarters, though) regards as part of a 'children' audience anyone between the age of 6 and 14 (AGB Hellas eds., 1996:100).

Despite difficulties in achieving consensus in terms of the exact boundaries of age groups for a 'children' audience, most of the audiovisual media people seem to agree on the variables that determine the viewing habits of - not just children but - overall TV audience in general. These variables are thought to be a) the age of the viewers, b) the sex/gender of the viewers, and c) the socio-educational class of the viewers (Luyken et al., 1991:114; Gottlieb, 1995:389; O'Connell, 1998:64). Davies adds a further two parameters: d) the availability of alternative activities for the viewers and, e) the time of the year and the time of the day that the programmes are broadcast (1989:42). For adults, it is generally assumed that preference for dubbing increases with age and decreases with the decrease in educational and socio-economic level (Luyken et al, 1991:114; cf. El-Sakran, 1997:98). But what about children?

What has been clearly proven about the variable of age and the audience group of 'children' is that children start to watch TV somewhere around the age of two and a half (Gunter & McAleer, 1990:100; AGB Hellas eds., 1996:100), with an increase in age resulting in an increase in viewing time, reaching an average of four hours daily at weekends for 40% of Greek youngsters aged between ten and twelve (AGB Hellas eds., 1996:100). In terms of gender, it has been proven that this variable affects the viewing habits of adult recipients but not those of children. As for the variable of socio-educational status, what has been shown is that Greek children of parents with a low socio-economic and educational status spend twice as much time watching TV than those whose parents belong to a higher socio-economic and educational class (Koronaiou, 1992:128). This is closely related to the variable of availability of other activities. Here, research findings suggest that children who enjoy recreational activities within the confines of the home also spend more time watching TV (Palmer, 1988:151); at the same time, families who can afford to spend more on outdoor activities for their children and families who live closer to areas with outdoor recreational facilities can provide alternatives to TV watching (ibid). Finally, in terms of broadcast time, it is easy to understand that programmes broadcast before 07:00/07:30AM cannot reach the full range of children sub-groups, because some of them are still asleep at that time of the day.

Some claim that lack of reading proficiency amongst children in general makes them favour revoicing (Luyken et al.,1991:136). Elsewhere, it is reported that it is children under six who watch mainly children's programmes, whereas children between the age of ten and twelve watch mainly adult material (Gunter & Svennevig, 1987:10; Stipp, 1993:301). The latter position recognises that the viewing habits of older children may be different, whereas the former does not recognise the distinction between older and younger children and treats them all as belonging to one broad age-group. If it is true, however, that older children watch more adult than children's material, one could expect the preference of the language transfer method for children between the age of ten and twelve to be closer to that of 'adults' than that of 'children', since their attitudes would be inevitably influenced by the norms which operate in the adults' programmes they mainly watch. As a result, one could expect Greek youngsters between the age of ten and twelve to be influenced by the predominant method of transferring TV programmes for adults and, therefore, favour subtitling rather than dubbing.

In Greece, the vagueness that surrounds the treatment of children as a broad audience group is emphasised by the views of people outside the audiovisual industry who lament the fact that children's TV programmes do not cater for the needs of individual children age-groups but are aimed indiscriminately at 'children' in general (Papageorgiou, 1981:5). What they propose is that one should distinguish between programmes targeted at younger children aged between five and eight, and others targeted at youngsters aged between nine and twelve (ibid). Even within the general category of 'children's audience', then, the age variable appears to play a significant role, since members of age sub-groups might be conditioned by different viewing habits, therefore favouring the one or the other method of language transfer.

Just as we claim that children, especially older ones, do not just watch children's programmes but also programmes aimed at adults, however, it is also possible to suggest that children's TV programmes are not viewed by children alone either. A survey carried out in Australia shows that only 7% of children watch TV on their own (Palmer, 1988:143). In Greece, most children in the household (78%) watch TV with other members of the family (AGB Hellas eds., 1995:33). This seems reasonable considering the fact that only 1% of TV sets are placed in children's bedrooms; 79% are placed in the lounge and another 16% in adults' bedrooms (AGB Hellas eds. 1996:32). As a result, private TV watching by children is rarely feasible. As for who decides what to be watched, 31% say that this is a decision they take together, and only 4.5% say that it is children who take the final decision (AGB Hellas eds., 1995:33). A broader survey conducted in 1996, however, states that "53% of the parents admit that they watch the programmes that the children like frequently or always, even if they would have preferred to watch something else" (AGB Hellas eds., 1996:101). At any rate, it is clearly the case that - mostly for the sake of controlling their children's viewing material - parents do watch TV with their children, a habit which decreases as children grow older (ibid:100). As a result, it is very difficult to assume that children's TV programmes are targeted at children alone, or that human agents do not also have adults in mind when they visualise their hypothetical audience, especially since reactions and feedback about the quality of children's broadcasts will come primarily from satisfied or dissatisfied parents. The figures speak for themselves:

Table 3.3.3.1 Average market shares[i] for overall children's TV programmes [source AGB Hellas]

AGE-GROUPS OF VIEWERS WATCHING CHILDREN'S PROGRAMMES	AVERAGE MARKET SHARES	
	1994-1995	**1995-1996**
Children	35.8	18.8
Young Men 15-24	22.6	19.1
Young Women 15-24	21.7	17.1
Men 25-44	20.4	12.4
Women 25-44	21.6	11.2

The figures for 1994-1995 indicate that children's TV programmes were watched by 35.8% of the children's audience, 22.6% of the audience of young men aged 15-24, 21.7% of the audience of young women aged 15-24, 21.6% of the audience of women aged 25-44 (i.e. potential mothers) and 20.4% of the audience of men aged 25-44 (i.e. potential fathers). For 1995-1996, the figures are even more indicative: children's TV programmes were watched by only 18.8% of the children's audience, 19.1% of the audience of young men aged 15-24, 17.1% of the audience of young women aged 15-24, 12.4% of the audience of men aged 25-44 and 11.2%, of the audience of women aged 25-44. If they were to decide on the language transfer method for children's TV programmes, then, commissioners would have to think about the opinions and the reactions of a broader range of viewers.

---

[i] The 'Average Market Share' is defined as the percentage of viewers of a specific programme in relation to the number of people watching TV at a specific time-point (AGB Hellas eds., 1995:107). For example, the figure '35.8' on the 'children' row, implies that 35.8% of the children that were watching TV at a specific time-point were actually watching a children's programme that was broadcast at the time. Similarly, the number '22.6' on the 'young men 15-24' row, indicates that 22.6% of the young men aged 15-24 who were watching TV at a specific time point were watching a children's programme that was broadcast at the time. The difference between 'TV Ratings' (or as commonly known 'Viewing Rates') and the 'Average Market Shares' is that the former are percentages measured against the total potential viewers, i.e. almost against the total population, whereas the latter are percentages measured against those members of the population who had their TV sets on at a given time-point.

Therefore, given the broader appeal of children's TV programmes, it is unreasonable to claim that the targeted recipients are children and children alone.

Before we go on to analyse the reception of the specific children's TV programmes broadcast in March 1995 and March 1996 it is important to stress a number of points which relate to the choice of language transfer method and the nature of children as a recipient group:

- First of all, dubbing demands less cognitive effort than subtitling on the part of young children and toddlers that have not yet developed a reading ability. The shift of cognitive effort - from listening to dubbed dialogues into reading subtitled dialogues - is heavier for younger children and toddlers than it is for viewers with developed reading abilities (Gottlieb, 1994a:102; Karamitroglou, 1996:35; O'Connell, 1998:65). A significant increase in cognitive effort would affect the level of enjoyment and minimise the appreciation of the visual and acoustic background.
- Subtitles enhance the reading abilities of young children and toddlers (Aaltonen, 1995b:387; Panourgia, 1998:5). Both age-groups are extremely vulnerable to linguistic phenomena surrounding them (Davies, 1989:11). This, together with the facts that the flash of subtitles at the bottom of the screen leads the viewer automatically to read them and that watching TV on a daily basis is equivalent to reading a massive amount of written material suggest that subtitling could serve as a good exercise for young chidren and toddlers to improve their ability to read texts in their own language (O'Connell, 1998:65; ITC (eds.), 1996:12).
- In countries like Greece, with no extended Teletext facilities, if commissioners had to cater for the needs and rights of the deaf and hard of hearing children too, they would have no choice but to subtitle. Switzerland is an example of a country with such a policy, where the state even refunds the broadcaster for the additional costs of language transfer (cf. Solholm, 1990:38).
- Due to reasons related to first language acquisition, children in general are better lip readers than adults (Fodor, 1976:53). As a result they are more able to spot and get discouraged by dubbed

programmes where the quality of lip-sync is not high. A commissioner who wants a dubbed children's programme to be successful, then, has to invest more time and money in order to achieve high-quality lip-sync.

- Research has shown that while watching TV it is sound that attracts and image that maintains children's attention on the screen (Gunter & McAleer, 1990:36). Especially for toddlers who tend to look away from the screen about 215 times an hour (ibid:4), the choice to dub would be more effective in terms of drawing their eyes back to the screen, since an acoustic change in the dubbed dialogues would attract their attention more easily than the visual flash of a subtitled image.

The picture of the viewing rates[i] for all children's programmes broadcast by the top 5 TV stations in Greece in March 1995 and March 1996 looks as follows:

---

[i] 'Viewing Rates' (or 'TV Rating') is defined as the percentage of viewers of a specific programme in relation to the total potential viewership, i.e. the number of people who own a TV set (AGB Hellas eds., 1995:106). For example, the figure '1.7' on the first row of the following table means that 1.7% of children that have a TV in their house were actually watching the cartoon series *Weejet* when it was broadcast. Similarly, the second figure '0.3' means that 0.3% of the total population in the country - who own a TV set - were watching *Weejet* when it was broadcast. For a comparison between the notions of 'Viewing Rates' and 'Average Market Shares' see footnote for table 3.3.3.1. It should also be noted that as 'overall' audience or 'total' viewers I do not only count the five age-groups of table 3.3.3.1 but also population over the age of 45, as classified and measured by the agency that measures viewing rates in Greece (AGB Hellas).

Table 3.3.3.2 Viewing rates for ANT1 children's series

TV STATION: ANT1 CHILDREN'S SERIES	**MARCH 1995**				**MARCH 1996**			
CARTOON	**SUB**		**DUB**		**SUB**		**DUB**	
	Chld	Ovrl	Chld	Ovrl	Chld	Ovrl	Chld	Ovrl
07:00 Weejet			1.7	0.3				
07:30 1995/1996 The Adventures of Gin Gin			2.7	0.4			2.2	0.4
08:00 Incredible Standmen			2.6	0.5				
08:30 The Adventures of Peter Pan			3.8	0.7				
09:00 The Magic Lantern			4.6	0.8				
09:30 Batman			6.6	1.3			7.9	1.5
10:00 Garfield	2.9	0.7						
10:30 The Jetsons			3.5	1.0				
11:00 1995 / 10:00 1996 Bugs Bunny and Friends	6.6	2.0			9.7	2.2		
07:00 Puppies in Action							1.0	0.2
08:00 Kalimero and Friends							2.9	0.5
08:30 Casper							5.1	0.8
09:00 Dragonball							6.9	1.1
09:30 Sailormoon							8.4	1.5
CARTOON TOTAL	**4.8**	**1.4**	**3.6**	**0.7**	**9.7**	**2.2**	**4.9**	**0.9**
LIVE ACTION								
10:30 VR Troopers							10.8	2.1
12:00 1995 / 11:00 1996 Power Rangers			10.7	2.5			13.8	2.7
LIVE-ACTION TOTAL			**10.7**	**2.5**			**12.3**	**2.4**

Table 3.3.3.3 Viewing rates for MEGA children's series

TV STATION: MEGA CHILDREN'S SERIES	MARCH 1995				MARCH 1996			
CARTOON	**SUB**		**DUB**		**SUB**		**DUB**	
	Chld	Ovrl	Chld	Ovrl	Chld	Ovrl	Chld	Ovrl
06:00 Laser Patrol	0.1	0.2						
06:15 Space Cats	0.2	0.2						
06:30 Kidd Video	0.6	0.2						
06:30 1995 / 07:45 1996 Smurfs			1.9	0.5			1.0	0.2
06:45 Yogi's Space Race	0.6	0.2						
06:45 The Simpsons	1.1	0.2						
08:00 Yo Yogi	3.5	0.7						
08:15 Scooby's All Star			4.7	0.9				
08:30 Flinstone Frolics			6.6	1.2				
08:30 Taz-Mania	4.3	0.9						
08:45 Young Robin Hood			6.2	1.2				
08:45 Saban's Adventures			3.0	0.7				
09:00 1995/1996 Mighty Max			9.9	1.9			6.2	1.0
09:15 1995/1996 Disney Club			8.1	1.9			8.5	1.7
11:00 Captain Planet			6.8	1.8				
11:15 Addam's Family	2.9	1.3						
07:30 Droopy Master Detective					0.4	0.2		
07:45 Two Stupid Dogs					0.5	0.1		
08:00 Tin Tin							2.0	0.4
08:00 Tale Spin							2.1	0.4
08:15 Flinstones							2.8	0.6
08:45 Darkwing Duck							3.1	0.8
10:15 My Little Pony Tale							8.4	1.8
CARTOON TOTAL	**1.7**	**0.5**	**5.9**	**1.3**	**0.5**	**0.2**	**4.3**	**0.9**
CART + L/ACTION								
11:15 Walt Disney Hourly Programme	4.1	1.6						
CART + L/ACTION TOTAL	**4.1**	**1.6**						

Table 3.3.3.4 Viewing rates for STAR children's series

TV STATION: STAR CHILDREN'S SERIES	**MARCH 1995**				**MARCH 1996**			
CARTOON	**SUB**		**DUB**		**SUB**		**DUB**	
	Chld	Ovrl	Chld	Ovrl	Chld	Ovrl	Chld	Ovrl
06:30 Rupert							0.1	0.1
07:00 Maya the Bee							0.5	0.1
07:30 Dennis The Menace							1.0	0.2
07:45 Popeye					0.6	0.2		
08:00 Woody Woodpecker					1.2	0.3		
08:15 Police Academy							2.3	0.4
08:30 Spiderman							2.7	0.6
08:30 Botsmaster							1.0	0.4
09:00 Fantom 2040							1.8	0.5
09:15 Lucky Luke							3.5	0.9
09:30 Iznogood							1.7	0.6
CARTOON TOTAL					**0.9**	**0.3**	**1.6**	**0.4**
LIVE ACTION								
10:30 Flipper	1.1	0.9						
10:45 Lassie	0.5	1.4						
06:00 White Fang					0.1	0.2		
12:00 Zorro					3.1	1.2		
14:20 Black Beauty					2.7	2.3		
LIVE-ACTION TOTAL	**0.8**	**1.2**			**2.0**	**1.2**		

Table 3.3.3.5 Viewing rates for SKY children's series

TV STATION: SKY CHILDREN'S SERIES	**MARCH 1995**				**MARCH 1996**			
CARTOON	**SUB**		**DUB**		**SUB**		**DUB**	
	Chld	Ovrl	Chld	Ovrl	Chld	Ovrl	Chld	Ovrl
07:30 Les Miserables	0.7	0.2						
08:00 Sky-toons			1.0	0.4				
08:15 Cartoon Festival	2.3	0.6						
08:30 Robotek			1.9	0.4				
09:00 Candy Candy			2.8	0.9				
09:30 Casper			3.0	0.7				
10:00 Rupert			4.3	0.9				
10:15 Prince Valiant			1.7	0.5				
10:30 The Defenders of the Earth			2.6	0.7				
11:00 Superforce			0.4	0.5				
14:00 Key West	0.6	1.4						
CARTOON TOTAL	**1.2**	**0.7**	**2.2**	**0.7**				
LIVE ACTION								
11:15 The Little Gladiators	2.0	0.5						
LIVE-ACTION TOTAL	**2.0**	**0.5**						

Table 3.3.3.6 Viewing rates for ET1 children's series

TV STATION: ET1 CHILDREN'S SERIES	**MARCH 1995**				**MARCH 1996**			
CARTOON	**SUB**		**DUB**		**SUB**		**DUB**	
	Chld	Ovrl	Chld	Ovrl	Chld	Ovrl	Chld	Ovrl
09:00 1995 / 08:00 1996 The Little Ones			0.8	0.2			0.6	0.1
09:30 Walt Disney Originals	0.9	0.3						
10:00 Smogeys			0.4	0.2				
10:30 The Incredible Melops	0.3	0.2						
16:30 Orson and Olivia			0.7	0.3				
17:00 Captain Hawk	1.3	0.6						
17:00 Jenny and Jenny			1.1	0.5				
17:30 Treasure Island	1.2	0.5						
08:45 Annette: The Alpes Girl							0.9	0.2
09:15 Star Trekkers					1.2	0.2		
11:15 Escape from Jupiter					1.4	0.2		
11:45 Become an Artist					1.0	0.2		
13:15 Spirou and Fantazio							1.4	0.4
13:15 Buzzy Bee							2.3	0.4
13:30 Casper and Friends							2.6	0.5
13:30 Taking off							2.1	0.5
13:45 Let's Go Higher							1.9	0.5
14:15 Pifs and Hercules							2.2	0.5
CARTOON TOTAL	**0.9**	**0.4**	**0.8**	**0.3**	**1.2**	**0.2**	**1.7**	**0.4**
LIVE ACTION								
08:30 Super Tarzan	0.3	0.3						
10:00 1995/1996 Circus	1.2	0.6			1.1	0.5		
11:40 Drama	0.2	0.2						
10:00 The Winners					0.6			
13:45 This is how the Chinese Call it							1.9	0.5
14:30 In the Rhythm of Love					1.4			
LIVE-ACTION TOTAL	**0.6**	**0.4**			**1.0**	**0.4**	**1.9**	**0.5**

Table 3.3.3.7 Overall viewing rates for children's movies

OVERALL VIEWING OF CHILDREN'S MOVIES	**TV STATION**	**MARCH 1995**				**MARCH 1996**			
CARTOON		**SUB**		**DUB**		**SUB**		**DUB**	
		Chld	Ovrl	Chld	Ovrl	Chld	Ovrl	Chld	Ovrl
Snooks	ET1, 12:30	0.9	0.2						
Tin Tin	ET1, 12:30	1.9	0.7						
CARTOON TOTAL		**1.4**	**0.5**						
LIVE ACTION									
Copycat	ET1, 12:30	1.1	0.4						
The Strongest Man in the World	MEGA, 08:00	0.3	0.5						
Cheetah	MEGA, 11.15	1.7	2.0						
The Seven Faces of Dr. Lao	MEGA, 11:00					1.3	1.7		
The Adventures of Huckleberry Finn	MEGA, 11:30					1.4	1.4		
LIVE-ACTION TOTAL		**1.0**	**2.0**			**1.4**	**1.6**		
CARTOON + L/ACTION									
Pete's Dragon	MEGA, 11:30					3.4	0.8		
CART + L/ACTION TOTAL						**3.4**	**0.8**		
MOVIES TOTAL		**1.2**	**0.8**			**2.0**	**1.3**		

Table 3.3.3.8 Overall viewing rates for children's TV programmes

VIEWING RATES FOR CHILDREN'S PROGRAMMES	**MARCH 1995**				**MARCH 1996**			
PROGRAMME TYPE	**SUB**		**DUB**		**SUB**		**DUB**	
	Chld	Ovrl	Chld	Ovrl	Chld	Ovrl	Chld	Ovrl
Children's movies (cartoons)	1.4	0.5						
Children's movies (l/action)	1.0	2.0			1.4	1.6		
Children's movies (cart + l/a)					3.4	0.8		
Children's movies (puppets)								
Children's series (cartoons)	1.8	0.6	3.3	0.8	2.0	0.5	2.9	0.6
Children's series (l/action)	0.9	0.7	10.7	2.5	1.5	0.7	8.9	1.8
Children's series (cart + l/a)	4.1	1.6						
Children's series (puppets)								
TOTAL AVERAGE[i]	**1.6**	**0.7**	**3.6**	**0.8**	**1.8**	**0.7**	**3.4**	**0.7**

An analysis of the tables above shows the following:

- Cartoon movies are not popular amongst total viewers (an average of only 0.5% of the overall potential viewership was watching them). They are relatively more popular amongst children (1.4%) but still not reaching a satisfactory level (see table 3.3.3.7). They are all broadcast subtitled, therefore complying with language transfer norms that are claimed to be predominantly applicable to adult programmes. Still, adult viewers are likely to be discouraged from watching such programmes because they can hardly identify with non-real cartoon characters that are obviously designed to

[i] Figures on this row are calculated according to the total number of products that contribute to each of the programme-types. As a result, programme types like cartoon series, for example, that dominate the number of children's TV programmes (see table 3.3.1.7), affect the total average at a greater scale.

appeal to children. In this respect, one cannot claim that it is the prospect of attracting adult- rather than children-audiences which motivates commissioners towards the choice of subtitling these specific products. What we can assume is that the viewing rates that children's cartoon TV movies are expected to attract in the first place are so low that human agents are reluctant to invest more money to have them dubbed.

- Live-action children's TV movies are even less popular amongst children (the figures are 1.0% in March 1995, and 1.4% in March 1996) (see table 3.3.3.7). In terms of total number of viewers, children's live-action movies seem to rate much better than cartoon movies (2.0% in March 1995, 1.6% in March 1996). Here, for reasons opposite to the ones that operate with adults in children's cartoon TV movies, it is children that show signs of indifference towards the colourless and real-life situations of live-action programmes that resemble adult-oriented material. Amongst adults, dubbing would prove less successful because it would give the impression that the movie is children-oriented. It is quite possible, then, that commissioners choose to subtitle children's live-action TV movies because they do not have children as the only potential audience in mind. The question then arises: how can we classify such material as children-oriented, when it attracts more adult viewers?
- The amount of available data for cartoon/live-action children's TV movies (only 1 programme in March 1996) does not allow us to draw any reliable conclusions (see table 3.3.3.7). At first glance, it seems that children liked it (3.4%), whereas overall viewership was low (0.8%). The only thing that could be reliably suggested is that these viewing rates still do not justify the risk to dub such productions.
- Children's cartoon TV series account for the largest section of the data available in this study. Not surprisingly, the viewing rates they achieve rise as the day progresses: from around 0.1% when some TV stations start their programmes at 06:00AM to around 9.0% for children and 2.0% for overall viewing during 09:00-10:00AM at weekends. With the exception of MEGA and SKY (see tables

3.3.3.3 and 3.3.3.5), the choice of transfer method does not appear to influence the choice of show time, and vice versa. This is quite surprising, since one would not invest ten times more money to dub a production that would be broadcast at a time of the day when, by definition, it is impossible to achieve high viewing rates, unless it is a multiple repeat of the same series and it is broadcast at that time just to fill in the time-slot.

- ANT1 TV has its two peak audience cartoon series in March 1995 with dubbed *Batman* (6.6/1.3%) and subtitled *Bugs Bunny and Friends* (6.6/2.0%) (see table 3.3.3.2). Both are very famous series, but - as already pointed out in section 3.3.1 - the latter is more of a classic and it is therefore subtitled. Surprisingly enough, the other subtitled cartoon series broadcast in March 1995, i.e. *Garfield*, does not manage to attract the expected overall viewership (only 0.7%), not to mention the children's viewership which is reduced at the peak time of 10:00, from 6.6% to 2.9%. TV station officials seem to have taken note of this record, since in March 1996 they go on with subtitling only *Bugs Bunny and Friends*, which interrupts the flow of dubbed cartoon series at 10:00 to achieve a quite satisfactory 9.7% viewing rate amongst children and 2.2% overall.
- MEGA CHANNEL restricts subtitled cartoon series to the period prior to 08:30AM. It has its peak audience cartoon series in March 1995 with *Mighty Max* (9.9/1.9%) and *Disney Club* (8.1/1.9%) both around 09:00AM and both dubbed (see table 3.3.3.3). Peak viewership for children's programmes in March 1996 is reached with dubbed *Disney Club* (8.5/1.7%) and dubbed *My Little Pony Tale* (8.4/1.8%) around 10:00AM. The low viewing rates for early-morning subtitled productions in March 1995 seemed to encourage TV station officials to cut down on the number of subtitled cartoon series significantly in the following year, and set the start of their daily children's programme flow later in the day. The only exception to the above was *Addam's Family* in March 1995, subtitled because of its macabre adult humour and broadcast at 11:15AM. It did not manage to attract high viewing rates, however,

(2.9/1.3%) and as a result was taken off the timetables the following year.

- Unlike the previous two TV stations which are larger, more popular and therefore with a more stable audience, STAR CHANNEL's audience, especially in 1994-1995, was more transient, consisting of viewers who would flick STAR on for a moment without knowing what was on and continue watching if they found something better than what was shown on ANT1 and MEGA. It is not surprising then that its viewership of children's TV cartoon series appears to fluctuate along the time scale (see table 3.3.3.4). The channel's big cartoon-series hit in March 1996 is a dubbed production, *Lucky Luke* (3.5/0.9%), famous in Greece through comics. The new subtitled episodes of previously subtitled cartoon series like *Popeye* (0.6/0.2%) and *Woody Woodpecker* (1.2/0.3%) do not seem to have been well-received; neither do the rest of the dubbed cartoon series. Despite the higher cost, though, most are still dubbed, given that in order to attract any consistent viewership for their children's programmes, the commissioners have to follow the already established children's preference for dubbing - at least as it is expressed through the viewing rates of the first two TV stations' big hits.
- The case of SKY TV is more or less similar to that of STAR CHANNEL in terms of size and stability of audience. Its top cartoon series is *Rupert*, achieving the figures of 4.3/0.9% at the peak viewing time of 10:00AM (see table 3.3.3.5). *Key West* which is broadcast at 14:00 is subtitled because it is not broadcast during the standard children's programmes time-slots but between programmes mainly targeted at adults. As a result, it attracts more adult than children viewers (0.6/1.4%).
- The state-owned ET1 presents the most complex (or least consistent) picture for March 1995, with subtitled cartoon series alternating with dubbed cartoon series both in the mornings and in the afternoons (see table 3.3.3.6). Peak viewing rates are reached with subtitled *Captain Hawk* (1.3/0.6%) but this does not indicate any tendency towards recipients favouring subtitled cartoon series in general, since the viewing rates for dubbed productions are not

far behind. As a result, in March 1996 we see that, following the example of larger private TV stations, there are more dubbed productions, broadcast in a new time-slot (weekdays 13:15-14:15) aiming to reach and attract a new audience without too much competition, at times when no other TV stations would be broadcasting children's programmes (see table 3.3.1.5). The results prove to be more encouraging, with peak viewing achieved by dubbed *Casper and Friends* (2.6/0.5%) around 13:30.

- Although the top children's cartoon TV series on most channels proved to be dubbed, we see that the overall movement towards dubbing more children's cartoon TV series in March 1996 (see table 3.3.1.7), as dictated by the March 1995 viewing-rate tendencies, was not justified by the overall new viewing rate figures. Table 3.3.3.8 indicates that the average viewing rates for dubbed cartoon series dropped from 3.3/0.8% in March 1995 to 2.9/0.6% in March 1996. By contrast, the fewer subtitled children's cartoon TV series seem to hold on to their position (1.8/0.6% in March 1995, 2.0/0.5% in March 1996). The high viewership of certain dubbed cartoon series is accompanied by low viewership of some other cartoon series. In other words, the viewers, children or adults, do not seem to be convinced that the best method of language transfer for children's cartoon TV series is actually dubbing. It is just sporadically that they show their appreciation of a specific dubbed cartoon-series programme; this, however, does not seem to be a result of the language transfer method chosen but of the overall promotion and quality of the programmes.
- Live-action series prove the most interesting case of all. The reason is that out of all children's TV programmes, the one with the highest viewing rates is a dubbed live-action series: ANT1's *Power Rangers* in March 1995 and March 1996 reaches the astonishing 10.7/2.5% and 13.8/2.7% respectively (see table 3.3.3.2). This is quite surprising if we consider that a survey conducted the same year by the same viewing rate company (AGB) on children's TV viewing stated that "the programme typology most viewed by children is cartoons (90%)" (AGB Hellas eds., 1996:100). The

result is even more surprising once we realise that this was the only dubbed children's live-action series in March 1995 (see table 3.3.1.7). The massive success of the series was obviously the motive for ANT1 dubbing another live-action series in March 1996, *VR Troopers,* which also reached astonishing viewing rates (10.8/2.1%). The rest of the (subtitled) live-action series, by contrast, record very low viewing rates, somewhere between 0.2/0.2% and 3.1/1.2% for both March 1995 and March 1996 on all other channels. These contradictory facts and figures suggest that there may be something other than the language transfer method alone involved in the success of the two ANT1 broadcasts. The answer lies in the boost given to the programmes by the toy industry that produces *Power Rangers* and *VR Troopers* merchandise. This toy industry supports and commissions the programmes, markets them in the best way possible and caters for the best quality dubbing available. In the section discussing the 'findings related to upper level human agents' we will examine the role of the toy industry and commissioners outside the audiovisual or general literary field in greater detail.

- The amount of available data for children's cartoon + live-action TV series (only one programme), does not allow us to draw any reliable conclusions. The *Walt Disney Hourly Programme* on MEGA is a series that contains a number of Walt Disney classics which, as we saw in the findings related to lower level products, are subtitled because of their status. As a result of this high status, we cannot claim that it is subtitling as a language transfer method that allows the programme to achieve the satisfactory rates of 4.1/1.6% (see table 3.3.3.3). At the same time, however, it is clear that subtitling does not appear to get in the way and the programme still achieves high viewing rate.
- The overall viewing rates for subtitled and dubbed programmes seem to support the initial hypothesis: namely that subtitled productions appeal more to adults than to children. In both March 1995 and March 1996, the ratio between children and total viewers for subtitled children's programmes is around 2.35/1 whereas for dubbed productions it rises up to around 4.67/1 (see table 3.3.3.8).

The overall rates of total viewers remain stable, whatever the language transfer method followed (around 0.7%). Within the range of only children viewers, however, dubbed children's programmes attract almost double the size of audience that subtitled programmes attract (3.5% vs. 1.7%).

- The overall viewing rates for children's TV programmes do not reveal the expected positive response to the overall tendency towards dubbing, as it was expressed in the findings related to lower level products on table 3.3.1.7. Following the mismatch that we already noticed in terms of more dubbed children's cartoon TV series and lower viewing rates for this specific genre, we notice that the overall rise in dubbed programmes in March 1996 is also accompanied by an overall drop of the viewing rates for both children and total viewers: from 3.6/0.8% to 3.4/0.7% (see table 3.3.3.8). At the same time, the overall viewing rates for subtitled children's TV programmes remain constant amongst both children and total viewers: 1.6/0.7% in March 1995, 1.8/0.7% in March 1996. It becomes clear, then, that recipients are less persuaded than human agents about the necessity for more dubbing and the overall successful prospects of this specific language transfer method.

3.3.4 Findings related to lower level human agents

Luyken et al. claim that there are three determinants affecting the choice of language transfer method: a) economic considerations (these are the most important), b) the audience's attitudes, and c) the suitability of the method for different television programme genres (1991:87). We have just discussed the audience's attitudes, and in the chapter devoted to findings related to lower level products we discussed the specific role of the various genres within children's TV programmes. But what about economic considerations? Television industry nowadays is not a charity funded organisation; considerable capital is invested and large numbers of employees depend on the TV stations' prosperity. The cost of a broadcast is extremely high, income from advertisements is always needed, and even in the case of state-owned TV stations the tax payers demand a top quality service. The choice of the language transfer method has a specific cost attached to it. This cost will be added to the cost of the programme's in-house production or outside purchase and together all these costs will have to be measured against the final viewing rates that were achieved and the income that the particular show managed to raise, in order to see if a particular broadcast was eventually profitable, and therefore successful. The cost of dubbing is 10 to 15 times more than that of subtitling, whereas the cost of narration/voice-over is two to five times more than that of subtitling (Luyken et al., 1991:94-105; Karamitroglou, 1996:48). If a specific programme is to be dubbed, the human agents/commissioners who will take that decision will have to be fully aware of the financial risk they are taking and fairly confident of the proportionally higher viewing rates that this specific choice of language transfer method will attract.

The structure of the audiovisual translation industry is different in every country, rather complicated, often quite cliquey, and even more often based on connections and networking. The audiovisual translation industry in different countries is built around different structures and based on different working habits (Barbe, 1996:257). French TV stations, for example, buy most of their programmes already translated from the local partners of the original production's company (Ganz- Blättler, 1995:251). Italian, German and Greek TV stations do not follow this pattern. This means automatically that whereas in France all the choices related to the translation of a specific programme are taken by the producers' associates, in Greece these producers' associates do not get so involved, and the translational decisions are mainly left to the TV stations that will broadcast the programmes they purchased. Some years ago, the role of the producer of the original programme used to be completely irrelevant to the audiovisual translation process. Nowadays it is becoming more and more significant but is still restricted to pre-translational considerations such as avoiding too many close-ups in order not to make dubbing difficult (cf. Dries, 1995a:4&31). In Greece, it is the role of the film distribution agencies that seems to be quite important, since most of the time they tend to intervene directly in the audiovisual translation process (cf. Delabastita, 1989:202) - less so in television but significantly in cinema - guiding or supervising choices at every step of the process.

Due to the oligopoly-based structure of the audiovisual translation market, commissioners throughout Europe tend to pay whatever price they are quoted for the audiovisual transfer of their programmes (Luyken et al., 1991:89). Audiovisual translators' unions strengthen the professionals' position in the industry and provide them with some voice of resistance (Dries, 1995a:11). In Greece, however, there are no such unions at all. As a result, commissioners will still pay the price they are asked, but they will not negotiate with the audiovisual translation studios or with the free-lance translators in terms of any choices to do with the language transfer method to be followed. They will rather impose these choices directly and with no further discussion. At the same time, however, they will not interfere too much with linguistic choices below the text level (cf. Gambier, 1994:280). All this, of course, provided that the TV stations do not have an in-house audiovisual translation department (cf. Vitkus, 1995:319). Greece seems to be wrongly classified as a country where TV stations do tend to have their own in-house translation departments (Luyken et al., 1991:93). The truth is that out of the whole range of TV stations operating on Greek territory, it is only the state-owned ET1 and the newly founded cable corporation FILMNET that have such departments. Clearly, then, when dealing with national norms and practices concerning the choice of language transfer method, it is not helpful to examine the role of the translation agencies; it is the norms and values of the film-distributors and the receiving TV networks that will have to be primarily investigated.

The following conclusions may be drawn from the responses to the questionnaire completed by employees of the top 5 Greek TV stations and the one cable TV station; these employees are responsible for the choice of the language transfer method to be followed for their foreign TV programmes.

- In most TV stations it is the administrative board of the overall programme flow who take the decision on how a children's TV programme will eventually be broadcast (MEGA, STAR, ANT1,

SKY). In ANT1, the more specific administrative board of foreign TV programmes has a say as well. In SKY, representatives from the departments of purchasing and trading take part in the meeting. In FILMNET, it is the director of general programme flow in association with the department of marketing and the in-house translation department who decide. Finally, in ET1 it is the department of foreign programme purchasing in association with the in-house department of audiovisual translation who take the decision. The particular structure of the committee that decides which language transfer method will be implemented is important for the following set of reasons: a) the fewer the people involved in the decision the more flexible the committee, the easier it is to change already established norms and habits and as a result, the more likely it is that the committee will vote for the more radical solution of dubbing; b) the more involvement on the part of departments of marketing, trading and purchase, the more likely it is for financial considerations to be raised and the less probable that a financially risky solution like dubbing will be finally implemented; and c) the more involvement from people from the audiovisual translation department, the more awareness of the special nature of the targeted children's audience and as a result, the more likely it is to decide on dubbing, the theoretically preferable method for children's TV programmes.

- All TV stations claim to prefer dubbing overall for their children's TV programmes. STAR, SKY and FILMNET, however, explicitly differentiate between children's TV programmes in general and those which are targeted at youngsters (ten to twelve years old) as well as adult audiences; for the latter, they claim that subtitling is preferable. For TV programmes in general ANT1, MEGA and STAR seem to base their choice of the language transfer method on a) the potential recipients of the programme; this means that for a potential children's audience they would most probably vote for dubbing; b) the time this programme will be broadcast; this means that a programme shown at non-peak audience times is less likely to be dubbed, but it also means that a programme broadcast at times when viewers are mostly adults is likely to be subtitled; and

c) the specific film-type and genre; this means that series film-types and cartoon genres are more likely to be dubbed. SKY also points to the importance of the language of the original, explicitly suggesting that if it is not English the programme has more chances of being dubbed. At the same time, they put emphasis on the feedback they get from viewing rates, meaning that if a dubbed programme does not eventually prove successful it might switch from dubbing to subtitling. ET1 raises the issue of the genre of the programme, as well as the original mode of discourse: if for example the original programme contains narration, the language transfer method of narration will be adopted for (the same parts of) the target programme as well. ANT1 and MEGA seem to be the most sensitive to the quality of dubbing, modifying their already expressed preference for this particular method to specify dubbing which achieves an ideal match of target voices with characters on the screen and which pays particular attention to the quality of the oral verbal material used (i.e. easily comprehensible, not offending children). In terms of broader subtitling norms that influence the commissioners' decisions, however, it is only FILMNET who explicitly justify occasional preference for subtitling some of their children's TV programmes due to the existence of a strong subtitling tradition in the country. This is the most straightforward acknowledgement of the existence of powerful norms in Greek audiovisual reality.

3.4 Norms and motivations at the Middle Level

3.4.1 Findings related to middle level products

One of the hardest tasks that a researcher has to face when investigating the language transfer of audiovisual products in general is, first of all, to classify these products into specific categories of film-types and genres. Luyken et al. stress the importance of such a classification, supporting that "specific forms of Language Transfer are more suited to particular programme-types of genre than others" (1991:129), going even further to claim that we might be better talking about genre-bound language transfer traditions and norms rather than country-bound language transfer traditions and norms (ibid). Unfortunately, no consistent classification of film/programme types and genres exists in the field of audiovisual media. Film/programme typologies vary from country to country and from scholar to scholar. Some scholars with a filmic background divide films/programmes into the following categories: a) series and serials, b) news and public affairs, c) movies, d) educational films/programmes, e) commercials, f) general entertainment films/programmes, g) children's films/programmes, h) features and documentaries, i) sports, j) plays, k) publicity films/programmes, l) religious films/programmes, and m) arts and music (Goodhart et al., 1975:5). Others working on "the transnationalisation of television in Europe" divide programmes into the following types/categories: a) drama/movies, b) light entertainment, c) music, d) sports, e) news, f) information, g) arts/humanities/science, h) education, i) religious, and j) other (Aaltonen, 1995a:287) with each category further sub-divided into more detailed programme-genres. Luyken et al., who come from an audiovisual translation background, divide programmes into the following categories, which are meant to fit the specific purposes of audiovisual translation studies: a) drama, b) educational programmes, c) entertainment programmes, d) information programmes, e) opera, f) puppet shows, cartoons and animation, g) religious programmes, h) science and arts programmes, and i) sport (1991:130-135).

The guiding motivations behind the last audiovisual-translation oriented classification lie in the hypothesis that:

> "where the main purpose of a production is to entertain and relax the audience, where generalised human reactions (taken from the world of reality or the fantasy world of crime and comedy) were the subject, then the dubbing was probably the best choice of Language Transfer. Where, on the other hand, a play, film or series attempts to portray life in a particular country, the language of that country is an essential part of that cultural experience and it should be preserved: in such cases subtitling might be the more appropriate form of language transfer" (Luyken et al., 1991:130).

In addition, it is noted that:

> "on the whole, subtitling does not seem to be suitable for educational programmes because it can only give a summary of the didactic explanations given in the programmes. On the other hand, revoicing may also have its problems, as its requirements could also conflict with the overriding educational/informational aims of the programme" (ibid:131).

Following the same logic in order to account for similar motivations in the classification of film types and genres for audiovisual translation purposes in particular, other audiovisual translational scholars have claimed that:

> "whenever the soundtrack contains discourse of an *informative* nature, *revoicing* should be considered. [...] But when we talk about human interest stories, TV fiction and feature films, that is *expressive* genres focusing on people, as opposed to objects or abstract phenomena, only *subtitling* will provide the authenticity needed" (Gottlieb, 1994a:103).

Some scholars stress the importance of distinguishing between genres where "language is central, people are central, or events are central" (Nedergaard-Larsen, 1993:221). Others stress that "long narrative or action scenes work well with a dubbed track" whereas "long personal exchanges are difficult to communicate with dubbing" (*TV World X/5*, 1987:38; cf. Adler, 1995:24). Others differentiate between genres within the same film type, as for example with 'I love you stories' where the viewers can guess the plot-line, thus a condensed form of subtitling would not interfere with film-watching, and 'crime stories' as well as 'espionage stories' where the eye of the viewer should be left free to focus on the picture in search of plot-essential visual information, and where dubbing would thus be preferable (de Linde, 1995:10). Finally, some writers stress the importance of distinguishing parts of genres even within the same audiovisual product, in cases for example where "songs that appear in films are often subtitled even when the rest of the film is dubbed, following the blanket principle that the music and the voices are always more important than the lyrics" (Zabalbeascoa, 1997:339).

All the above can be seen as attempts to develop a consistent classification of audiovisual products into specific film types and genres, but in fact they make the task of developing such a classification more complicated. How can we tell for sure when a product is 'expressive' or 'informative'? Who can tell whether its purposes on broadcast were 'didactic'? How can we know if its aim was to 'entertain' rather than to 'inform' the audience? In this respect, the landscape of audiovisual products remains fuzzy. In addition, most of the above comments seem to derive from speculation and/or hypothetical considerations rather than factual evidence. So, what happens in reality? Do all these parameters play an important role in the choice of the language transfer method in the end?

In Greece, people working in the audiovisual media do not seem to agree on a consistent audiovisual product typology either. AGB, as the company that measures viewing rates for all TV programmes, is obliged to construct such an audiovisual product typology. Their typology consists of the following programme types: a) series, b) films, c) light entertainment, d) arts/culture, e) news/information, f) children's programmes, g) sports, and h) other (AGB Hellas eds., 1995:37; 1996:37). At first glance, this typology does not seem to suit the purposes of investigating audiovisual translation, as outlined by the views of the scholars quoted above. It clearly has a number of drawbacks. First of all, following the classification of 'children's programmes' into various film/programme types, one would necessarily have to distinguish between 'adult movies' and 'children's movies' instead of establishing a broad category of 'films'. Similarly, one would also want to distinguish between 'adult series' and 'children's series' instead of establishing a broad category of 'series'. Furthermore, the category of 'arts/culture' appears to be too vague, since it can include 'informative' (or 'educational') documentaries as well as 'music' (or 'opera' or 'ballet') programmes, two types of programmes which - according to the audiovisual translation scholars quoted above - are fundamentally different with respect to what they consider as the 'optimum'(?) language transfer method that should be implemented. Bearing all these considerations in mind, I decided to develop my own typology of audiovisual products by adding to the children's programmes typology (as described in section 3.3.1) the following set of categories which attempt to account for adult audiovisual products: a) adult movies, b) adult series/serials, c) light entertainment, d) documentaries, e) sports, f) news/information, and g) music/opera/ballet. With the assistance of various people working with various types of audiovisual media, I managed to classify each one of the actual products in my data into one of the categories above. This is a classification of film/programme *types*. A rough description and a brief analysis of the specific film/programme's *nature* - namely its theme, humour, cinematic style, narrative style etc. rather than simply its *genre* - was sought for specific products that were seen to divert from the established norm. It would be interesting to see whether there are any consistent patterns where specific genres within the same film/programmes types do affect the choice of language transfer method. Once again, it should be stressed that the above typology is restricted not only to audiovisual translation, but specifically to the present research into the norms and motivations which lie behind the choice between subtitling and revoicing in Greece.

Apart from these considerations of film types and genres, there are certain objective parameters related to the status and nature of an audiovisual product which also play an important role in deciding whether the product is to be subtitled or revoiced. Products that are rich in dialectal or other idiomatic language are harder to subtitle, because they have no standard written form (cf. Zabalbeascoa, 1997:341). Physical linguistic features pose another problem. For example, the Japanese are reported to favour subtitling in Western markets simply because spoken Japanese is very hard to match with the lip movements of Western languages (*Screen Digest*, July 1992:153; cf. Fodor, 1976:79). Similarly, Greeks may not favour the dubbing of certain Western European (Germanic) languages but favour the dubbing of other similarly articulated Mediterranean languages. Thirdly, soap operas are difficult to dub because they consist of continuous close-ups of people talking to each other (Bakewell, 1987:16; Kilborn, 1993:645). In addition, the difficulty of getting hold of post-scripts for a sufficient number of consecutive episodes often leads to inconsistency in constructing character profiles, when for example the character that was initially perceived as a hero turns out to be the villain after a short number of episodes (Bakewell, 1987:17). Finally, the use of pivot language translations instead of original post-production scripts creates serious obstacles in dubbing, since the dubbing director cannot be fully aware of the exact original phonetic structure of the original dialogues and will have to rely solely on his/her ears in order to reconstruct a phonetic transcription of the original dialogues from scratch (cf. Gottlieb, 1994a:118; cf. Luyken et al., 1991:181).

It has been initially claimed that Greece is a traditionally subtitling country, meaning that the norm in the language transfer of audiovisual products is to opt for subtitling. It is time now to examine whether this is actually true, to what extent it is true and, most of all, to see whether the norm is so strong as to influence the language transfer method used for children's TV programmes. In the following tables we can see the number of adult programmes that were broadcast by the top 5 TV stations and the one cable TV channel in all possible language transfer methods, namely a) subtitling, b) dubbing, c) narration, d) narration + subtitling, and e) free commentary, in March 1995 and March 1996:

Table 3.4.1.1 Adult TV programmes on ANT1

TV STATION: ANT1	**LANGUAGE TRANSFER METHOD USED**									
	Subtitling		**Dubbing**		**Narration**		**Nar+Sub**		**F/Com**	
PROGRAMME TYPE	M'95	M'96	M'95	M'96	M'95	M'96	M'95	M'96	M'95	M'96
Adult movies	76[i]	74[ii]								
Adult series/serials	15[iii]	9[iv]								
Light Entertainment										
Documentaries							1[v]	1[vi]		
Sports										
News/Information	2[vii]	2[viii]								
Music/Opera/Ballet										
TOTAL	**93**	**85**					**1**	**1**		

[i] 65 from English, 7 from French, 3 from Italian (2 of which through English) and 1 from Brazilian/Portuguese

[ii] 67 from English, 3 from French and 4 from Italian (all of which through English)

[iii] All from English

[iv] All from English

[v] *The Cousteau Library*

[vi] *The Great Moments of Our Century*

[vii] *CBS News, ANT1 Satellite News*

[viii] *CBS News, ANT1 Satellite News*

Table 3.4.1.2 Adult TV programmes on MEGA

TV STATION: MEGA	**LANGUAGE TRANSFER METHOD USED**									
	Subtitling		**Dubbing**		**Narration**		**Nar+Sub**		**F/Com**	
PROGRAMME TYPE	M'95	M'96	M'95	M'96	M'95	M'96	M'95	M'96	M'95	M'96
Adult movies	59[i]	78[ii]								
Adult series/serials	11[iii]	13[iv]								
Light Entertainment										
Documentaries							1[v]	1[vi]		
Sports										
News/Information										
Music/Opera/Ballet										
TOTAL	**70**	**91**					**1**	**1**		

[i] 57 from English, 1 from French and 1 from Italian (through English)

[ii] 77 from English, 1 from Italian (through English)

[iii] 1 was initially dubbed (*Days of Our Lives);* all from English

[iv] All from English

[v] *The Making of...*

[vi] *The Making of...*

Table 3.4.1.3 Adult TV programmes on STAR

TV STATION: STAR	**LANGUAGE TRANSFER METHOD USED**									
	Subtitling		**Dubbing**		**Narration**		**Nar+Sub**		**F/Com**	
PROGRAMME TYPE	M'95	M'96	M'95	M'96	M'95	M'96	M'95	M'96	M'95	M'96
Adult movies	58[i]	59[ii]								
Adult series/serials	24[iii]	29[iv]								
Light Entertainment	1[v]	1[vi]								
Documentaries	1[vii]	3[viii]						1[ix]		
Sports										
News/Information							1[x]	1[xi]		
Music/Opera/Ballet										
TOTAL	**84**	**92**					**1**	**2**		

[i] All from English

[ii] 58 from English and 1 from French

[iii] 22 from English, 2 from Portuguese/Brazilian (*Corazone Salvaje, Right to Love*)

[iv] 26 from English, 2 from French (*Hélèn et les Garçons, Miracle of Love*), 1 from Portuguese/Brazilian (*La Duena*)

[v] *The 1995 Oscar Awards*

[vi] *The 1996 Oscar Awards*

[vii] *African Safari*

[viii] *The Making of: ..., Great Events, Mysteries of the Universe*

[ix] *Hotel Paradise*

[x] *Lifestyles of the Rich and Famous*

[xi] *Lifestyles of the Rich and Famous*

Table 3.4.1.4 Adult TV programmes on SKY

TV STATION: SKY	**LANGUAGE TRANSFER METHOD USED**									
	Subtitling		**Dubbing**		**Narration**		**Nar+Sub**		**F/Com**	
PROGRAMME TYPE	M'95	M'96	M'95	M'96	M'95	M'96	M'95	M'96	M'95	M'96
Adult movies	30[i]	14[ii]								
Adult series/serials	7[iii]									
Light Entertainment	1[iv]	1[v]								
Documentaries										
Sports										
News/Information										
Music/Opera/Ballet										
TOTAL	**38**	**15**								

[i] All from English

[ii] All from English

[iii] 4 from English, 2 from French, 1 from Spanish

[iv] *Crystal Maze*

[v] *Colpo Grosso* (Italian)

Table 3.4.1.5 Adult TV programmes on ET1

TV STATION: ET1	**LANGUAGE TRANSFER METHOD USED**									
	Subtitling		**Dubbing**		**Narration**		**Nar+Sub**		**F/Com**	
PROGRAMME TYPE	M'95	M'96	M'95	M'96	M'95	M'96	M'95	M'96	M'95	M'96
Adult movies	27[i]	19[ii]								
Adult series/serials	3[iii]	7[iv]								
Light Entertainment										
Documentaries	4[v]	6[vi]					1[vii]	2[viii]		
Sports										
News/Information										
Music/Opera/Ballet										
TOTAL	**34**	**32**					**1**	**2**		

[i] 24 from English, 2 from French, 1 from Norwegian (through English)

[ii] 16 from English, 1 from French, 1 from Spanish, 1 from Italian

[iii] All from English

[iv] 1 from Spanish (*The Secrets of the Sand*)

[v] *Gabrielle, Portraits of Artists, Noam Chomsky and the Media, Alabra Stories* (Spanish)

[vi] *The Truth About Lies, Body Mechanics, Portraits of Artists, 100 Years of Hollywood Westerns, La monteé des femmes au pouvoir* (French), *Plaidoyer pour les femmes* (French)

[vii] *The incredible horrific life of Lenny Riffenschtal* (German)

[viii] *The National World/National Geographic:...* (2 individual episodes)

Table 3.4.1.6 Adult TV programmes on FILMNET

TV STATION: FILMNET	**LANGUAGE TRANSFER METHOD USED**									
	Subtitling		**Dubbing**		**Narration**		**Nar+Sub**		**F/Com**	
PROGRAMME TYPE	M'95	M'96	M'95	M'96	M'95	M'96	M'95	M'96	M'95	M'96
Adult movies	115[i]	164[ii]								
Adult series/serials	10[iii]									
Light Entertainment	1[iv]	1[v]								
Documentaries	3[vi]	8[vii]								
Sports									14[viii]	7[ix]
News/Information	2[x]	1[xi]								
Music/Opera/Ballet	4[xii]									
TOTAL	**135**	**174**							**14**	**7**

---

[i] 114 from English and 1 from French

[ii] 162 from English and 2 from French

[iii] All from English

[iv] *1st Annual Actors Guild Awards*

[v] *2nd Annual Actors Guild Awards*

[vi] *Australian Cinema IV, Century of the Cinema, Hollywood Golden Night*

[vii] *World's Funniest Commercials, Marilyn, Elvis, Sophia, Hollywood:...* (3 individual episodes), *The Hour of the Champions*

[viii] Programmes include multiple broadcasts of: UK Soccer, Italian Soccer, German Soccer, UK Soccer Highlights, German Soccer Highlights, Eurogoals, Transworld Sport, Latin Futbol, Futbol Mundial , Top Rank Boxing, Global Wrestling, Drag Racing, ATP Golf Tour, Speedweek

[ix] The first 7 of the programmes listed in the previous footnote

[x] *The Making of the Oscars, Oscars 1995: Pre- and Post-Shows*

[xi] *Academy Awards Post Show*

[xii] *Barbara Streisand and Elvis Presley, The Temptations, Artistry of Torvill and Dean, Whitney Houston in Concert*

Table 3.4.1.7 Overall TV programmes (children's and adult)

OVERALL TV PROGRAMMES	**LANGUAGE TRANSFER METHOD USED**									
	Subtitling		**Dubbing**		**Narration**		**Nar+Sub**		**F/Com**	
PROGRAMME TYPE	M'95	M'96	M'95	M'96	M'95	M'96	M'95	M'96	M'95	M'96
Children' TV programmes	33	21	28	35						
Adult movies	365[i]	408[ii]								
Adult series/serials	70[iii]	58[iv]								
Light Entertainment	3	3								
Documentaries	8	17					3	5		
Sports									14	7
News/Information	4	3					1	1		
Music/Opera/Ballet	4									
TOTAL	**487[v]**	**510[vi]**	**28[vii]**	**35[viii]**			**4[ix]**	**6[x]**	**14[xi]**	**7[xii]**

The following conclusions may be drawn from the tables presented above:

- No adult TV programmes are dubbed. The only TV programmes that are dubbed are those aimed at children (see table 3.4.1.7).

---

[i] 95% from English, 3% from French
[ii] 96.5% from English
[iii] 93% from English, 3% from Brazilian/Portuguese, 3% from French
[iv] 93% from English, 3.5% from French
[v] **91.4%** of total TV programmes
[vi] **91.4%** of total TV programmes
[vii] **5.2%** of total TV programmes
[viii] **6.3%** of total TV programmes
[ix] **0.8%** of total TV programmes
[x] **1.1%** of total TV programmes
[xi] **2.6%** of total TV programmes
[xii] **1.2%** of total TV programmes

- Adult movies are invariably subtitled. Therefore, any speculation regarding film genres and their role in the choice of the language transfer method is not relevant for Greek audiovisual reality. 'Crime' stories, 'espionage' stories, 'action' movies, 'long narrative' movies are not judged as belonging to different film genres but as simply constituting one broad film/programme type of 'adult movies'.
- The same holds for adult series/serials: they are invariably subtitled too. The various genres of adult series/serials, for example 'sitcoms', 'soap operas', and 'detective' series, are treated as belonging to one broad film/programme type. As with adult movies, then, the Greek audiovisual translation market does not differentiate between various genres of adult series/serials either.
- All light entertainment products are invariably subtitled. Although the size of the sample might not look satisfactory enough to draw reliable conclusions (only 3 products per year), the fact that they come from 3 different TV stations (STAR, SKY and FILMNET) suggests that the norm in Greece is to subtitle light entertainment programmes.
- Music/opera/ballet products are - as expected - invariably subtitled. As the original soundtrack plays an important role in this film/programme type, its integrity must be maintained.
- All sports programmes are delivered in free commentary. Since the data comes from one TV station only (FILMNET), it is possible that this reflects the policy of a specific channel. More data must be investigated in the video context before any broad conclusions can be drawn. But the fact that most sports TV programmes have to be ready for broadcast a very short time after the original event (e.g. a football game is broadcast recorded but only a few hours after it was actually played) makes free commentary an attractive method of language transfer.
- News/information programmes are predominantly subtitled. The only exception is a series of informative episodes which consist of review-like show-biz reports (*Lifestyles of the Rich and Famous* on SKY, see table 3.4.1.3). Since the items of news are relatively old in the first place, this allows the commissioners enough time to

provide the method of narration. Furthermore, the sequential nature of the programme suggests that it may be seen more like a series of documentary-like episodes investigating the lives of celebrities.

- The only instance of significant variation in terms of language transfer method can be observed in the case of documentaries. For documentaries, both narration and subtitling are theoretically justified since both allow the presence of the original soundtrack to provide an impression of authenticity (Kilborn, 1993: 643). It is interesting to note, however, that no documentaries were delivered in narration alone (see table 3.4.1.7). The frequent overlap of the off-screen narrator's voice and the voices of characters on the screen (Luyken et al., 1991:134), explains the motivation for the combined language transfer method: in the transferred version, the narrator's voice is in the target language whereas the words of the characters on screen are conveyed via subtitles. All the products delivered in this double-mode had this hybrid structure in the original too. On the other hand, however, not all the documentaries that were subtitled consisted of only off-screen or only on-screen voices. The choice of a particular method is not even theme-bound. We cannot say for example that documentaries which deal with art/cinema - like FILMNET's - tend to be subtitled, since documentaries with a similar theme - like MEGA's - tend to be delivered in the double narration+subtitling mode (see tables 3.4.1.6 and 3.4.1.2). The same holds for other themes like history (narration+subtitling on ANT1, subtitling on STAR) or geography (subtitling on STAR, narration+subtitling on ET1) (see tables 3.4.1.1, 3.4.1.3 and 3.4.15). We can say, then, that there is no consistent pattern or a specific strategy related to the products themselves that motivates the choice of language transfer method in the case of documentaries. The case of *The Making of:...* provides particularly good evidence of the inconsistency in this area: the same documentary – which describes the way specific cinema films are framed - is subtitled on STAR but delivered in narration+subtitling on MEGA (see tables 3.4.1.3 and 3.4.1.2).
- Looking at the overall figures for products broadcast on these six Greek TV stations it is reasonable to suggest that the claim about

Greece being a predominantly subtitling country seems justified, at least in the area of television, since 91.4% of the foreign programmes were subtitled in both March 1995 and March 1996 (see table 3.4.1.7). This overwhelming percentage, which is indicative not only of the number of products but also of the air-time occupied by subtitling, cannot but have an impact on language transfer commissioners. Their choice of language transfer method will always be influenced by the existing norm of subtitling.

To claim that a country is a predominantly subtitling one means that the norm to subtitle audiovisual products is not restricted to television but applies to other audiovisual modes as well. Television and norms related to the language transfer of TV programmes will definitely have a direct influence on children's TV programmes. But the field of audiovisual media is not divided into clear-cut categories. Views and attitudes overlap: different audiovisual media are often influenced by the views of the same people. As a result, norms that are found to account for the language transfer method chosen overall or for specific children's products in other audiovisual media will inevitably influence the choice of language transfer method in children's TV programmes too. Thus, it would be interesting to see what happens with the cinema-films as well. Here, the number of products would be too small if the data was restricted to a specific month of the year. Data from the top 6 cinema-film distribution agencies for the two full cinematic years that contain March 1995 and March 1996 were therefore collected. The language transfer picture for the cinema-film products looks as follows:

Table 3.4.1.8 Language Transfer method for cinema-films in 1994-1995

CINEMA-FILM DISTRIBUTION AGENCY	CINEMATIC YEAR: 1994-1995 CHILDREN'S MOVIES								ADULT MOVIES	
	CARTOON		LIVE ACTION		CART + L/ACTION		PUPPET			
	SUB	DUB	SUB	DUB	SUB	DUB	SUB	DUB	SUB	DUB
Prooptiki	2[i]	2[ii]							44[iii]	
Spentzos Cinema	1[iv]								28[v]	
Rosebud									22[vi]	
Nea Kinissi									19[vii]	
OVO									-	
ELKE	3[viii]	1[ix]	1[x]		1[xi]				42[xii]	
TOTAL	**6**	**3**	**1**		**1**				**155**	

[i] *The Lion King, 101 Dalmatians*

[ii] Same as the subtitled (double release)

[iii] 40 from English, 2 from French, 1 from Italian, 1 from Spanish. Also 1 Greek original (no language transfer)

[iv] *Asterix in America* (French through English)

[v] 25 from English, 1 from French, 1 from Spanish, 1 from Hungarian (through English). Also 2 Greek originals (no language transfer)

[vi] 6 from English, 11 from French, 1 from Italian, 2 from Chinese (through English), 1 from Chinese (through French), 1 from Romanian (through French). Also 2 Greek originals (no language transfer)

[vii] 10 from English, 4 from French, 3 from Italian, 2 from Japanese (through English)

[viii] *Asterix and Cleopatra* (French through English), *Asterix and the Gauls* (French through English), *Lucky Luke in Daisy Town* (French)

[ix] *Thumbelina*

[x] *Richie Rich*

[xi] *The Pagemaster*

[xii] 41 from English, 1 from French. Also 1 Greek original (no language transfer)

Table 3.4.1.9 Language Transfer Method for cinema-films in 1995-1996

CINEMA-FILM DISTRIBUTION AGENCY	**CINEMATIC YEAR: 1995-1996 CHILDREN'S MOVIES**								**ADULT MOVIES**	
	CARTOON		**LIVE ACTION**		**CART + L/ACTION**		**PUPPET**			
	SUB	**DUB**	**SUB**	**DUB**	**SUB**	**DUB**	**SUB**	**DUB**	**SUB**	**DUB**
Prooptiki	3[i]	3[ii]							54[iii]	
Spentzos Cinema			1[iv]						19[v]	
Rosebud									22[vi]	
Nea Kinissi									12[vii]	
OVO									20[viii]	
ELKE			1[ix]						35[x]	
TOTAL	**3**	**3**	**2**						**162**	

From the two tables above, the following conclusions may be drawn:

- Adult movies are invariably subtitled. As in the case of TV-films, then, genre does not appear to play any role at all in the choice of language transfer method for cinema-films.

---

[i] *Pocahontas, Sleeping Beauty, Toy Story*

[ii] Same as the subtitled products (double release)

[iii] 50 from English, 2 from French, 1 Spanish, 1 Chinese (through French). Also 2 Greek originals (no language transfer)

[iv] *Power Rangers*

[v] 16 from English, 1 from Spanish, 1 from Japanese (through English), 1 from Serbian (through English). Also 3 Greek originals (no language transfer).

[vi] 6 from English, 10 from French, 1 from Italian, 2 from German (through English), 1 from Romanian (through French), 1 from Polish (through English), 1 from Chinese (through English). Also 2 Greek originals (no language transfer)

[vii] 8 from English, 1 from French, 1 from Spanish (through English), 1 from Italian (through English), 1 from German (through English). Also 1 Greek original (no language transfer)

[viii] 9 from English, 4 from French, 1 from Spanish, 1 from Portuguese (through French), 1 from Russian (through English), 1 from Finnish (through English), 1 from Polish (through French), 1 from German (through English), 1 from Chinese (through English)

[ix] *Free Willy 2*

[x] 33 from English, 2 from French. Also 2 Greek originals (no language transfer)

- The number of live-action children's cinema-films is not sufficient to allow us to draw reliable conclusions about the language transfer method chosen (one product in 1994-1995 and two in 1995-1996). As in the case of live-action TV children's movies, live-action children's cinema-films are all subtitled. The norm that requires live-action adult movies to be subtitled appears to influence live-action children's cinema-films too. What is striking, though, is that the cinema-film version of the most popular children's TV programme, the dubbed live-action series *Power Rangers*, is released subtitled by Spentzos Cinema (see table 3.4.1.9) revealing an inconsistency between the two audiovisual media. At the same time, however, this emphasises the individual status of cinematic as opposed to television products and proves the necessity for them to be studied separately. The financial risk involved in changing the language transfer method for the cinematic version of the most popular children's TV programme must have been carefully considered by commissioners at Spentzos Cinema. A number of potential scenarios can provide possible motivations for this change in language transfer method: a) the structure of the cinema audience may have been considered different from that of TV audience; in other words the number of children who would be attracted by the film may not have been thought significant in financial terms; b) the role of the language transfer method (dubbing) in the success of the series may not have been considered significant; in other words the commissioners may have believed that subtitling would not affect the attitude of the audience and that the success of the televised series would attract the necessary number of viewers irrespective of the language transfer method; c) the cinematic mode may have required a change in the language transfer method; in other words, the commissioners may have thought that the audience would still prefer to watch a subtitled cinema production because Greek audiences are used to watching subtitled rather than dubbed cinema products in general. All these possible scenarios are investigated further when we talk about findings related to recipients and human agents at the middle level (see sections 3.4.3 and 3.4.4).

- The number of cartoon + live-action children's cinema-films does not allow us to draw any reliable conclusions (only one product in 1994-1995). As in the case of live-action children's and adult cinema-films, the only cartoon + live-action cinema-film was subtitled too, therefore not deviating from the subtitling norm.
- The only types of cinema-films that were released dubbed were cartoon children's cinema-films (three in 1994-1995 and three in 1995-1996). Five out of these six products were actually double-releases, i.e. the same product was released with subtitles as well. This double-release phenomenon, however, cannot be claimed to be the norm in the broader context of Greek cinema but is rather a tactic favoured by the specific distribution-agency, namely Prooptiki. The only cartoon children's cinema-film that was released in a single dubbed copy was *Thumbelina* (by ELKE), a cinema-film with theme and humour aimed at toddlers rather than youngsters. On the other hand, cartoon children's cinema-films with theme and humour that would appeal to youngsters rather than toddlers (*Asterix* cinema-films, three released by ELKE and one by Spentzos Cinema) were released in a single subtitled copy. Even in cartoon children's cinema-films, then, it is clear that the norm tends towards subtitling. This would support the norm already seen to operate at the lower level: the norm that wants cartoon children's TV-films to be subtitled too (see table 3.3.1.7). Moreover, the stronger the norm in cartoon-type films in general, the more it will influence choices in cartoon-type series, since this serves to make the audience accustomed to watching subtitled cartoon dialogues. This influence from children's cartoon movies, then, can explain the otherwise unusual decision to subtitle certain cartoon TV series (as seen in section 3.3.1).
- 93.3% of the overall foreign cinema-films released in 1994-1995, and 95.2% of the overall cinema-films released in 1995-1996 were subtitled. This indicates the strength of the subtitling norm in the Greek audiovisual context and reinforces the characterisation of Greece as a predominantly subtitling country.

Having dealt with TV and cinema, the last audiovisual mode that is left to discuss is that of video. The situation with video data collection is slightly more complicated than that of TV and cinema. Data on video releases may be collected for sell-through or rental figures. Rental figures would not give a clear view of films that were released at a specific time-point, since it would consist of products that were released once but then released again for video clubs, perhaps even years after their original release. Sell-through figures would provide a more reliable picture since they would relate to products that are launched onto the market at a specific time-point not just to video clubs for rental, but to the public for full purchase as well. However, some video distribution agencies had considerable difficulty tracing the exact date of an original release through their archives. In addition, the video-release year does not have a three months break, like the cinematic one, but lasts twelve months with some releases overlapping in two consecutive years. As a result, I decided to draw up a cumulative table with data for 1994-1996 instead of two tables for two separate years. In this respect, the opportunity to discuss the diachronic evolution of norms is lost but, on the other hand, the findings become more reliable. Data was collected from the top 4 video distribution agencies that dominate the Greek video market. The typology that was established for TV programmes, distinguishing between children's and adult productions, was maintained. The picture of the language transfer method for video sell-through releases looks as follows:

Table 3.4.1.10 AUDIOVISUAL Video sell-through releases

VIDEO DISTRIBUTION AGENCY: AUDIOVISUAL	**VIDEO SELL-THROUGH 1994-1996 LANGUAGE TRANSFER METHOD USED**				
	Sub	**Dub**	**Nar**	**Nar+Sub**	**F/Com**
PRODUCT TYPE					
Children's movies (cartoons)	10[i]	14			
Children's movies (l/action)	2[ii]	2[iii]			
Children's movies (cart + l/a)					
Children's movies (puppets)	1				
Children's series (cartoons)	7[iv]	28			
Children's series (l/action)					
Children's series (cart + l/a)					
Children's series (puppets)					
CHILDREN'S TOTAL	**20**	**44**			
Adult movies	27				
Adult series/serials					
Light Entertainment					
Documentaries	2[v]		20[vi]		
Sports			6[vii]		
News/Information					
Music/Opera/Ballet	4				
ADULT TOTAL	**33**		**26**		
OVERALL TOTAL	**53**	**44**	**26**		

[i] 8 products (*Aladdin, Snow White and the Seven Dwarfs, The Aristocats, The Return of Jafar, The Lion King, Thumbelina, 101 Dalmatians, Sleeping Beauty)* in a double release, 2 products in a subtitled version only (*Batman: The Mask of the Phantasm, The Dog Who Gets No Respect*)

[ii] *Free Willy, Dennis the Menace*

[iii] *Benji, For the Love of Benji*

[iv] *The Little Mermaid:...* (4 individual episodes), *Police Academy:...* (2 individual episodes), *Ariel's Gift*

[v] *The Making of: JFK* (2 individual episodes)

[vi] *Predators of the Wild* (14 individual episodes), *The Greek Islands* (6 individual episodes)

[vii] 6 individual keep-fit products

Table 3.4.1.11 HVH video sell-through releases

VIDEO DISTRIBUTION AGENCY: HVH	VIDEO SELL-THROUGH 1994-1996 LANGUAGE TRANSFER METHOD USED				
	Sub	**Dub**	**Nar**	**Nar+Sub**	**F/Com**
PRODUCT TYPE					
Children's movies (cartoons)		28[i]			
Children's movies (l/action)	2[ii]	1[iii]			
Children's movies (cart + l/a)		1[iv]			
Children's movies (puppets)					
Children's series (cartoons)		15			
Children's series (l/action)					
Children's series (cart + l/a)					
Children's series (puppets)					
CHILDREN'S TOTAL	**2**	**45**			
Adult movies	20				
Adult series/serials	4				
Light Entertainment					
Documentaries	12[v]				
Sports					
News/Information					
Music/Opera/Ballet					
ADULT TOTAL	**36**				
OVERALL TOTAL	**38**	**45**			

[i] 1 (*Asterix Conquers America*) from French through English

[ii] *Andre, Babe*

[iii] *Babe* (double release)

[iv] *The Pagemaster*

[v] *National Geographic* series of documentaries (12 individual episodes)

Tables 3.4.1.12 VIDEOSONIC video sell-through releases

VIDEO DISTRIBUTION AGENCY: VIDEOSONIC	**VIDEO SELL-THROUGH 1994-1996** **LANGUAGE TRANSFER METHOD USED**				
	Sub	**Dub**	**Nar**	**Nar+Sub**	**F/Com**
PRODUCT TYPE					
Children's movies (cartoons)		12			
Children's movies (l/action)	17	1[i]			
Children's movies (cart + l/a)					
Children's movies (puppets)					
Children's series (cartoons)		3[ii]			
Children's series (l/action)		5[iii]			
Children's series (cart + l/a)					
Children's series (puppets)					
CHILDREN'S TOTAL	**17**	**21**			
Adult movies	73				
Adult series/serials					
Light Entertainment					
Documentaries	13[iv]		41[v]		
Sports	2[vi]		11[vii]		
News/Information	1[viii]				
Music/Opera/Ballet	2[ix]				
ADULT TOTAL	**92**		**59**		
OVERALL TOTAL	**109**	**21**	**59**		

[i] *Pippi Longstocking*

[ii] *Santa:...* (3 individual episodes)

[iii] *Power Rangers* (5 individual episodes)

[iv] *Lonely Planet* (13 individual episodes)

[v] 33 miscellaneous Geographical/Animal Kingdom, *Planet Earth* (7 individual episodes), *Lover's Guide*

[vi] *100 Years of Olympics* (2 individual episodes)

[vii] 1 aimed at children (*Barbie*, children's 'keep-fit'), 10 learn-how-to-play-basketball products. Also 8 Greek originals (no language transfer)

[viii] *Oscar's Great Moments*

[ix] Also 1 Greek original (no language transfer)

Table 3.4.1.13 SPENTZOS VIDEO video sell-through releases

VIDEO DISTRIBUTION AGENCY: SPENTZOS VIDEO	**VIDEO SELL-THROUGH 1994-1996 LANGUAGE TRANSFER METHOD USED**				
	Sub	**Dub**	**Nar**	**Nar+Sub**	**F/Com**
PRODUCT TYPE					
Children's movies (cartoons)					
Children's movies (l/action)					
Children's movies (cart + l/a)					
Children's movies (puppets)					
Children's series (cartoons)					
Children's series (l/action)					
Children's series (cart + l/a)					
Children's series (puppets)					
CHILDREN'S TOTAL	-	-			
Adult movies	122[i]				
Adult series/serials					
Light Entertainment					
Documentaries					
Sports					
News/Information					
Music/Opera/Ballet					
ADULT TOTAL	**122**				
OVERALL TOTAL	**122**				

[i] 121 from English, 1 from Spanish. Also 1 Greek original (no language transfer)

Table 3.4.1.14 Overall video sell-through releases

OVERALL VIDEO PRODUCTS	VIDEO SELL-THROUGH 1994-1996 LANGUAGE TRANSFER METHOD USED				
	Sub	**Dub**	**Nar**	**Nar+Sub**	**F/Com**
PRODUCT TYPE					
Children's movies (cartoons)	10	54			
Children's movies (l/action)	21	4			
Children's movies (cart + l/a)		1			
Children's movies (puppets)	1				
Children's series (cartoons)	7	46			
Children's series (l/action)		5			
Children's series (cart + l/a)					
Children's series (puppets)					
CHILDREN'S TOTAL	**39**	**110**[i]			
Adult movies	342				
Adult series/serials	4				
Light Entertainment					
Documentaries	27		61		
Sports	2		17		
News/Information	1				
Music/Opera/Ballet	6				
ADULT TOTAL	**382**		**78**		
OVERALL TOTAL	**421**[ii]	**110**[iii]	**78**[iv]		

From the tables above the following conclusions may be drawn:

- There is considerable variety of video-product types, as in the case of TV and unlike the mode of cinema. The norms operating in television may thus be expected to exert a strong influence on the choice of language transfer method in videos.

---

[i] **74%** of all children's video products

[ii] **69%** of all video products

[iii] **18%** of all video products

[iv] **13%** of all video products

- Starting with adult video products, all adult movies, adult series and music/opera/ballet products are invariably subtitled (see table 3.4.1.14). Bearing in mind the existing subtitling norm for TV and cinema (for movies only), we may speak of a very strong norm that cuts across all audiovisual modes.
- The only news/information product (a film-type not really common to video products) was released subtitled (*Oscar's Great Moments* by VIDEOSONIC, see table 3.4.1.12). Interestingly enough, it is almost identical to FILMNET's TV broadcast *Oscar's 1995: Pre- and Post-Shows* (see table 3.4.1.6) in both theme and structure. This TV programme was also subtitled. The consistency of the established norm, therefore, seems to be maintained.
- As in the case of TV documentaries, video documentaries reveal a variation in the language transfer method chosen by the various commissioners of video products. This time, however, the choice is between subtitling and narration (and not narration+subtitling), and the commissioners appear to favour the latter (see table 3.4.1.14). The theme/genre of most video documentaries is 'geography'. This thematic coherence, however, does not appear to clarify the choice of the language transfer method to be followed. On the contrary, it blurs the picture even further since, once again, the suggestion that the genre of the product guides the choice of language transfer method does not seem to hold true. We might, then, talk about a video-distribution-agency-bound language transfer strategy: AUDIOVISUAL favours narration, HVH favours subtitling, and VIDEOSONIC leans slightly towards narration. Each agency has its preference with regard to the optimal method of language transfer for video documentaries. Interestingly enough, however, the video equivalent of the TV documentaries *The making of:...* - broadcast on TV by MEGA and STAR in different versions (subtitling / narration+subtitling) - is released subtitled by AUDIOVISUAL. Two parameters might have influenced the above decision: a) the fact that AUDIOVISUAL in general seems to favour subtitling (see table 3.4.1.10), and b) the fact that the process of language transfer in the case of STAR channel, which broadcast the documentary subtitled, takes place at the in-house

translation studios of AUDIOVISUAL. The TV-documentary broadcast preceded the video release chronologically. The decision to maintain the language transfer method initially chosen (or dictated by STAR commissioners) for the TV-documentary would be both financially wise, since it would save time and labour, and would also be consistent with what the viewers have already become accustomed to by watching the subtitled TV version.

- Unlike sports TV programmes, video sports products are released mainly in narration. It would seem, however, that the theme/genre and the relative time of public release for these video sports products are quite different from those of their TV counterparts. All the video sports products released are instructive rather than entertaining in orientation: 'learning how to keep fit' (by AUDIOVISUAL, see table 3.4.1.10), and 'learning how to play basketball' (by VIDEOSONIC, see table 3.4.1.12). This is the first time that the theme/genre of an audiovisual product appears to play a role in the choice of language transfer method. In any case, unlike sports TV programmes, the fact that the programmes do not have to be broadcast immediately after the event means that they do not require an immediate language transfer process. As a result, the video distribution agencies have more time to implement the language transfer method they consider most appropriate.
- Moving on to children's video products, we see that these are the only video products that are dubbed. A few children's videos are subtitled, but they only represent 26% of the total children's video releases, while dubbed releases account for no less than 74% (see table 3.4.1.14), a much higher percentage than the average of dubbed children's products on TV (46% in March 1995, 63% in March 1996; see table 3.3.1.7) or cinema (27% in 1994-1995, 37.5% in 1995-1996; see tables 3.4.1.8 and 3.4.1.9). Since the choice to subtitle or to revoice children's TV programmes is part of the broader audiovisual picture and is inevitably influenced by decisions taken in other audiovisual modes, this clear tendency towards dubbing children's video releases counterbalances the tendency to subtitle children's cinema products. Children's TV programmes, then, seem to be positioned in the centre of a

magnetic field, metaphorically speaking, with decisions concerning language transfer method being subject to the influence of the other two audiovisual modes. At the same time, however, this influence is filtered, re-diverted and channelled back to the modes of cinema and video, leading to a constant interaction between all three modes.

- The only children's product type where subtitling seems to be the favoured method is live action movies. This is understandable given that the same product type on TV or cinema is invariably subtitled. Children's live action video movies that are released dubbed are either a) dubbed versions of a double video release (as in the case of *Babe* by HVH, see table 3.4.1.11), or b) new versions of older products that were also broadcast dubbed on TV (as in the case of *Pippi Longstocking* by VIDEOSONIC, see table 3.4.1.12, whose series were broadcast dubbed on ET1 years ago), or finally c) they are clearly aimed at toddlers rather than older children (as in the case of *Benji* and *For the love of Benji* by AUDIOVISUAL, see table 3.4.1.10).
- Children's live action video series on the other hand are invariably dubbed. Not surprisingly, all products belong to the same series (5 individual episodes) of the most popular (dubbed) children's TV product *Power Rangers*, released on video by VIDEOSONIC (see table 3.4.1.12). As we previously saw, however, the cinema-film version of the same series was released with subtitles by Spentzos Cinema (see table 3.4.1.9). This proves first of all the need to distinguish between series and movies. It also proves, though, that the choice of the language transfer method for video products is motivated by existing norms in television rather than in cinema.
- Unlike TV and cinema, the norm for children's cartoon video movies requires that they are dubbed (see table 3.4.1.14). As a matter of fact, all the subtitled releases come from AUDIOVISUAL. Eight out of the ten subtitled children's cartoon movies are subtitled versions of a double release (see table 3.4.1.10). The motivations behind the subtitled release of the other two products (*Batman: The Mask of the Phantasm* and *The Dog Who Gets No Respect*) is hard to explain. Their theme and humour

do not appear to be aimed particularly at older children. Clearly, though, the commissioners of the specific video products believed that they would not appeal to younger children so much. Interestingly enough, however, the TV series' version of one of these products, *Batman*, is broadcast dubbed by ANT1 with relative success (see table 3.3.3.2). The three cartoon movies that had been already released in the cinema in a double version (*The Lion King, 101 Dalmatians, Sleeping Beauty* by Prooptiki, see tables 3.4.1.8 and 3.4.1.9) were released in a double version on video too (by AUDIOVISUAL see table 3.4.1.10). Another movie, however, which was only dubbed (*Thumbelina*, by ELKE, see table 3.4.1.8) was this time released in a double version on video (by AUDIOVISUAL, see table 3.4.1.10). This suggests that the mode of video allows greater flexibility in the choice and implementation of the language transfer method.

- Children's cartoon video series are dubbed (see table 3.4.1.14). Once again, all the subtitled releases come from AUDIOVISUAL (see table 3.4.1.10). None of the seven subtitled products (4 episodes of *The Little Mermaid*, 2 episodes of *Police Academy* and 1 of *Ariel's Gift*) appears to be aimed especially at older children. As a result, there can be no other explanation than that the commissioners of these subtitled cartoon children's video series did not believe that they could attract a large enough audience of younger children to justify dubbing expenses. The trend was already clear with one of these series, *Police Academy*, which was broadcast dubbed on TV by STAR without great success (see table 3.3.3.4).
- For children's cartoon + live-action or puppet video movies no reliable conclusions can be drawn (only one product per category). It is interesting to note, however, that the cartoon + live-action movie that was released dubbed by HVH is the video version of the cinema-film *The Pagemaster*, released subtitled by ELKE (see tables 3.4.1.11 and 3.4.1.8). We see therefore that although these two audiovisual distribution agencies are affiliated, the different audiovisual mode they serve is strong enough to draw a distinction

between their trends: HVH seems to favour dubbing whereas the parent agency seems to favour subtitling in general.

3.4.2 Findings related to middle level audiovisual mode

So far we have been talking of an intersection between norms operating in the three audiovisual modes as if the audiovisual translation process is the same for television, video and cinema. Limitations related to the specific audiovisual mode, however, restrict the potential for natural influence as they provide a tight framework within which this interaction between norms from TV, video and cinema can take place.

It has often been observed that a cinema-film is re-subtitled before it is broadcast on TV (*EBU Review*, 1987:12). This happens in response to a number of audiovisual-mode specific technical, financial and cultural parameters. Yves Gambier points out four reasons for producing different subtitles for TV, cinema and video (1994:275). First of all, TV, video and cinema products are imported, distributed and their translation commissioned by different agencies. As a result, copyright law and local legislation might require compensation, accreditation or alteration since the product represents someone's intellectual effort and property (Krogstad, 1998:57&59). In Greece, specific legislation for subtitling- and revoicing-copyrights does not exist at all; the whole issue depends on the good will of the commissioners to respect the work of the translators (cf. Papadakis, 1998:69). Secondly, the translation process itself requires different working conditions for TV, video and cinema. As we have already seen, various TV stations in Greece have their own in-house audiovisual translation departments. This allows the translators to be in constant touch with the products' commissioners; translating for the cinema, however, means doing something that a distribution agency commissions you to do, outside the agency's premises. Thirdly, the speed of cinema picture is slower than the speed of TV and video picture. Adapting an audiovisual translation means cueing it on the original product in terms not just of seconds but even of individual frames. Cinema products have 24 frames per second; TV and video products have 25 - hence the fact that the same cinema movie is usually shorter on TV (Ivarsson, 1992:40, Minchinton, 1993:3.1). Finally, the size and definition of the cinema screen is different from the size and definition of the TV (and video) screen. Cinema screen is larger, thus enhancing reading speed (cf. de Linde, 1995:9). At the same time, TV's digital technology provides the potential for better image analysis; but a jammed broadcast signal that spoils the quality of the image also slows down the reading speed. Luyken et al. point out as an additional reason for distinguishing between subtitling for TV, cinema and video the variety of the technical processes involved (1991:42). Chemically and optically inserted subtitles are used for cinema; electronic insertion is used for television (only lately in cinema by state-of-the-art subtitling studios). However, in certain countries - but not in Greece - the methods of inserting subtitles chemically and optically are also used for television. In such cases, Beta or VHS video systems cannot be used. The obligatory use of 16mm gauge TV-films, as opposed to that of 35mm gauge cinema-films (Armes, 1988:82), interferes with the quality of TV subtitles even further, since the smaller gauge has less 'grains' on its photographic emulsion and, as a result, the outline and definition of subtitles are considerably blurred (Minchinton, 1963a:42). Electronically inserted subtitles are generally of better quality and enhance reading speed. All the above indicate that any programme - including children's programmes - delivered subtitled on TV does not necessarily have to be delivered subtitled in the cinema or on video, nor the other way round.

Dubbing for TV, cinema and video also has its own individual limitations. Technically, first of all, the 'unilinear' method for projection which is mainly used for TV and video requires fewer retakes than the 'loop projection' method used for cinema (Luyken et al., 1991:79). This cuts down on the time required to dub which in turn brings costs down. On average, the price of dubbing is higher for cinema than it is for TV and video because the former demands more accuracy and higher lip-sync quality since the size of the cinema screen makes lip-sync defects more visible (Dries, 1995a:14; Fodor, 1976:61). Again, all the above indicate that any programme -

including children's programmes - which was delivered dubbed on TV does not necessarily have to be delivered dubbed on cinema or video, nor the other way round.

None of the above audiovisual-mode specific subtitling and dubbing constraints seem to directly guide or consciously motivate the choice to dub or to subtitle children's TV programmes in Greece. In a number of other European countries, however, the audiovisual mode is directly associated with the norms that dictate the choice between subtitling and revoicing. Some Eastern European countries like Poland, Latvia, Estonia, and Lithuania, for example, subtitle their cinema products but broadcast their TV programmes in narration (Dries, 1994-95:36; Vitkus, 1995:317-318). Even in Western Europe, though, the audiovisual mode itself tends to play a gradually increasing role: France and Spain, two traditionally dubbing countries for example, are reported to be gradually restricting their dubbing traditions to television only, with subtitling daily gaining ground amongst cinemas (Dries, 1995b:237). The advent of a new audiovisual mode has also been observed to signal the advent of a new audiovisual transfer method: in Belarus, for example, everything used to be dubbed by the communist regime in order for the original voices to be completely erased (Baranitch, 1995:309). When the mode of video, which was illegal at the time, appeared in the early 1980's though, it brought along the new language transfer method of narration as it was both cheaper and quicker than dubbing (ibid). In our computerised era, we have to be prepared for the advent of a new audiovisual mode that is directly linked with the use of the Internet (cf. Cattrysse, 1998:7; cf. Lambert, 1998.14). It is already possible to watch large chunks of audiovisual products on our computer screens. So far, I am not aware of any commission to translate such audiovisual products. Nevertheless, the future is not far away and we should not be surprised to see a brand new language transfer method in the field of audiovisual translation competing with the already existing ones for domination of the new audiovisual mode.

For television at least, digital broadcasting technology nowadays appears to favour subtitling (James, 1998:244; cf. Bicknell, 1998:39). It is not just the increasing use of teletext that will offer greater public access to this specific language transfer method. The introduction of the new 16/9 (or 9 x 16) TV-screen resolution - as already seen on Channel 4 in the UK - has allowed for a different approach to the issue of subtitles, since they can be placed under the filmic image, no longer obscuring the visual image (cf. Ivarsson, 1992:163; cf. Ivarsson, 1995b:423). In Greece, the only TV station that possesses the system (state-owned ET3, based in Thessaloniki and not in Athens) has not used it in association with inserting subtitles on screen, since the foreign products it broadcasts are transferred and processed in Athens in the traditional screen-resolution way. Technology has also worked in favour of revoicing. The use of each of the two sound channels in a stereo broadcast can give the viewer the choice to receive the revoiced version through the one sound channel and the original through the other. This system has been implemented in Greece by the cable TV station FILMNET which broadcasts most of its sports programmes in free-commentary through the one channel and in the original source-language commentary through the other. What I can personally see as playing a crucial role in future revoicing, however, is the use of digital image processing. With the help of simple computer equipment it is already possible to change the lip-movements of the actors on screen while keeping the rest of their facial and body motions intact (Giles, 1997: 47; cf. Reeve, 1995:419). This technique has already been implemented in Japan on Japanese-made cartoons where the mouth movements of the cartoon characters are digitally processed to fit the new dialogues in Western languages (most often to a French scenario). When they reach European markets, such Japanese cartoon products that are not actually the primary originals but digitally processed copies. I can see in the near future each individual country re-processing the mouth movements of these cartoon characters in a way that would fit the desired transferred script. Such a development which would definitely affect the choice between subtitling and revoicing cartoon children's products however, would also affect from that point on the totality of children's products in general.

Apart from all the above technical, financial and cultural limitations in the use and choice of the language transfer method, there is a new set of limitations that derives from the social ritual which is associated with watching a product on TV, in the cinema, or on video in particular. The projection of the cinema image on a large screen, in a darkened auditorium where spectators have gone voluntarily to watch a filmic production for approximately 90 minutes, sometimes even without leaving their seats (Harvey, 1996:242), enhances the reading speed of subtitles. In addition, the fact that their attention is so focused on the image and that they pay in order to get into the auditorium means that they demand high quality viewing. Whatever the language transfer method chosen, then, cinema viewers demand very high quality performance and as we have seen, this is harder and more costly to achieve in dubbing. In addition, the 'event' of cinema-going is associated with a deliberate attempt to escape from reality, a sense that is highlighted both during film-watching and especially when spectators leave the auditorium (Turner, 1988:110). As a result, the attempted recreation of illusionary reality meant to be achieved by the use of dubbing may not be particularly appealing precisely because viewers go to the cinema to escape from this reality. Watching a subtitled film that constantly challenges this sense of reality by reminding them that they are not experiencing a real-life event taking place on the screen but something prepared in advance for them does not spoil their sense of ease and comfort because they do not go to the cinema expecting to see such immediate real-life situations. Greek audiovisual reality seems to support these observations, since the norm for cinema-film products is clearly in favour of subtitling.

Television, on the other hand, attempts consistently to present itself as 'live' and 'unmediated' (Armes, 1988:127; Rath, 1988:32, Ivarsson, 1992:75). Subtitling spoils this attempt; revoicing supports it. Watching television is a popular pass-time because watching moving images is associated with a sense of ease, relaxation and availability for distraction (Barwise & Ehrenberg, 1988:19); in other words, TV watching is a 'laid-back' activity. The increased cognitive effort in the visual process of subtitles conflict with this attitude to TV watching. Additionally, distractions from various sources around the house also mean that subtitles have to stay longer on the TV screen (Minchinton, 1987:280). Greek audiovisual reality does not support these observations for television as much as it supports those related to cinema: revoicing is not significantly more popular on Greek TV than it is in cinema (revoiced products were found to occupy 8.6% of total TV products and 5.7% of total cinema products on a two years' average; see tables 3.4.1.7, 3.4.1.8 and 3.4.1.9).

Video may provide more cinematic narrative than TV but it does not replicate the experience of the darkened cinema auditorium (Turner, 1988:97). As a result, video watching habits seem to resemble TV more than cinema. Although Greek audiovisual reality does not support the above observations for TV, it appears to support the 'easy-watching' principle for video (revoiced products were found to occupy 31% of total video products; see table 3.4.1.14).

Even specific film/programme-types within the same medium are influenced by the social ritual that accompanies the medium itself. Soap operas on television are a good example. The attempt of television to present itself as 'live' and 'unmediated' interacts with the attempt of the specific programme-type of soap opera to mimic and portray real life situations (cf. Brown: 1994:72). Soap opera is a programme type specifically designed for television. The use of dubbing makes sense in terms of the attempt to sustain reality, as mentioned above; the use of subtitling would spoil this attempt (cf. Ganz-Blättler, 1995:249). In Greece between 1994-1996, however, soap operas (as adult series) were invariably subtitled. It is only recently (during 1997) that some viewer-testing experiments were carried out by SKY and some other minor channels, who took the risk to broadcast some of their soap operas dubbed.

In terms of chronological precedence of one audiovisual mode over the other, we could safely say that for movies, the only film-type that cuts across all three modes, cinema precedes both TV and video; a movie will first be released in the cinema and then become available for use on TV and video (cf. Corner, 1987:22). There are other cases, however, where TV series inspired the consecutive production of a cinema movie with the same protagonists. We have already come across cases where the same product appears on two different modes. Intertextuality would demand these products to be delivered in the same language transfer method; in this respect, the factor of chronological precedence would suggest that choices made during the initial translation process will be followed in the translation of the other two modes. As we have seen so far, instances where these rules of intertextuality and chronological precedence were respected were significantly fewer than the instances where these rules were violated. Examples of compliance with the principle of intertextuality include the cartoon children's series *Police Academy*, initially broadcast subtitled on TV and subsequently released subtitled on video, as well as three cartoon children's movies (*The Lion King, 101 Dalmatians* and *Sleeping Beauty*) which were released in a double version first in the cinema and then on video. The rest seem to ignore the principle of intertextuality. Live-action children's series *Power Rangers* was broadcast dubbed on TV, subsequently released dubbed on video, but the cinema-film under the same title was later released subtitled. Cartoon series *Batman* was broadcast dubbed on TV, but later released subtitled on video. Cartoon + live-action children's movie *The Pagemaster* was released subtitled in the cinema, but in the subsequent video release it was dubbed. Cartoon movie *Thumbelina* was released dubbed in the cinema, to be later released in a double version on video. Artistic documentaries *The Making of:...* were broadcast subtitled by one TV station, in narration+subtitles by another, to be later released subtitled on video. The diverse patterns of overlap between film-types and audiovisual modes makes it difficult to identify a consistent pattern of influence. Each audiovisual mode has its own status and independence and works with its own individual criteria. Normative influence between the various audiovisual modes is, therefore, considerably restricted. It does exist, but not as an undifferentiated repertoire: every mode has its own dynamic.

A few things that have to be stressed and added to the overall picture of middle-level audiovisual modes have to do with comparative financial aspects. Logically, the mode with the stronger financial backing should be able to impose its norms on the other two more easily. The fact that viewers are involved in watching TV for an average of 1,000 hours a year per person implies that the finances of TV are of much greater importance than those of the other two modes (cf. Harvey, 1996:238). In Greece, however, there are a few other parameters that interfere with the way the relative finances of the three audiovisual modes impact on patterns of influence. The massive boom in private TV in the early 1990's created chaos in the audiovisual industry, which is still recovering from the aftermaths. At the moment there are about 20 non-pay local and national TV channels transmitting in Athens alone. However, the top 5 TV stations collect about 80% of total viewership. The rest of the small local private TV stations, some of which operate even without a licence, broadcast movies they rent or buy from video clubs illegally, without paying any copyright fees to the producers or distributors, since broadcasting and property rights legislation in Greece is somewhat vague and difficult to enforce (cf. Carr, 1991b:I-8). All this started alongside a governmental project to liberalise mass media in general and offer free satellite service to all citizens. This was a major blow not just for video clubs and consequently for video as an audiovisual mode (ibid:I-8), but for cinema and the other TV channels too. There was no need for the viewers to go to the video clubs and hire the tapes; they would be broadcast free - sooner or later - on one of these local private or foreign satellite channels. There was no need to go to the cinema even; the broadcast of so many TV channels and movies could very easily satisfy their individual interests and quench their thirst for movies. It dealt a blow to the large - and legal - TV stations in particular, since they would see their viewing rates drop and new competitors arrive with a budget amazingly lower than theirs to threaten and disrupt the market. Today, this free-satellite project has been considerably restricted to a few music channels and a serious attempt is made to control illegal practices in the small local channels. TV and cinema show encouraging signs of recovery with cinema-ticket figures rising sharply again, and viewing rates for the large and legal TV channels climbing to reflect the considerably higher quality of service they offer in comparison to the rest of these small local channels. Video, though, has not yet shown such encouraging signs of recovery (cf. Papadakis, 1998:66). As a summary of all the above, we can suggest that in Greece it is TV and cinema norms that exert stronger control over video norms and not the other way round.

3.4.3 Findings related to middle level recipients

The present study is interested in the choice of the language transfer method for children's TV programmes in particular. Given the individual nature of each of the three audiovisual modes as described in the previous section, one might question the relevance of investigating choices of language transfer method in the other two audiovisual modes. The point is, however, that we cannot name a whole country 'predominantly subtitling' or 'predominantly dubbing' just by investigating the mode of television. Although it is human agents who initiate a shift in the dominant language transfer method of a particular audiovisual mode, it is the recipients who dictate the fate of that norm through their *overall* attitudes to language transfer methods. In this respect, the overall attitudes of the recipients of audiovisual products should be closely investigated.

When investigating data and attitudes of the television audience in particlular, a number of parameters have to be taken into account. First of all, the use of house recording video equipment can distort viewing rates. In the UK, for example, it has been shown that for households with children, children's TV programmes rank at the top of TV programmes recorded for later viewing (Gunter & Svennevig, 1987:10). In theory, then, such instances of recorded material should be added to the already measured viewing rates to give a clear picture of the number of individuals who have watched the actual programmes. In Greece, no similar surveys are consistently carried out.

Two closely related phenomena that also seem to blur the picture of viewing rates are 'repeat viewng' and 'audience duplication' (cf. Goodhart et al., 1975:125-126). 'Repeat viewing' refers to consecutive viewing of successive episodes of the same programme (usually a day or a week later); 'audience duplication' refers to consecutive viewing of programmes along the time scale, i.e. of programmes that follow what we have already been watching simply because we had the television on. Earlier studies in the UK have indicated that repeat viewing can reach a level of 55% (ibid), i.e. 55% of the viewers of one episode one week will watch it again the following week. Unfortunately, I am not aware of any studies in Greece on either of the two phenomena. What must be stressed, however, assuming these two phenomena prove relevant, is that viewing rates alone are not a totally reliable source on which to base any conclusions, let alone conclusions related to the recipients' preference for certain programmes in terms of the specific language transfer method used.

It is often claimed that "subtitling is the most widely spread form of language transfer in countries with a small population and small viewer figures" (Aaltonen, 1995b:384; cf. Whitman-Linsen, 1992:18). Nevertheless, various exceptions to the above statement have already been found, including countries like Hungary, the Slovak Republic and Bulgaria for example, where dubbing is the predominant language transfer method on TV, and other Eastern European countries where narration is favoured (Dries, 1994-95:36). I would regard the above statement, therefore, as a case of unfortunate over-generalisation. The economics of a country undoubtedly play a significant role in the choice of the language transfer method, but the accustoming of the audience with an existing norm in terms of language transfer method plays an even more significant role. Especially in countries where one language transfer method is used for TV and another for cinema or video, one has to be very careful to specify what medium s/he is talking about, since an overall attempt to portray such a country "as a subtitling or a dubbing country for good means that one is paying less attention to the audience and its wishes" (Dries, 1995b:237).

The difference between TV and cinema audiences has been stressed by various scholars. Hood says:

> "the television audience differs from a theatre or cinema audience in its nature, composition and reactions. Theatre and cinema audiences are made up of men and women who, as an act of volition, have decided to go to a particular place on a particular day at a particular time to see an entertainment of their own choosing. They are active audiences [...] The television audience is a statistical fiction. It exists only in the sense that its members, who are to be reckoned in millions, hear and see the same things at the same second in time. In economically advanced countries it consists of discrete groups - two or three people watching in the privacy of their own homes - or of individuals.[...] It is a passive audience which

> sits at home and expects to be amused, informed, or - more rarely - educated" (1967:36).

All these factors have an impact on the choice of the language transfer method for each of the audiovisual modes. The fact that we pay to go to the cinema makes us more demanding in terms of the quality of the product on offer (cf. Armes, 1988:139), including the quality of language transfer. At the same time, however, the TV viewer can be equally demanding: unlike the cinema spectator who is caught in a mass reaction and subconsciously becomes a submissive, less critical acceptor of whatever s/he is offered in his/her particular cinema-visit, the TV viewer has the chance to press the button on the remote control and flick to another channel if the quality of what is shown fails to meet the standards that s/he has set (Hood, 1967:37). In this respect, it is easier to manipulate and control cinema audiences than it is to hold the attention of TV audiences. Even for TV, then, an equally high standard of performance, including language transfer method, needs to be maintained. It is simply that the voluntary nature of the cinema audience makes it easier for the human agents to assess what has to be served and how it should be served. The random nature of TV audience, where quite often viewers have to compromise with other fellow viewers in the house in order to reach a consensus on what to watch, makes it more difficult for the human agents to assess the nature of what has to be served.

So, if cinema audience is not as random as TV audience and therefore more easily accessible, how can one ensure that the language transfer method caters for the needs of such a specific audience? It has been proven that cinephiles/cineastes, for reasons of artistic perception, prefer subtitled versions; the rest of the adult audience prefer whatever method happens to represent the norm of the country. In countries like Greece then, where subtitling is the overall predominant norm, there is no need to dub adult cinema-films at all. In other countries where there is a struggle between the language transfer methods for each of the various audiovisual modes or where revoicing is the overall predominant norm, there is still a need to provide subtitled versions for those cinephiles/cineastes, the loyal cinema-goers. In predominantly dubbing Italy and Spain, subtitled cinema-film versions are screened in "small private film clubs or 'art' cinemas" (Myers, 1973:57), "almost exclusively for intellectuals and film festivals" (Zabalbeascoa, 1994:93). Cinephiles claim that they prefer subtitling because they believe that dubbing distorts the artistic impression of the original film (*American Film*, April1983:6), not because there is something inherently wrong in this specific language transfer method, but "largely because of the shoddy careless way it's done" (Moskowitz, 1979:1). We can assume, then, that a rise in the quality standards of dubbing would lead to a rise in the cineastes appreciation of this particular method. However, if there is nothing inherently wrong in the method, where does this generalisation that 'dubbing is done in a careless way' stem from? In other words, why is it that dubbing is so frequently 'done in a careless way' and is thus associated with this sense of disbelief? One has to admit that it is really difficult to achieve high quality dubbing standards that would please the language transfer demands of the cinephiles (Whitman-Linsen, 1992:85; cf. Li, 1998:156). Similarly, one has to accept that it is easier to achieve high standards of language transfer performance with subtitling since this language transfer method appears to meet the artistic demands of the cinephiles. This existing bias on the part of the cinephiles against dubbing and their preference for subtitling has led to the perpetuation of the norm to subtitle films. As a result, commissioners are very reluctant to offer a dubbed film to cineastes, because they know that even if it managed to meet the high quality language transfer standards they set, it would have to confront their already established bias against this specific language transfer method. And in a vicious circle, this perpetuation of the norm of subtitling strengthens the impression that subtitling is the only method that can truthfully and faithfully serve the artistic intentions of a cinema-film.

In the US, anonymous cineastes have convincingly argued that since the 'average viewer' goes to see an imported foreign film exactly because it is not an English-speaking production, every released foreign film is actually aimed at a cineaste (*American Film*, April 1983:6). The attempt to attract more viewers by providing dubbed versions in English is therefore pointless in the American audiovisual market (ibid). In Greece of course the situation is quite different. Still, what emerges from all the above is that even in the Greek audiovisual market it would be easier to track the needs and attitudes of cinema audience and specifically cater for them than it would be for TV or video audience, exactly because it is easier to construct a profile of the 'average' cinema viewer.

Studies in the UK, the US and Australia have indicated that "the majority of those who attend movies [...] are between 12 and 24 years [...] bearers of a college education" and belonging to a social class that can afford cinema-going as an "élitistic activity" (Turner, 1988:95). So, if a cinema-film is to be released and targeted to a particular sub-group of the potential general audience, and given the general make up of the cinema audience as described above, language transfer commissioners can trace the language transfer needs and attitudes of the targeted sub-group and choose a language transfer method accordingly. It is certainly easier than constructing profiles of sub-groups of the broader TV-audience which is not so well-defined in terms of age, education and socio-economic background. It is also true that it is easier to influence the tasks of sub-groups whose attitudes you know. Promotion and advertising of cinema-films play an integral role in defining a targeted sub-group. Unlike TV where, as we said, one just switches on and watches, and therefore no particular advertising is required, cinema-film attendance is strongly conditioned by the success of advertising and promotion of the respective film products (cf. Turner, 1988:99). As a result, commissioners of the cinema-film's language transfer method have to be sure that their estimation of the targeted sub-group of recipients is actually compatible with the product's promotion, so that their choice does not conflict with the advertising propaganda. For children's products, this becomes especially important, since it is easy for the language transfer commissioners to assume that a product is aimed solely at young children or toddlers, for example, while the advertising campaign sets out to attract a broader audience of older youngsters and teenagers.

We saw when discussing findings related to lower level recipients that one of the basic variables that affect the viewers' choice of a language transfer method, that of the viewers' gender, has not been shown to be directly associated with children as recipients of audiovisual products. Amongst adult viewers, though, it appears to play an important role. Morley claims that when investigating TV viewing at home "one is by definition investigating something which men are better placed to do wholeheartedly, and which women seem only to be able to do so distractedly and guiltily, because of their continuing sense of their domestic responsibilities" (1986:147), a result which is clearly based not on any biological fact but rather on a social definition of masculinity and power control (ibid:150). This however has direct and extremely important implications for the language transfer method to be chosen for TV programmes aimed at women rather than men (like soap operas for example). The fact that it is difficult for women to sit down and watch a TV programme non-stop, from the beginning to the end, since at the same time they often have to do other things around the house, does not allow them to coherently follow anything that flashes on and off the screen, including subtitles (O'Connell, 1998:66; Papadakis, 1997). Revoicing, then, appears to suit the social role of women better, since at least they are able to follow the plot by listening to the orally transferred dialogues. Other reports have indicated that, because of similar social conventions related to 'masculinity', men tend to prefer 'factual' programmes (like documentaries for example), whereas women tend to go for 'fictional' programmes (like soap operas) (Morley, 1986:162). Men's preference for 'factual' programmes is framed by a sense of guilt that TV-watching in general is a second-rate activity, i.e. second after 'real' leisure activities that demand men being more energetic (ibid:165). This finding has direct implications for the language transfer method to be followed too, since subtitling and narration which retain the original dialogues can provide a platform of authenticity and credibility for the transferred dialogues, suggesting that what is transferred is transferred in a strict 'factual' way closer to the original, and is not a freer, more 'artistic' or 'fictional' version of the original dialogues (cf. Gunter, 1982:6). Men need to feel that they can always check on the quality of language transfer, especially if they have a vague knowledge of the original language. Dubbing deprives them of such an ability, leaving them feeling powerless and weak, in direct conflict with their socially constructed role of control and masculinity. As we said earlier, gender has not been proven to play any role in the case of children. However, I can see the possibility (subject to further investigation) that the more the children are attached to one of the parents, and the older they become, the more they are likely to acquire his or her views, attitudes and habits, in a conscious or subconscious way. It would not be surprising if research indicated that girls who grow up to acquire their social feminine role prefer dubbing even during their early teens. Similarly, boys may well prefer subtitling even during their early teens and may start assuming their social role of masculinity quite early on, especially in a society that tends to attribute such social roles to its members during childhood.

Another factor related to the position of women in our society concerns the fact that quite a few years after the introduction of video in most homes, many women still do not know how to operate this piece of equipment, relying solely on their husbands or children in this respect (Morley, 1986:158). As a consequence, women are found to contribute less to making decisions related to hiring videotapes (ibid:159). This is extremely important for the choice of the language transfer method in video products, since it implies that the potential video audience is made up primarily of males or children. Language transfer commissioners of video products can therefore target their audience and choose the specific language transfer method accordingly.

In addition to the findings above, studies on reading behaviour in relation to subtitles have shown that women look at subtitles longer than men do, but no explanation for this phenomenon has yet been offered (d'Ydewalle et al., 1991:654). Whatever the reason, longer reading time means more cognitive effort, less time for the rest of the visual image, and as a result, feelings of unease and depreciation are experienced. This is another argument and possible motivation for revoicing audiovisual products aimed primarily at women. However, just as with previously discussed motivations and arguments in favour of revoicing, we see that the norm of subtitling in Greece remains strong and has not yet been influenced by such considerations.

Less speculative considerations are also found to play a part in the choice of language transfer method. Unlike the UK, teletext technology in Greece is still in its infancy (cf. Roffe & Thorne, 1994:254). Since very few households in the country are equipped with teletext receiving TV sets, the size of teletext receiving audience is small. It is natural for TV commissioners, then, to be reluctant to experiment with the possibility of transmitting the revoiced version through one of the stereo channels, the original through the other and subtitles through teletext, giving viewers the opportunity to combine the last two facilities into what would be a conventional broadcast of interlingual subtitling. The only way to broadcast a subtitled version in predominantly subtitling Greece is the traditional way, i.e. with 'open' subtitles applied to the translated copy, rather than with 'closed' subtitles encoded in a digital teletext message. As a result, the viewers' lack of access to 'advanced' technological equipment seems to block any attempt on the part of TV commissioners to gradually alter the subtitling norm by providing a simultaneous revoiced alternative.

There are other European countries, however, with more serious problems of social and technological development. In Latvia for example, the choice of narration instead of subtitling for TV programmes is motivated by the fact that the quality of the recipients' TV sets is so poor as to interfere with the reception of subtitles on screen (Vitkus, 1995:318). In addition, the percentage of elderly population with eyesight problems in the same country is reported as 25% (ibid). As a result, even if TV commissioners were thinking of providing subtitled TV programmes, the eventual choice of narration is dictated by socio-technological problems rather than the recipients' preferences as such.

So far, a large part of this section on findings related to middle level recipients has been devoted to comparisons of audiences and situations in various countries. But what is the specific viewing profile of the Greek TV, cinema or video audience? Starting with the mode of TV, for both 1994-1995 and 1995-1996, adult female TV audiences (aged 25 and over) were found to be quite keen on viewing Greek entertainment programmes. Children's audiences in general were found to be keen on watching domestic sitcoms (AGB Hellas eds.,

1995:52; AGB Hellas eds., 1996:54). This preference for - and familiarity with - hearing Greek language on TV could, in theory, encourage some human agents to believe that foreign programmes aimed at these specific audience groups can afford to be delivered dubbed. As we have seen already, out of the total volume of foreign broadcast TV material it was only some children's programmes that were eventually dubbed. In 1997, SKY channel decided to experiment with dubbing certain soap operas (aimed at the adult female audience), but no specific data is available yet on the success or failure of this experiment[i].

As far as the rest of the Greek TV-audience groups are concerned, we see that adult male viewers (aged 25 and over) as well as young male and female viewers (aged 15-24) seem to be quite keen on watching foreign programmes (ibid). Since they do not follow programmes with Greek language on TV, then, their preference for - and familiarity with - reading subtitles would make it rather difficult to promote dubbing in programmes aimed at them.

Greek cinema audiences, like large Western audiences, consist basically of young people aged 15-24 (Koronaiou, 1992:113). Young people from urban areas were found to be more frequent cinema-goers than their fellow young people from rural areas (ibid). Cinema fans - the cineastes who go to the movies at least twice a month - proved to belong to the upper-middle social class (ibid:114). Due to social reasons related to the fact that Greek families are stricter with their daughters than they are with their sons when it comes to going out for fun and entertainment, young males tend to go to the movies more often than young females (ibid:120). But even when they do go out, young females tend to favour more easy-to-follow movie genres that demand less cognitive effort (like romances, musicals etc.), whereas their male counterparts tend to favour movie genres that demand more mental effort, constant attention and conscious thinking (like thrillers, detective stories etc.) (ibid:120-121). The fact that the overall Greek cinema audience has a profile closer to that of male urban upper-

[i] A similar experiment carried out by MEGA three years before did not prove successful and the language transfer for the particular soap opera (*Days Of Our Lives*, see table 3.4.1.2) was turned from dubbing to subtitling after a few episodes.

middle class audience can justify and at the same time motivate the decision on the part of language transfer commissioners to follow the norm of subtitling.

Unfortunately, no data was available on the profile of Greek video audience. What has been already said about video watching habits in general, lying somewhere between TV watching habits and cinema watching habits, suggests that the profile of Greek video audience combines characteristics of both these audiovisual modes.

The only survey so far that has addressed the particular issue of Greek adult recipients' preference for subtitling or dubbing[i] was conducted in 1978. The fact that it was conducted about 17 years before the present research restricts considerably the applicability of its results. In 1978, 45.55% of the Greek adult TV audience stated that they favour subtitling for their foreign TV programmes, whereas 42.70% stated that they prefer dubbing (Doulkeri, 1992:104). Men were found to favour subtitling (50.34%), whereas women were found to favour dubbing (44.80%) (ibid). Young audiences between the age of 15-24 appeared to be the most keen on subtitling (60.15%), whereas elderly audiences of 65+ were the most keen on dubbing (64.35%) (ibid:105). They were even able to justify their preferences, the former claiming that TV-subtitling gives them the opportunity to practice "their English" - and not a foreign language in general (!) - whereas the latter complained that they found reading subtitles "not easy" (ibid:106). Recipients with just primary-school educational qualifications mostly favoured dubbing (56.31%), whereas those who had a university degree mostly favoured subtitling (64.41%) (ibid:105). Finally, manual workers, housewives and pensioners appeared to favour dubbing in particular (around 51%), whereas students and office-workers favoured subtitling in particular (around 48%) (ibid:106). A quick look at this survey suggests that its findings are fairly similar to more up-to-date surveys conducted in other Western European, predominantly subtitling countries (cf. Luyken et al., 1991:111-127). The survey made reference to the same parameters that were found to play a role in the recipients' preference for the one or the other method in these predominantly subtitling Western

[i] No other forms of revoicing were included.

European countries and came up with quite similar results. What is interesting to note here is that the percentage of adult recipients who preferred subtitling on TV (45.5%, as opposed to 42.7% who preferred dubbing), which is by all accounts quite marginal, does not justify the present (1994-1996) data on TV-programmes which shows an overwhelming tendency in favour of this particular language transfer method (91.4% of the overall TV programmes, see table 3.4.1.7). Neither do the variations amongst viewers' preferences according to their age, education or social class - quite often in favour of dubbing - seem to justify the absolute lack of any kind of dubbed material aimed at adult recipients (see table 3.4.1.7). For these two self-contradicting norm+motivation patterns above, four possibilities can act as plausible scenarios: a) the language transfer commissioners are not aware of the facts that this survey points to, b) the language transfer commissioners are in fact aware of these facts but try to neglect them for some reason, c) the findings of the 1978 survey are totally irrelevant to present Greek audiovisual reality and a new survey on recipients' preferences would indicate that they favour subtitling, and d) a combination of all of the above. The fourth scenario looks the most plausible to me: it is true that certain language transfer commissioners are not in tune with the preferences of the Greek TV audience, others try to ignore the demand for dubbing and opt for the cheaper method of subtitling. At the same time, in a kind of vicious circle, today's Greek audiences are indeed of higher socio-educational status than the 1978's audiences and therefore they are expected to be more in favour of and conditioned by the dominant norm of subtitling.

All the findings so far indicate that the profile of Greek TV or cinema audiences is not that distinct from the profile of audiences of other predominantly subtitling Western European countries. As a result, it does not seem inappropriate to apply to Greek audiences the same comments that were made in relation to Western European audiences. In an attempt to generalise across the two modes of TV and cinema in Greek audiovisual reality, we may note that there is a link between: a) the fact that young audiences are keen on watching foreign programmes on TV, b) that they constitute the bulk of cinema audience, c) that the release of Greek cinema film productions is restricted to 4% in 1994-1995 and 6% in 1995-1996 (see footnotes in tables 3.4.1.8 and 3.4.1.9), and d) that products from both TV and cinema which are aimed primarily at these young audiences are subtitled. Children's audiences are just one age-step before young audiences; children's audiences are the ones who will become young audiences in a few years' time. It is therefore reasonable to expect that the norms and motivations related to the choice of the language transfer method for products aimed at young audiences will exert a strong influence on the norms and motivations related to the choice of the language transfer method for products aimed at children's audiences, especially if these products are aimed at older children who are not far removed from young audiences.

In the absence of a survey on Greek recipients' present attitudes towards the choice of language transfer method, the only ways we might infer comparative conclusions are by: a) looking at the relative viewership of double cinema-film releases for the mode of cinema, b) looking at the relative viewership of double video-film releases for the mode of video, and c) comparing relative viewing rates of TV programmes that belong to the same programme type and present a variation in the choice of the language transfer method used, for the mode of television. Starting with TV, the two TV programme types that presented a variation in the choice of the language transfer method - apart from children's TV programmes with which we dealt analytically in the previous chapter - are news/information programmes and documentaries (see table 3.4.1.7). The viewing rates for products which belong to these two programme types are as follows:

Table 3.4.3.1 Comparative viewing rates of TV programme-types with language transfer variations

PROGRAMME TYPES WITH LANGUAGE TRANSFER VARIATIONS	**TV STATION**	**VIEWING RATES PER LANGUAGE TRANSFER METHOD**			
DOCUMENTARIES		**Subtitling**		**Nar + Sub**	
		MAR'95	MAR'96	MAR'95	MAR'96
The Cousteau Library	ANT1, 05:30			0.1	
The Making of:...	MEGA, 00:15			2.7	
African Safari	STAR, 03:20	0.4			
Portraits of Artists	ET1, 20:00	0.4			
Noam Chomski and the Media	ET1, 01:00	0.2			
Gabrielle	ET1, 14:00	0.7			
Alabra Stories	ET1, 18:30	0.5			
The incredible horrific life of Lenny Riffenschtal	ET1, 00:30			0.4	
The Great Moments of Our Century	ANT1, 05:00				0.1
The Making of:...	MEGA, 01:00				1.4
The Making of:...	STAR, 01:20		2.0		
Great Events	STAR, 09:40		0.2		
Mysteries of the Universe	STAR, 09:40		0.1		
Hotel Paradise	STAR, 01:30				0.7
The Truth About Lies	ET1, 18:50		0.3		
Body Mechanics	ET1, 19:20		0.6		
Portraits of Artists	ET1, 16:20		0.4		
100 Years of Hollywood Western	ET1, 22:00		1.5		
La monteé des femmes au pouvoir	ET1, 16:20		0.3		
Playdoyer pour les femmes	ET1, 19:50		0.2		
The National World (documentary 1)	ET1, 16:30				0.5
The National World (documentary 2)	ET1, 17:30				0.2
TOTAL		**0.4**	**0.6**	**1.1**	**0.6**
NEWS/INFORMATION					
CBS News	ANT1, 06:20	0.3	0.3		
ANT1 Satellite News	ANT1, 06:45/06:00	0.3	0.2		
Lifestyles of the Rich and Famous	STAR, 07:45			0.2	0.3
TOTAL		**0.3**	**0.3**	**0.2**	**0.3**
OVERALL TOTAL		**0.4**	**0.5**	**0.9**	**0.5**

No specific conclusions about the recipients' preference for the choice of either subtitling or narration+subtitling can be safely drawn from the above table. The decision to watch a particular programme seems to be very strongly determined by: a) when the programme is broadcast (programmes broadcast early in the morning are expected to attract viewing rates lower than those of programmes broadcast during peak-audience times), b) the TV station that broadcast the programme (programmes broadcast by the more popular ANT1 and MEGA are expected to attract higher viewing rates than those broadcast by STAR or ET1, because of the phenomenon of 'audience duplication' which would be stronger for the first two TV stations), and c) the theme of the programme (viewing rates for documentaries *The Making of:...* and *100 Years of Hollywood Western* which have 'cinema' as their theme are four to five times higher than those of the rest of the documentaries). The only conclusion that can be cautiously expressed would be in favour of subtitling rather than narration+subtitling as a result of the 2% that *The Making of:...* receives when broadcast subtitled by the less popular STAR, in comparison with the 1.4% that the same documentary receives when delivered around the same time of the day in narration+subtitling by the more popular MEGA. *The Making of:...* is a series of individual documentary programmes which present backstage information on the way a particular film was shot. If, then, the film which was discussed in the documentary on STAR was better known than the one discussed in the documentary on MEGA, the correspondent viewing rates cannot be taken as indicative of any preference for subtitling but are rather a result of the particular theme of the programme.

Prooptiki was the only cinema-film distribution agency to release some of its products in a double version (see tables 3.4.1.8 and 3.4.1.9). All these products were cartoon children's cinema-movies. The policy of film distribution agencies for cinema and video in Greece is not to reveal exact figures for the viewership of their products. Therefore, the only way to reach any conclusions on the audience's appreciation of the one or the other language transfer method used, was to obtain oral estimates of the relative percentage out of the total viewership that each of the two versions finally received (on numbers of tickets for cinema, and number of sell-through copies sold for video). The relative percentages for Prooptiki's double cartoon children's cinema-film releases are as follows:

Table 3.4.3.2 Prooptiki's cartoon children's cinema-film double releases

PROOPTIKI'S CARTOON CHILDREN'S DOUBLE RELEASES	CINEMATIC YEAR	RELATIVE PERCENTAGE OF VIEWERSHIP PER LANGUAGE TRANSFER METHOD	
		Subtitling	**Dubbing**
Lion King	1994-1995	30%	70%
101 Dalmatians	1994-1995	30%	70%
Pocahontas	1995-1996	30%	70%
Sleeping Beauty	1995-1996	30%	70%
Toy Story	1995-1996	40%	60%
TOTAL		**32%**	**68%**

The overall relative percentages indicate a clear preference on the part of viewers for the dubbed version. Since the above products are cinema-films aimed at children, the dominance of dubbing does not come as a surprise. As expected, children attended the easy-to-process dubbed version screened in the afternoon, whereas adult recipients watched one of the movies for their own pleasure (rather than because they had to accompany children) in the evening. What is surprising to note, however, is that although the percentages of viewership for cartoon children's cinema-films are in line with the overall percentages of children's TV programmes and strongly in favour of dubbing, they still do not seem to persuade the language transfer commissioners of cartoon children's TV movies to broadcast these movies dubbed as well (both cartoon children's TV movies shown in March 1995 were broadcast subtitled, see table 3.3.1.7). This is even more surprising if we note that the above percentages relate to cinema, where the norm of subtitling is even stronger. *Toy Story* that shows a more balanced distribution of viewership should not be taken as an indication of lack of preference for dubbing but rather as a special case of a - pioneering in its making and widely advertised - movie that managed to attract not just children but also large adult audiences who naturally chose to attend the late evening or night shows, when the subtitled copy was shown.

Video double releases come from AUDIOVISUAL and HVH and are all children's movies, most of them cartoon, with one live-action (see tables 3.4.1.10 and 3.4.1.11). The relative percentages of viewership for these specific products are as follows:

Table 3.4.3.3 Children's video-film double releases

CHILDREN'S VIDEO DOUBLE RELEASES	**DISTRIBUTION AGENCY**	**RELATIVE PERCENTAGE OF VIEWERSHIP PER LANGUAGE TRANSFER METHOD**	
CARTOON MOVIES		**Subtitling**	**Dubbing**
Aladddin	AUDIOVISUAL	35%	65%
Snow White and the Seven Dwarfs	AUDIOVISUAL	30%	70%
The Aristocats	AUDIOVISUAL	30%	70%
The Return of Jafar	AUDIOVISUAL	30%	70%
The Lion King	AUDIOVISUAL	35%	65%
Thumbelina	AUDIOVISUAL	25%	75%
101 Dalmatians	AUDIOVISUAL	35%	65%
Sleeping Beauty	AUDIOVISUAL	30%	70%
TOTAL		**31%**	**69%**
LIVE-ACTION MOVIES			
Babe	HVH	60%	40%
OVERALL TOTAL		**34%**	**66%**

As with children's cartoon cinema-movies, children's cartoon video-movies indicate an audience preference for the dubbed version (around 70%-30% in favour of dubbing in both cases). The movie with the strongest preference for dubbing, *Thumbelina*, has a fairy-tale-like filmic style and theme that appeals to toddlers rather than older children. However, it does not seem to be the theme or the filmic style of the movies that influences the preference for subtitling these products but rather the advertising promotion and the previous success of the same movies when they were released in the cinema. *Aladdin, The Lion King and 101 Dalmatians* had stronger advertising and promotional support, and managed to reach higher box-office ratings compared to the rest of the cartoon movies at the time they were released in the cinema. Video provided an opportunity for those adults who had heard so many things about the films but had not managed to see them in the cinema to watch them in their homes, away from noisy children's audiences in cinema auditoriums. These adult recipients are responsible for the high pro-subtitling percentages. As for the live-action movie *Babe*, it seems that the live-action filmic convention discouraged children from watching it, thus raising the proportion of adults amongst the overall audience and, with it, the percentage of subtitled vs. dubbed copies sold.

3.4.4 Findings related to middle level human agents

The accustoming of the audience with one particular language transfer method has been found to be the most important reason, so far, for motivating language transfer commissioners to support the continued domination of a certain method and therefore maintain the existence of an already established norm. The issue of the accustomed audiences, however, is not restricted to the application of norms that affect the choice of language transfer method; it is so strong that sometimes it affects the use of certain conventions even within the same method. Viewers from predominantly dubbing areas in the US, for example, have found dubbing in Italy annoying because it did not emphasise lip-sync as much as it did the quality of the dubber's voice (Myers, 1973:57). If the use of different conventions within the same language transfer method was found to create feelings of unease and lack of enjoyment, one can imagine the unease experienced by viewers when they are confronted with language transfer methods different from those they are accustomed to. Human agents as language transfer commissioners do not want to generate such feelings in the recipients since this would bring the viewership down, with obvious financial consequences. Respect for the recipients' viewing habits is the number one priority for human agents and the strongest motivation for the choice of a particular language transfer method. This explains and justifies the choice of dubbing as the dominant TV language transfer method in countries with relatively small population like the Czech Republic, Slovakia, Bulgaria and Hungary (Dries, 1994-95:36). Instead of opting for the cheaper, quicker and less complex method of subtitling, TV agents in these countries cannot risk going against the audience's preference for dubbing and therefore continue to support the existing norms.

Human agents can have a number of personal principles and priorities (textual or professional) which they rank in a hierarchical scale and attempt to satisfy as many of them as they can when choosing the language transfer method for a specific audiovisual product (cf. Zabalbeascoa, 1994:91). Sometimes, though, there are cases beyond the human agents' control that impose unavoidable constraints and leave no alternative for the language transfer method to be chosen. On Latvian TV channel LTV, for example, apart from the fact that subtitling costs more than revoicing (cf. Lyuken et al., 1991:95), there are only four subtitling machines and sometimes there is no time to subtitle all the programmes that human agents feel should be subtitled (Vitkus, 1995:318). Similar problems can occur with original soap opera episodes that would be dubbed under normal circumstances, but they arrive at the TV studios so close to transmission time that dubbing is not feasible (cf. Minchinton, 1987:281). A strike organised by the dubbers' syndicate can also leave the commissioners no alternative but to release/broadcast an audiovisual product in another language transfer method. Greece has no such dubbers' or subtitlers' syndicates. In Italy, however, a dubbers' strike in 1983 caused serious problems in the audiovisual industry (*The Hollywood Reporter*, 15 March 1983:12). A few films were released subtitled. The majority of films, however, were not released at all. In this case, human agents in Italy were not just worried about the risk they were taking by deviating from the audience's preferences; they were mostly afraid of the collapse of the whole established audiovisual translation industry if they chose to introduce a new, alternative language transfer method (ibid). In Germany, dubbing was reportedly introduced in the mid 1930's by the leading local film importing company UFA, as an antidote to the unemployment crisis amongst actors (Vöge, 1977:120), and with the support of local cosmopolitan cineastes who were allowed the pleasure of choosing during private screenings which foreign films should be released at all (*Film Weekly*, 24 September 1938:14), dubbing passed on as the predominant language transfer method in the country and was maintained as such from thereon. Today, opting for subtitling would deal too hard a blow to all these people employed in the dubbing industry, with immense economic implications for the whole German audiovisual industry (cf. Dries, 1995a:10). On the other hand, however, a similar blow to the subtitling industry, if the idea of dubbing was to be introduced in a predominantly subtitling country like Greece for example, would not be so detrimental, exactly because the financial investments in personnel and equipment are not as high for subtitling studios as they are for dubbing studios.

In most countries of the world, the audiovisual translation industry seems to be small and cliquey, "with the same small number of people circulating around the jobs" (Fawcett, 1996:80). This realisation enabled us to initially hypothesise that norms and motivations, as well as people's attitudes and ideas, penetrate all three audiovisual modes and, as a result, consistency in the behaviour of language transfer commissioners is to be expected (ibid). Greek audiovisual reality per se does not appear to form an exception to the above. The exception seems to come from the legal and professional framework in which audiovisual translation in Greece is seen to operate. We mentioned already the lack of copyright laws for the intellectual product of subtitling or revoicing. We also mentioned the lack of specific dubbers' or subtitlers' syndicates. There appears to be some provision in Greek law regarding "the hiring of specialised scientific personnel, text-editors, and the organisation of seminars" (Hellenic Republic, Ministry of Press and Mass Media eds., 1995:40). Even this legal provision, however, does not appear to be enforced. It is revealing that, within the whole area of the audiovisual translation industry, only the in-house departments of two TV stations demand as a prerequisite from their personnel a 'degree in Translation'[i]. Most other audiovisual translation employers (studios, companies, agencies) are satisfied even with a First Certificate in the English language for their 'specialised'(?) personnel of subtitlers and revoicers (*Cinema*, 1993:74; Papadakis, 1998:66). Even if we allow for the fact that academic courses in audiovisual translation are non-existent in Greece and have only been recently offered elsewhere in Europe, the organisation of training seminars for the personnel of new or experienced audiovisual translators - as stated in the national law above - should not remain as a mere recommendation on paper. Fawcett suggests that audiovisual translation as a form of mass communication has the ability to exercise power over society as a whole (1996:82), and he adds that "this particular exercise of power comes from the translation commissioner bowing to legal, economic, and political constraints and the influence of pressure groups, but the practitioners themselves exercise a form of power by controlling entry to the profession" (ibid:83; cf. Hempen, 1998:53-54). Unfortunately, in Greek audiovisual reality, the position of the practitioners within the audiovisual translation industry is so weak that the power they can exert is considerably limited.

The discussion of findings related to lower level human agents (section 3.3.4) offered a glimpse of the attitude of commissioners of TV programmes. In order to complete the picture we need to consider the views and attitudes of language transfer commissioners for cinema and video products as well. Based on the questionnaire that was circulated to human agents, the following conclusions may be drawn:

- In the case of cinema-film distribution agencies, the decision to release a movie dubbed or subtitled is taken by the Director of the company (for Spentzos, Nea Kinissi and Rosebud), the Marketing Department (for ELKE and OVO) or both plus the Sales Department (for Prooptiki). What is worth noting, however, is that when it comes to children's movies in particular, the two agencies that release most of the children's movies (Prooptiki and ELKE)

[i] This is not a Greek phenomenon. Ivarsson (1992:10) reports similar processes of employing unqualified subtitlers in Sweden and Whitman-Linsen (1992:115) condemns the similar process of hiring such unqualified dubbers in Germany.

consult the original film production company abroad before deciding on the method of language transfer. If the original film production company does not wish to invest a large amount of money in promoting a children's movie, then the movie will be released with subtitles. If, however, the original film-production company is willing to increase the promotion budget by paying the cost of dubbing, then the movie will be dubbed as well and released in a double version (cf. Papadakis, 1998:70).

- Unlike cinema-film distribution agencies, video distribution agencies do not report any insight from the original film production companies abroad. It is the Marketing Department (for Videosonic), the General Manager (for Spentzos Video) or both (for Audiovisual and HVH) who decide upon the language transfer method. Considering that no impact from original film production companies was reported by language transfer commissioners for TV either, it would seem that foreign companies are concerned first and foremost about the release of their products in the cinema. This makes sense since a movie will first be shown in the cinema. It is the success or failure of this initial release that will determine the fate of the movie's consequent release on video or TV. As a result, original film production companies do invest in the language transfer of a cinema children's movie and will have it dubbed as well as subtitled, in order not only to attract more children viewers but also to promote the movie among the Greek audience and the media in general. In this respect, and despite the fact that overall financial aspects for TV are higher than those for cinema or video, the budget for language transfer for cinema in particular appears to be more generous because the release is more significant, especially where children's products are concerned. In other words, more attention and consideration is devoted to the choice of language transfer method for children's movies in the case of cinema than in the case of TV or video.
- No cinema- or video-product distribution agency has its own in-house translation department, with the sole exception of AUDIOVISUAL video distributors. Interestingly enough, however, AUDIOVISUAL do not report any involvement of this in-house

department in the choice of language transfer method. All cinema-film distribution agencies have their own individual free-lance subtitlers with whom they most frequently co-operate, except for Rosebud which, like the rest of the video-film distributors, co-operate with various independent subtitling companies and free-lancers. When it comes to dubbing, however, all agencies - except for AUDIOVISUAL again - use other studios that specialise in dubbing for the translation of their products. Especially for children's cinema movies, it is the original film production companies who have the last word in the choice of the dubbing studio, quite frequently asking for tapes of sample voices before approving those that will be finally used on their original products.

- All cinema and video distribution agencies who release children's products stress two factors as determining the possibility for a product to get dubbed: a) the target audience (i.e. if a product is aimed at children then it might be dubbed), and b) the product's budget (i.e. products with high budget due to high viewership expectations might be dubbed). This appears to be a consistent and straightforward pattern.
- When it comes to commissioners' personal attitudes concerning the optimum method of language transfer for children's products, however, the audiovisual translation landscape is rather less clear. A range of contradicting opinions creates a picture that explains the inconsistency we noted in terms of the choice of language transfer method for children's products, not only for cinema or video but also for TV. Surprisingly enough, commissioners from the only video-distribution agency that does not release children's products (Spentzos Video) seem to favour dubbing. Commissioners from cinema-distribution agencies with no children's products, are less in favour of dubbing: people from OVO and Rosebud believe that children's movies should not deviate from the general principle that dictates transparency in the translation of audiovisual products in order to maintain the highest possible degree of faithfulness to the original, and therefore subtitling is preferred. Commissioners from Nea Kinisssi (again with no releases of children's products) support subtitling as well, this time however because of the bad

quality of dubbed products, implying that an improvement in dubbing standards would improve their appreciation of the method too. When it comes to agencies that do release children's products, commissioners from two of the video-distribution agencies (HVH and AUDIOVISUAL) prefer dubbing. Those from VIDEOSONIC, however, say that they prefer subtitling, on the same artistic/aesthetics grounds that govern the attitudes of cinephiles. Commissioners from two of the cinema-distribution agencies who release cinema children's movies (Prooptiki and Spentzos) cautiously favour dubbing, stressing at the same time the importance of high quality transfer at every level of the dubbing process. Commissioners from ELKE, however, claim that they prefer subtitling and go for dubbing only when it is dictated by the original film-production companies.

To summarise the attitudes of cinema and video language transfer commissioners towards the optimum method for children's audiovisual products, fans of dubbing and fans of subtitling exist for both audiovisual modes. Both dubbing and subtitling seem to have some strong and faithful supporters. There are also supporters of each method who are more cautious in their preferences. Some fans of dubbing seem apologetic about deviating from the general national norm of subtitling and about betraying the aesthetic features of the original product. At the same time, some fans of subtitling seem apologetic about the need on the part of children's audiences to access a product aimed primarily at them without having to undergo a more complicated cognitive reading process. All these views relate to TV too. The inevitable interference of such contradictory attitudes explains the fuzzy picture that emerges in relation to the choice of language transfer method for children's TV programmes. Only two conclusions may be reliably drawn: a) the choice of the language transfer method for children's TV programmes in Greece is not as straightforward as is suggested by some audiovisual translation scholars in other European countries, and b) the dominant national norm of subtitling which applies to all audiovisual modes and the motivations for upholding it influence the choice of language transfer method in the special case of children's TV programmes.

3.5 Norms and motivations at the Upper Level

3.5.1 Findings related to upper level products

So far, we have been occupied with normative issues directly related to specific children's TV programmes (at the lower level), or with normative issues indirectly influencing these specific products via the interaction between all kinds of audiovisual modes, products, recipients and human agents that operate within the audiovisual framework (at the middle level). This framework, however, needs to be further broadened to account for norms and motivations that derive from the general, national literary (and extra-literary) culture/system.

Research in the Netherlands, which is another predominantly subtitling country, indicates that resistance to subtitled programmes, whenever it exists, does not derive from linguistic or other difficulties inherent in subtitling as a language transfer method, but from the fact that the subtitled products themselves are foreign, i.e. it derives from cultural prejudice (Van der Weel, 1990:23). The decision to release/broadcast foreign audiovisual products subtitled rather than dubbed evokes stronger cultural prejudice because the foreign linguistic aspects of the original product are kept intact. Expressing the same idea from the point of view of dubbing, Fawcett stresses that strong, powerful nations are keen on dubbing because through this particular language transfer method they can manipulate, suppress and inferiorise a product from a 'minor' culture, dress it in their own language and make it fit into their own culture (1996:84). It appears, then, that prestige and relative dominance between cultures in general play a significant role determining the choice of language transfer method (cf. Delabastita, 1989:209). It is beyond the scope of the present thesis to attempt an investigation into the totality of the cultural aspects that indicate or lead into the relative prominence of one target system over the other. But a brief consideration of some of the narrower *literary* aspects of the target culture/system might be helpful in terms of providing guidelines for a more detailed sociological investigation at a later date.

The size, strength and power of the anglophone market today hardly need emphasising (cf. Dries, 1995a:6; Luyken et al, 1991:3). The course of events which led to this situation is best summarised by Guback as follows:

> "towards the end of the era of the silent movies, the American film industry dominated the world market. World War I had been a dramatic turning point for the US because it had changed its status from a debtor to a creditor nation. The motion picture was one product to benefit from this situation. European film industries were either disrupted or forced out of business, creating a vacuum, soon filled by a massive wave of American pictures. From 1913 to 1925 American film exports increased fivefold to Europe and tenfold to the reminder of the world. Such a policy, of course, was a blow to foreign producers who suddenly found their own home markets glutted with American pictures. As a result of the war, American distributors were able to gain control of foreign territory without competition. And by the time capital was once more available for production abroad, American films had obtained almost complete control of foreign markets." (in Ballester, 1995:160)

Similarly, the market for written literature has been dominated by anglophone products. Venuti suggests that quite often it was human agents of the target system, i.e. foreign publishers themselves, who "exploited the global drift towards American political and economic hegemony in the postwar period, actively supporting the international expansion of Anglo-American culture" (1995:15). Greece was no exception to this rule. On the contrary, being a nation of travellers, always open to new, innovative elements and interaction with foreign cultures, the penetration of anglophone products inevitably reached its peak within the Greek culture. Despite its relatively small market/audience size, Greece ranks at the top of the table of European countries with the highest number of language transfers for foreign cinema-films between 1985 and 1989 (Luyken et al., 1991:13). And if the number of total language transfers is not so impressive since other European countries like Spain or Italy show equally high figures (around 400), in Greece the number of products translated from English in particular (around 350 out of these 400) is almost double the European average (ibid). This characteristic of the Greek culture is arguably not an instance of 'xenomania' in general, but rather an instance of specific and consistent 'Anglo-mania'.

Around 8 years after the above findings were reported, the picture of language transfers for cinema- and video- products in Greece is still indicative of the same phenomenon of 'Anglo-mania':

Table 3.5.1.1 Greek vs. foreign cinema and video-products

AUDIOVISUAL MODE	NUMBERS OF PRODUCTS RELEASED IN THE YEARS 1994-1996	
	Greek	**Foreign**
Cinema	16[i]	336[ii]
Video	10[iii]	609[iv]

As the table above indicates, Greek cinema- and video-products account for a very restricted percentage of total cinema- and video-releases. The figures for local releases (4.5% for cinema, 1.6% for video) reinforce the picture of general 'xenomania' in Greece; the figures for English-speaking products amongst the foreign releases (74.4% for cinema, 99.7% for video) suggest a strong tendency towards 'Anglo-mania' (cf. Carr, 1991a:I-5). For TV, however, things seem to be different:

[i] **4.5%** of total cinema-film releases

[ii] Of which 74.4% have English as the original language on screen

[iii] **1.6%** of total video-product releases

[iv] Of which 99.7% have English as the original language on screen

Table 3.5.1.2 Greek vs. foreign TV programmes

TV STATION	**HOURS OF ORIGINAL PROGRAMMES PER WEEK**			
	MARCH 1995		**MARCH 1996**	
	Greek	**Foreign**	**Greek**	**Foreign**
ANT1	86	82	101	67
MEGA	94	51	104	56
STAR	75	72	78	74
SKY	83	57	139	6
ET1	95	32	80	38
FILMNET	7	161	10	158
TOTAL	**440**[i]	**455**[ii]	**512**[iii]	**399**[iv]

The mode of TV, as we saw in the findings related to middle level audiovisual mode, is more direct, live and unmediated. TV is the carrier of news, information and local affairs as well as a source of entertainment and leisure passtime. In that respect, it is a more important part of the local culture and activities than cinema and video, because it is supposed to portray real-life local events primarily. Greek legislation demands at least 25% of TV airtime to be devoted to "products with Greek as the original language" (Hellenic Republic, Ministry of Press and Mass Media eds., 1995:40) [my translation]. Local TV stations seem to respect this rule in general: 49.1% of the overall airtime in March 1995 and 56.2% in March 1996 is dedicated to Greek productions. This reflects a choice on the part of both TV-commissioners and the public, since the former would never risk investing such a high percentage of airtime in Greek products if they thought that this would not appeal to the general public. At the same time, however, it explains and justifies the mismatch we discovered between the expressed preference of a large part of the Greek TV audience for dubbing and the overwhelming norm of

[i] **49.1%** of total TV programmes

[ii] Of which 91.4% have English as the original language on screen

[iii] **56.2%** of total TV programmes

[iv] Of which 90.4% have English as the original language on screen

subtitling. TV is a popular medium that appeals primarily to the broad masses. Dubbing costs are high for TV programmes. A large part of the audience prefers dubbing (see section 3.4.3). Still, educated upper-middle class viewers prefer subtitling. In order to satisfy the latter group, foreign products are broadcast subtitled. Since dubbing is out of the question for financial reasons, and in order to satisfy the need of the former group to hear their national language on TV, the airtime that would otherwise be devoted to dubbed foreign products is devoted to products with Greek as the original language. The 'pro-dubbing' group prefers dubbing not because of the qualities of the specific language transfer method but as a reaction to the invasion of foreign products in their home culture, as we saw at the beginning of this section in the case of the Netherlands. Increasing the airtime of local productions solves the problem and caters for the preferences of both 'pro-subtitling' and 'pro-dubbing' groups. By increasing the airtime of Greek products and maintaining subtitling for foreign imports, both the cultural prejudices against foreign products and the feelings of 'Anglo-mania' are catered for.

What happens with children's TV programmes though? Is the balanced pattern of Greek vs. foreign productions maintained for children's TV programmes as well? The table below suggests the opposite:

Table 3.5.1.3 Greek vs. foreign children's TV programmes

GREEK & FOREIGN CHILDREN'S PROGRAMMES	**NUMBER OF PRODUCTS BROADCAST**					
	MARCH 1995			**MARCH 1996**		
PROGRAMME TYPE	**Greek**[i]	**Foreign**		**Greek**[ii]	**Foreign**	
		Sub	**Dub**		**Sub**	**Dub**
Children's movies (cartoons)		2				
Children's movies (l/action)		7			6	
Children's movies (cart + l/a)					1	
Children's movies (puppets)						
Children's series (cartoons)	1	17	27		8	32
Children's series (l/action)	5	6	1	4	6	3
Children's series (cart + l/a)		1				
Children's series (puppets)	1			2		
TOTAL	**7**[iii]	**33**[iv]	**28**[v]	**6**[vi]	**21**[vii]	**35**[viii]

In most European countries (Finland, Holland, Belgium, Germany, Italy and the UK) locally made children's TV programmes are reported to account for 90% of the overall airtime (Papageorgiou, 1981:6). In Greece, local children's TV productions account for no more than 10% of total broadcasts. It is also worth noting that all local children's TV productions are broadcast by the state-owned ET1. ET1 has the resources - and the legal obligation - to co-operate with other state-owned institutions, like the Centre of Greek Cinema and the Centre of Children's Education, to produce local material cost-effectively (cf. Papadakis, 1998:67). All other private TV stations seem to have neither the resources nor the willingness to produce children's TV programmes that would only attract the criticism of the

[i] All broadcast by the state-owned ET1
[ii] All broadcast by the state-owned ET1
[iii] **10.3%** of total children's programmes in March 1995
[iv] 32 with English as the original language on screen (97%), 1 with French
[v] 26 had English as the original language (92.8%), 2 had French
[vi] **9.7%** of total children's programmes in March 1996
[vii] All of which with English as the original language on screen
[viii] 32 had English as the original language (91.4%), 3 had French

local media in terms of quality. Private TV stations are conscious that children's programmes can attract much more serious criticism than sitcoms and TV-shows. In addition, they are aware that high standards require the employment of a number of pedagogical, educational and other consultants, which would make the relevant products economically unviable. And so they opt for filling children's airtime-slots with the foreign products that are readily available in the global market. This has direct implications for the choice of language transfer method. As we saw, TV commissioners attempt to cater for audiences wishing to hear their own language on screen not by opting for dubbing foreign products but by increasing the number of local broadcasts. With children's TV programmes, however, they have no such alternative. Especially if they need to address an audience of younger children who cannot follow subtitles easily, TV commissioners have no alternative but to opt for foreign children's programmes and have them dubbed[i]. This motivation justifies and reinforces the norm of dubbing that we identified for children's TV series in particular (see table 3.3.1.7).

The presence of so many foreign children's products in the Greek audiovisual market - or rather the absence of local productions - customises the vulnerable and easily moulded attitudes of the children's audience. When children start to understand the difference between the notions of 'foreign' and 'local', around the age of ten or twelve, this accustoming starts to develop into 'xenomania'. Older children gradually become fans of foreign products in general. As they grow into an adult audience, and with the level of literacy in the country rising considerably, although initially used to dubbing, children gradually turn into strong advocates of subtitling. This happens exactly because dubbing itself is not associated with the idea of an 'optimum method of language transfer' but with the idea of suppressing foreign material and language on Greek screens. Since these children, however, become keen on the idea of watching 'foreign' material at quite an early age, and given the availability of original

[i] The cost for dubbing a foreign programme might be higher than that of subtitling but it is considerably lower than the cost of an own-production.

adult productions, as they become older they choose subtitling for imported adult material in order to retain the feeling that they are actually watching something 'truly foreign'. As a result, one can expect in the near future that the number of foreign productions on TV will remain constant, if not rise even higher, subtitling will continue to be the norm for products aimed at adults, and dubbing will come to represent a stronger norm for children's programmes, as it is the language transfer method that future adults will have been accustomed to. In other words, the gap between dubbing children's foreign material and subtitling adult foreign material is expected to increase. What might become weaker, however, is the concept/definition of 'children's audience', and as a result, the concept/definition of products aimed at 'children'. The growing adaptation of adult attitudes and habits by older children is bound to narrow down the notion of 'children's products' to those products targeted at the age-group 2-10 or 2-12 instead of the current 3-14. More children's programmes aimed at the age-group 10-14 or 12-14 are likely to be subtitled in future. And here the question arises: can a children's programme restrict itself so much as to address itself to the narrow age-group of 2-10 or 2-12 and still survive financially? Or should it widen its scope to address the marginal 10-14 / 12-14 age-group as well? And if it is decided that the definition of the target audience needs to be broadened up, which language transfer method will be chosen? Dubbing for the younger age group or subtitling for the older age group? Such products which seem to fluctuate between these two age groups will always appear to disturb what would otherwise be a clear cut, straightforward set of norms.

But is this 'xenomania', or rather 'Anglo-mania', a trait of the general Greek literary culture or is it restricted to the audiovisual market, a mere side effect of TV, or even more, of cinema and video? The following table, which summarises the situation for local literary productions vs. foreign imports, might help clarify the issue[i]:

---

[i] Unfortunately, the latest available data on local literary productions was for 1993. It should also be noted that the annual inflation rate in Greece at the time was around 9%. This should be taken into consideration when drawing analogies between the economic figures of 1993 and 1995.

Table 3.5.1.4 Local vs. foreign literary productions

WRITTEN LITERARY MATERIAL	LOCAL PRODUCTIONS (1993)		FOREIGN IMPORTS (1995)	
	Quantity (in tons)	**Value (in million drcs)**	**Quantity (in tons)**	**Value (in million drcs)**
BOOKS				
Fiction and Scientific	5301[i]	1777	4073[ii]	9604
Dictionaries and Encyclopaedias	684	1258	123[iii]	293
Other	3207	370	188	370
TOTAL	**9192[iv]**	**3405**	**4384**	**10267**
NEWSPAPERS & MAGAZINES				
Released at least 4 times per week	431272	36153	3323	4425
Released less than 4 times per week	126583	19717	2434	5107
TOTAL	**557855[v]**	**55870**	**5757[vi]**	**9532**
OVERALL TOTAL	**567047**	**59275**	**10141**	**19799**

When it comes to newspapers and magazines, the percentage of local productions is overwhelming (98.9%). This makes sense given that imported products in this case would not relate to current local affairs and therefore cannot possibly appeal to the Greek readers as much as products in the local language. Still, the value of imports for foreign newspapers and magazines is high for the relatively small Greek market. The situation is more interesting for books. The local products here only account for 67.7% of the total market, but Greek fiction and

[i] **56.5%** of total Fiction and Scientific book circulation
[ii] Of which 68.8% from UK and US
[iii] Of which 74.0% from UK and US
[iv] **67.7%** of total book circulation
[v] **98.9%** of total newspaper & magazine circulation
[vi] Of which 35.2% from UK and US

scientific books in particular account for even less (56.5%). We see, therefore, that it is academic thinking in Greece which is under the strongest influence from foreign material. It is the educated audience that generates this 'xenomania' and not the broad masses, who express their preference for local products by supporting local newspapers and magazines. Not surprisingly, it is UK and US products again that dominate foreign literary and scientific book imports, appearing at the top with 68.8%. The most startling figure, though, relates to foreign book imports which account for over 250% of the market investment in Greek books.

To summarise, 'xenomania' and 'Anglo-mania' seem to be characteristic of the literary market too. The figures noted for the audiovisual market then are not specific to it but reflect a general phenomenon, a general trait of the Greek culture. It is only the 'mass-media' end of the audiovisual and literary markets - namely TV, newspapers and magazines – which reveals a preference for Greek products. This comes as a reaction to the general bombardment of foreign influences, influences that pose a threat to national identity. In that respect, TV, newspapers and magazines act as a means of sub-conscious popular self-defence against foreign invasion.

Robyns divides nations according to the way they respond to foreign elements in a given culture: a) 'imperialist' nations deny and transform foreign elements, b) 'defensive' nations acknowledge foreign elements but still transform them, c) 'transdiscursive' nations do not oppose foreign elements radically and do not transform them, and d) 'defective' nations demand these foreign elements and do not transform them (in Ballester, 1995:175, footnote). Taking the data presented in the above tables into account, I would classify Greece somewhere between 'transdiscursive' and 'defective'. Some Greek scholars see this as a major weakness and lament the absence of local audiovisual productions for children in particular (Papageorgiou, 1981:5). Others are more optimistic but still nationalistic: they acknowledge foreign interference and the phenomenon of 'xenomania' in Greek culture, but they appear content that at least "the national cultural creation occupies the first place amongst the choices of the youth, despite the expansion of the foreign, and especially the Anglo-saxon culture" (Koronaiou, 1992:149) [my translation]. It has to be noted that three quarters of the bibliographical references in the book that contains the above comment are foreign.

The strongest proof that Greece lies actually somewhere between the 'transdiscursive' and the 'defective' category comes not only from the mild legal enforcement on the balance between local and imported productions (as we saw before, the law states that only 25% of TV airtime has to be devoted to local productions), but also from the complete absence of any legal enforcement on the language transfer method to be chosen for imported audiovisual products. In Germany and Italy, especially between the two World Wars, the state catered for the language method to be chosen just as it used to cater for the circulation of local children's literature (cf. Even-Zohar, 1996b:28). In 1925, Germany imposed a law according to which distributors were allowed to release one foreign film for every release of a local production (Ballester, 1995:163). This idea of balanced releases was gradually adopted by France, Italy and the UK as well, but only in the form of balanced screen time (ibid). World War II changed the situation and put a stop to these protective measures because for financial reasons the number of local productions dropped considerably and could not satisfy the demands of the local markets any more. More American films had to be imported (ibid). Restrictions on the earnings of American film distributors - as a means of protecting the local audiovisual industry - were implemented in France and the UK but these did not appeal to smaller countries like Switzerland, Belgium, the Netherlands, Ireland and the Scandinavian countries because the latter did not have a strong local audiovisual industry to protect (ibid:164). Greece belongs to this last group of countries where, even if protective measures had been taken, local production could not have been strengthened (cf. ibid; Minchinton, 1987:279). The American audiovisual invasion, however, put the notions of 'national identity' and 'social integrity' under threat. As a result, certain European countries decided to take further action, this time related to the choice of the language transfer method for foreign imports. In Italy and Spain, legislation immediately specified that all imported films should be released dubbed (Vöge, 1977:120). In

Germany, dubbing was subtly promoted and supported by the regime (ibid). Spain, however, soon decided to abolish the law that demanded all foreign products to be dubbed (*Motion Picture Herald*, 19 April 1947:42). But Spain had several other problems of national coherence which it attempted to solve by "suppressing peripheral regions to its own national ideology" (Ballester, 1995:174). It appears, however, that this decision still came rather late: as peripheral regions - like Catalonia for example - were gaining in strength, they tried to preserve their own regional integrity by dubbing not just 'foreign' products but those from Spain as well (Agost, 1995:195; Bassols et al., 1995:411; Kilborn, 1993:644). Wales was a similar case where products used to be dubbed from English into the local Welsh language (Kilborn, 1993:644). The 1990 Broadcasting Act, however, changed the scene and demanded an increase of subtitled programmes on TV to account for 50% of the total airtime by the end of 1998 (Roffe & Thorne, 1994:253). In other former Soviet Union countries (e.g. Latvia and Belarus) the communist regime used to control the whole film translation process, opting for narration or dubbing into Russian "due to ideological reasons to prevent the listeners from hearing undesirable words or expressions (like swearing)" (Baranitch, 1995:309). When these countries gained their independence, new laws had to be established in order to promote the local vernacular, demanding even products from Russia to be revoiced or at least subtitled into the new State Language (Vitkus, 1995:318).

The idea of dubbing (or revoicing) in order to protect national identity and social integrity, however, has certain drawbacks. First of all, it is practically impossible to sustain the illusion of watching a local production, since cultural and other visual and aural mismatches will always interfere with this illusion (Bakewell, 1987:16; Kilborn, 1993:645; Fodor, 1976:76; Whitman-Linsen, 1992:17). Viewers are always aware that the original product is foreign. Secondly, dubbing has been proven to undermine the national language, since it requires 'twisting' the local vernacular (e.g. by introducing anglicisms) to make it fit the foreign audio-visual image as far as both lip-sync and cultural mismatches are concerned (Ross, 1995:48; Herbst, 1995:259; Goris, 1993:173). As a result, the national identity itself is again endangered, since corrosion starts from the inside, from a language transfer method that presents itself as an advocate of the preservation of the national vernacular. Finally, dubbing seems to threaten original local productions more than subtitling. In Egypt in 1947, local film directors, actors and producers protested against the dubbing of American and other films into Arabic and called upon the Ministry of Social Affairs to pass a law that would forbid the release of dubbed foreign films, precisely because "allowing foreign companies to release Arabic dubbed versions of their films threatens dangerously the existence of the Egyptian motion picture industry" (*Motion Picture Herald*, 22 February 1947:43). This view of dubbed imported films threatening domestic productions seems reasonable given that local industry "renders its enemies its best gun: language" (Ballester, 1995:176).

3.5.2 Findings related to upper level audiovisual mode

Sociologists classify the reasons that motivate people to use the media under four main categories: a) information, b) entertainment, c) personal identity, and d) integration and social interaction (Brown, 1994:69). Audiovisual media seem to fit into this classification. People can watch TV, go to the movies or hire a videotape in order to fulfil one or several of the above functions. Nevertheless, each audiovisual mode with its individual constraints and different watching habits plays a separate role in people's lives. TV has its own way of emphasising the last two functions of 'integration' and 'social interaction'. Unlike the other two audiovisual modes, TV is not just a window on the world but to many people it is "the most important source of knowledge of their own culture and language" (Luyken et al., 1991:28). As a result, "there are in television clear limits to the extent to which audiences are willing to watch foreign-language programmes, [something which is] evidenced by the fact that home-language programmes almost always achieve higher rates than foreign ones, and that the actual knowledge of foreign languages is, amongst the wider television audiences, much less than might be expected" (ibid:24).

In most developing countries, like Greece, the mode of TV was imported in the form of foreign technological or financial investment, introducing a new western-like habit in the local life style: that of TV-watching (cf. Koronaiou, 1992:32). Some people believe that such a technological and financial dependence could not but lead into a form of "cultural dependence and decomposition of traditional society" (ibid) [my translation]. The advent of cinema and video had similar effects; their impact and penetration into local societies, however, was not as deep as that of TV, since the latter was a mass-medium with a broad social appeal. This is why reactions against foreign elements in cinema and video are not as passionate as those against TV. In Greece, TV is often condemned as being responsible for the "demolition of the national cultural identity [and the carrier of phenomena such as] cultural imperialism, internationalism and the westernisation of the local way of life" (ibid:33) [my translation]. Cinema and video host more foreign productions than TV. It is TV, however, that attracts most of the criticism because, apart from its massive appeal, its ability to report local activities renders it - at least in theory - as the representation of local heritage, the guardian of national identity. Other Greek scholars, however, acknowledge that there are other more important parameters that reinforce this openness of Greek society to imported life styles, such as emigration, urbanisation and the return of expatriots (ibid:34).

The advent of TV was accompanied by a reorganisation of the traditional means of acquiring information and entertainment. TV started gradually to replace radio. The role of the press, in contrast, was not significantly affected (Gunter & Svennevig, 1987:11). Cinema was only initially influenced by this development, when traditional cinema-goers acquired the habit of TV-watching, but it is gradually reclaiming its position (ibid). TV watching had serious effects on written literature too. Watching soap operas, for example, replaced reading romance fiction (Morley, 1986:38). Similarly, documentaries replaced consulting encyclopaedias and cartoons replaced the reading of comics. Undoubtedly, audiovisual products had a clear advantage over written literature: they called for the application of two senses, namely the visual and the aural, minimising, however, the use of imagination. Still, the two habits of reading literature and watching audiovisual products have been proven to share a great number of similarities. Even in the case of cinema-watching, which involves a completely different social habit, it has been proven that "the set of reactions that we unconsciously attach to the privacy of the reading experience is automatically blended with the kind of reactions we have to the more public nature of the filmed dramatic experience" (Grillo & Kawin, 1981:28). This similarity of experiences is eventually maximised when we are actually watching subtitled audiovisual productions since in both cases most of the verbal meaning is reconstructed through the analysis of written linguistic symbols (cf. Kovacic, 1998:126). The influence of written literature on subtitles comes also from the fact that it enhances them with quasi-scientific credibility since a "written word stands for more than things just acoustically heard" (Aaltonen, 1995b:387; cf. MacDougall, 1995:83; cf. Giles, 1997:48). It has been suggested that, in many aspects, the role of the audiovisual translator is "nearly the same as that of the literary translator" (Hochel, 1985:4) and this type of remark indicates that the relationship between written literature and audiovisual products is perceived to be quite close. Taking all the above into account, it is not unreasonable to treat the study of norms related to audiovisual products as part of a larger study of norms related to general written literature, especially in the case of subtitling. Nevertheless, there are certain fundamental differences between reading literature and watching audiovisual products, differences that derive primarily from the polysemiotic nature of films as well as the immediate conditions of reception and interpretation that do not allow back-tracing of dialogues[i] (Gambier, 1994:278; Gottlieb, 1994a:101&106).

Greek scholars often claim that watching TV destroys the habit of reading literature and brings down the level of literacy, especially

---

[i] Video-products are an exception since viewers can stop the videotape and replay a specific part whenever they like.

amongst children (Papageorgiou, 1981:4). Surveys conducted in other countries present contradictory results (Gunter & McAleer, 1990:11). The most conclusive reports, however, seem to indicate that TV-watching mainly replaced radio-listening and cinema-going. A temporary replacement of book-reading occurred among children when TV was first introduced but this was soon adjusted and returned to previous levels (ibid:12&14; Davies Messenger, 1989:141). Nor was any relationship found between TV-watching and the children's level of literacy (Davies Messenger, 1989:167). What was found, on the contrary, was that the habits of TV-watching and book-reading are complementary rather than mutually exclusive: it was discovered that children who watch a lot of TV also read a lot (ibid:171). As a result, TV-watching is seen to provide "a different form of satisfaction which can both complement and help to promote reading" (ibid).

Irrespective of the findings above, the fact remains that TV-watching performs a vital function in modern society. In Finland for example, the 3,000 foreign TV programmes shown every year were calculated to correspond approximately to 200 novels of 300 pages each (Gambier, 1994:273). In Greece the situation is quite similar. As a result, and taking the economics of the audiovisual industry into account as well, I cannot see any reason why the norms of written literature should be considered superior, dictating or motivating the norms of audiovisual media. I believe that norms in both fields are strong and the influence of one over the other does not take the form of domination-subordination but of mutual interaction. As a result, I find the attempt of traditional literary translation scholars to marginalise audiovisual translation and place it outside the field of translation studies rather futile. Audiovisual translation deserves more attention from translation scholars, and this is already beginning to happen.

To sum up, it is interesting to note that the attitude of the first silent movie audience towards the advent of verbal - oral or written - language on the screen was quite negative (Metz, 1974:49). Initially, a compromise had to be made by using 'intertitles' inserted between images, a precursor of the actual subtitles adapted on the image. The idea of sound as a potential carrier of oral messages accompanying the image, however, came as a major threat to what viewers considered to be the essence of cinema: "the image is like a word, the sequence like a sentence, for a sequence is made up of images like a sentence of words" (ibid:51). Although one might regard this as an exhortation against revoicing, this is not the case. What the first cinema audience found disturbing was the subordination of the image to any kind of language that would interfere with the visual aesthetics, and not to oral language alone. With the fast development of high-quality techniques for inserting sound on the silent image revoicing as a language transfer method for recreating the dialogues in a multitude of languages came to be seen as a logical step (Vöge, 1977:121). Subtitles interfere with the image more than revoicing. Still, the idea/concept of revoicing as imposing sound on the image developed negative associations, leading to bias against this particular language transfer method amongst those who used to be fans of cinema (Whitman-Linsen, 1992:18). It is therefore possible to see this bias against dubbing amongst modern cinephiles as a consequence of the rejection of the idea of sound subordinating the image.

3.5.3 Findings related to upper level recipients

Similarities between the audiovisual framework and the general literary framework arise from the postulation of 'ideal' audiences, i.e. the process of conceptualising target recipients (Kovacic, 1995, 376). With any of the audiovisual modes, however, and especially with television, it is much more difficult to locate the target recipients because this conceptualised audience has to be drawn from a wider range of the total population (Luyken et al., 1991:155). Nowadays, audiovisual products have a broader and stronger appeal than other literary products. But this does not mean that the recipients of audiovisual products have more control over the other factors involved in the audiovisual process, let alone over human agents / commissioners of audiovisual products. As with literary commissioners in the case of literature, it is the network of human agents involved in the audiovisual industry that manipulates audiences, and not the other way round. As Hartley says, audiences are "created, organised, and maintained *by* networks, and not vice versa" (1989:239). And he continues:

> "indeed, the real relations of broadcasters are not with audiences as such but with other professionals in the industry: with advertisers, funding agencies, suppliers and - it's about as close as they get - with audience research organisations. In this context, the 'power' of the audience is contained within the networks themselves, taking the fictionalised form of ratings and those of imaginary, paedocratized representations of the audience that the networks promote through the industry. Networks minimise their risks by stabilising not demand but supply, but neither networks nor producers know what will 'sell'. They don't know who they're talking to and they don't 'give the public what it wants' because they don't know what the public wants. This structural uncertainty [...] means that networks and producers alike are afraid of the audience: afraid of offending it, of inciting it, of inflaming it - above all, of losing it". (ibid)

It is this 'stabilisation of supply' that results in the retention and perpetuation of existing normative situations. In this respect, it is the network of human agents who are reluctant to upset the existing, stabilised landscape of norms, and not the recipients themselves. But this in itself suggests that recipients are not powerless before the network of audiovisual commissioners. As a matter of fact, and despite the fact that it is the 'supply' of products that will reflect the perpetuation or the evolution of a norm, it is always the 'demand' for a certain kind of product that guides the supply. In other words, the recipients' right and obligation to 'demand' certain products gives them power and control over the network of human agents as well. Thus, the pattern of influence is bi-directional. Although the formulation and final appearance of a norm is the result of the human agents' actions and decisions, the decisions themselves are shaped and motivated by the recipients, their demands and their opinions.

The interaction of the public with situations in other - mostly neighbouring - countries and the habits of other audiences across the national borders are also important. This inter-national exchange of ideas appears to be responsible for the prominence of dubbing in countries like Hungary, Slovakia and the Czech Republic: both recipients and the network of human agents there seem to be conditioned by existing, strong dubbing norms in neighbouring

Germany (cf. Dries, 1995a:10). Greek reality, on the other hand, does not seem to be so influenced by neighbouring traditions: Turkey in the East, Italy in the West and even Bulgaria in the North are predominantly dubbing countries - at least when it comes to TV. This is further proof that, for the Greek community, relations with other countries are not based on 'xenomania' in general but on 'Anglo-mania'. The Greek public is not interested in the attitudes of foreign countries in general, but in the habits of Anglophone countries in particular.

This phenomenon of 'Anglo-mania' can also be found in the field of second language learning. The number of young people between the ages of 15-28 who are holders of the First Certificate in English as a Foreign Language exceeds 60%, a figure that puts Greece at the top of the European countries in the respective table[i]. It is natural, then, for these young educated people who constitute the majority of the Greek cinema audience to prefer to watch more Anglophone products since they feel they can understand them better as a whole (cf. Luyken et al., 1991:4). And in a vicious circle, the more Anglophone products they watch the more they get conditioned by these products and the stronger their Anglo-mania grows. Since, however, they feel that they need to get as close to the foreign product as possible the choice of the language transfer method should be based on the consideration that access to the original source language is maintained. Only subtitling can allow this (cf. Myers, 1973:58; cf. *American Film*, April 1983:6). The choice of subtitling for Greek cinema products, then, comes as a natural response to public demand. In a similar fashion, one can extend this chain of motivations to account for the situation in the other two audiovisual modes, assuming the products are targeted at the same audience of young educated recipients.

A survey conducted in 1978 indicated that the Greek public favours local TV productions rather than foreign TV productions

---

[i] This figure is unofficial, quoted by the National Federation of Foreign Language Schools and is based on an internal unofficial survey that they conduct on an annual basis regarding the relative success and failure of students who take the Cambridge and Oxford First Certificate exams.

(Doulkeri, 1992:103). The difference between the two groups was not huge: 45.36% for Greek-product supporters vs. 39.64% for foreign-product supporters, with Greek products having a stronger appeal amongst viewers of the lower socio-educational classes (ibid). In the questionnaires that accompanied the same survey, many of the viewers from all walks of life expressed the need to study "our own Greek history and not the English one, [...] the geography of our own land" (ibid) [my translation]. This, in addition to the already expressed preference of a large number of viewers for dubbing rather than subtitling, suggests the same conclusion that was reached in the Netherlands: that pro-dubbing attitudes derive from cultural prejudices and the desire for more local productions rather than anything else pertaining to the language transfer method alone (see also section 3.5.1). What has to be stressed, however, is the inconsistency between the opinions voiced by many people and their actual daily behaviour, their western habits and the ease with which they adopt new, foreign social customs (Koronaiou, 1992:152).

So, what did the Greek TV audience choose to watch during the two years covered in our present investigation? Was it Greek or foreign productions? The following table contains average data[i] on the preferences of specific age-groups amongst the total population:

Table 3.5.3.1 Market shares for Greek vs. foreign TV programmes

AGE GROUP OF VIEWERS	**AVERAGE MARKET SHARES PER PROGRAMME TYPE (FOR 1994-1996)**			
	Adult TV Series		**Adult TV Movies**	
	Greek	**Foreign**	**Greek**	**Foreign**
Children	27.8	26.2	51.0	43.4
Young men 15-24	21.3	33.4	40.8	44.4
Young women 15-24	29.6	49.2	49.5	46.6
Total viewers' average	**28.5**	**29.0**	**45.2**	**38.0**

[i] The data is presented in relative 'market shares' that indicate how many of the particular group of viewers with their TV-sets on at a specific time point, were actually watching one particular TV programme.

From the table above, the following conclusions can be drawn[i]:

- On average, the Greek audience prefers to watch Greek rather than foreign adult TV programmes. The figure is greater for movies (45.2% vs. 38.0%) than it is for series (28.5% vs. 29.0%). The figure for Greek movies is a result of the high status and the broad appeal of some classic Greek movies made during the 'golden years' of the Greek cinema (1955-1975) and shown over and over again. Greek series that have to cope with the continuous production of new episodes do not attract high market shares because of their relatively low quality, which is a sign of the decline in the current Greek audiovisual industry.
- Young audiences between the age of 15-24 prefer foreign productions. This is no surprise since we have already noted a similar tendency amongst the cinema audience which consists of the same young recipients. The hypothesis that young - and nowadays highly educated - audiences prefer foreign audiovisual products in general is, therefore, justified for TV as well.
- Young women show a marginal preference for Greek rather than foreign movies (49.5% vs. 46.6%). However, when it comes to series - women's favourite programme type - they show a clear preference for foreign productions (29.6% vs. 49.2%).
- Young men are more consistent in their TV watching habits. Their preference for foreign products is more straightforward and covers both adult series (21.3% vs. 33.4%) and movies (40.8% vs. 44.4%). This finding is emphasised by the fact that their market shares are lower than those of the total viewers' average for Greek productions, whereas they are higher for foreign productions, movies or series. In other words, young men do not simply show a preference for foreign products but also a lack of interest in Greek products.

---

[i] The validity of the results is achieved by the balanced distribution between Greek and foreign airtimes throughout both years, as table 3.5.1.2 indicates. In other words, none of the high or low market shares can be accounted for the small or large amount of airtime dedicated to Greek or foreign, series or movies, broadcast by Greek TV stations.

- As expected, children seem to favour Greek adult productions in terms of both adult series (27.8% vs. 26.2%) and movies (51.0% vs. 43.4%). Since children have not yet developed any cultural prejudice in favour of or against Greek or foreign products, we should view this finding simply as a sign of their desire to watch programmes with Greek spoken language on the screen and not as a reaction to any 'foreign invasion'. If we also bear in mind that 91.4% of the adult foreign programmes are broadcast subtitled (see table 3.4.1.7) we can assume that children do not favour foreign programmes precisely because they cannot follow subtitles as easily as they can follow foreign revoiced or Greek original productions. If this is true, children's TV-programme commissioners should perhaps reconsider their views and use revoicing for more children's programme types and not just cartoon series.

A more detailed investigation into the watching habits of the children's audience, however, indicates that the picture is more complex than it initially appears and that the commissioners' decision to use subtitling for some children's TV programmes might be justified after all, at least to a certain extent, since various age groups within the general category of children have significantly different watching habits:

Table 3.5.3.2 Viewing habits of different age groups within the children's audience

ADULT TV PROGRAMMES MARKET SHARES	**CHILDREN'S AUDIENCE (UP TO 12 YEARS)**	
	Up to 10 years	**10-12 years**
Greek adult movies	39.2	55.6
Foreign adult movies	3.7	24.0
Greek adult series	23.4	31.7
Foreign adult series	3.6	9.9

As the table above indicates, children viewers up to 10 years old[i] strongly favour Greek productions (39.2% vs. 3.7% for movies, 23.4% vs. 3.6% for series). It is the preferences of older children which seem to influence the commissioners of children's TV programmes. Since foreign movies and series do appeal to older children, commissioners are encouraged to choose subtitling, at least for those programmes targeted at youngsters rather than toddlers. The threshold of children's accustoming with reading subtitles has been discovered to lie around the age of ten: at this age, reading subtitles becomes "a habit that can be acquired: the more one reads, the faster one can read" (*EBU Review*, November 1987:12). As already discussed, older children are accustomed to reading subtitles through watching adult productions (see table 3.4.1.7). Subtitled children's programmes aimed at such older children would therefore not reduce overall market shares, because older children would not be put off by subtitling. It is the market shares of young children / toddlers that perhaps would be affected and rise accordingly if these children's programmes were broadcast dubbed. However, this rise could not affect the overall market shares and balance the extra dubbing expenses, because a) these products would not be particularly designed and targeted at toddlers and as a result their themes would not be attractive, and b) the low market shares for toddlers indicate that their contribution to the overall viewing of TV programmes in general is insignificant.

3.5.4 Findings related to upper level human agents

In various countries, the press plays a significant role in the choice of language transfer method by criticising the one or the other method (Vitkus, 1995:320). In Greece, the role of the press in this respect is considerably restricted. Nowhere in the regular film reviews

---

[i] Unfortunately, the survey (conducted by AGB Hellas in 1996) does not extend its scope to youngsters aged 12-14 who are still considered by the same company members of the 'children's audience'. All points indicate that for this particular age-group, the market shares of foreign products would be even higher.

on newspapers and magazines, nor in any other press material do we find extensive critiques on the choice or the overall quality of the language transfer method used for any foreign audiovisual product (Papadakis, 1998:66). Yet, people everyday, amongst each other, do criticise the language transfer of various audiovisual products, i.e. basically subtitling, commenting primarily on the quality of the linguistic aspects of the transfer, criticising the subtitler and criticising 'mismatches' between linguistic items of the original dialogues and their translation on screen (cf. *Cinema,* 1993:73). However, due to the fact that for decades now the norm of subtitling has been firmly established in the country, the public does not appear to be troubled by the very issue of the choice between subtitling and revoicing. Subtitling is taken for granted and even in the case of children's products dubbing has not become a topic of discussion; it is viewed as the exception to the subtitling rule.

These public views and pre-occupations do not leave the human agents /audiovisual-product commissioners unaffected. In any case, the agents themselves are part of the general public and their opinions cannot but be shaped alongside the opinions of the public. Still, their specific involvement in the business makes them more sensitive to certain issues and aspects of the language transfer process. Before they choose the method to be followed, human agents have a list of hierarchically structured principles and ideas in their minds, and they try to satisfy as many of them as they can. In the present investigation, so far, we examined certain principles and ideas related to children's TV products in particular (at the lower level, see section 3.3.4). We also examined principles and ideas related to other products of the same TV mode, as well as products of the other two audiovisual modes (at the middle level, see section 3.4.4). Apart from these product-type specific or audiovisual-mode specific principles and ideas, however, there are broader issues that cut across all audiovisual product types and all audiovisual modes and allow us to see the debate of subtitling vs. revoicing from a wider translational perspective. These are already formulated opinions, an outcome of the thinking and pre-occupation of various scholars and practitioners around the globe. Human agents in Greece are aware of or at least they can sense and understand some of these global opinions. These opinions are sometimes in favour of subtitling and sometimes in favour of revoicing. Since dubbing is the most widespread form of revoicing, these views are most often presented as a contrast between subtitling and dubbing in particular rather than between subtitling and revoicing in general. The present thesis is concerned with the choice between subtitling and revoicing children's TV programmes. Since however the only form of revoicing we encountered for such children's TV programmes was actually dubbing (see table 3.3.1.7), these global opinions that point out the pros and cons of either method do not restrict the scope of the thesis. The individual merits and drawbacks of subtitling and dubbing, as seen from a general theoretical point of view, can be summarised in the following arguments:

- High quality dubbing is very hard to achieve, especially in countries with no dubbing tradition (Vöge, 1977:121; Zabalbeascoa, 1996:236, Li, 1998:156). Counter-argument: 'bad' translations can be traced in all forms of language transfer. Subtitling can be of equally low quality. Lip-sync faults can be equally measured against defective cueing and clumsy subtitles layout (Ivarsson, 1992:18; Krogstad, 1998:62; cf. Dries, 1995a:3; cf. de Linde, 1997:172).
- Dubbing protects and promotes the local language and culture (Roffe & Thorne, 1994:253). Counter-argument: dubbing is often full of 'anglicisms' and distortions of the local language (Herbst, 1995:259; Ross, 1995:48; Whitman-Linsen, 1992:108).
- Dubbing reflects imperialistic cultural intentions (Goris, 1993:171; Vaughan, 1990:4; Giles, 1997:47; Coll, 1998:204). Counter-argument: subtitling equally reflects cultural submission, weakness and vulnerability to foreign cultural invasions (Goris, 1993:172).
- Subtitling is didactic, in both increasing literacy amongst the target audience and presenting foreign cultures in a more authentic form (Delabastita, 1989:213). Counter-argument: the level of literacy in current western societies is already high and does not need a further boost. In addition, the primary aim of most audiovisual productions is not to educate but to entertain recipients.

- Subtitles condense and therefore inevitably distort original dialogues (Kovacic, 1994:245). Counter-argument: not everything needs to be translated. Incomprehensible and insignificant elements can be left out to allow more time for the eye to appreciate the visual aesthetic aspects of the product (Goris, 1993:171; Vöge, 1977:121).
- Dubbing distorts original dialogues by altering the translated material to fit the original lip-movements (Ivarsson, 1992:17; Myers, 1973:56). In this respect, it is 'unfaithful' to the original (Gottlieb, 1994a:102; cf. Ascheid, 1997:35). Counter-argument: this happens only in the case of close-ups, and not with every shot, so that the overall changes in the original script are minimal (Goris, 1993:182). At any rate, subtitling, which condenses dialogues, can also be regarded as 'unfaithful' to the original (Myers, 1973:58).
- Subtitles create a boring and lulling effect on the viewers, partly because of their pace on the screen and partly because of their staccato method of serving small chunks of meaning (MacDougal, 1995:88). Counter-argument: subtitles provide the viewers with something additional to watch, introducing an extra element of vitality - that of 'reading'- and modifying the passive alertness with which we watch dubbed products or products in our original language, not to mention the constant flashes which are bound to increase attention on the screen (Grillo & Kawin, 1981:25).
- Dubbing is more homogeneous than subtitling, since it is an oral translation of an oral text (Goris, 1993:171). Counter-argument: when translated, dubbed dialogues too are first taken down on paper, to be later converted back to oral language. At any rate, one wonders if it is worth producing an oral rather than a written translation after all since the former requires considerably more time and money (Dries, 1995a:17).
- Subtitling can lead to misconceptions and misinterpretations of a character's personality if viewers are not completely familiar with the foreign culture and its particular kinetic and paralinguistic features (Herbst, 1995:258). Counter-argument: a new imposed dubbed dialogue with new target culture familiar paralinguistic and phonetic features can create a credibility gap between itself and the

visual elements on screen if the latter appear foreign and the former is target culture bound (Nedergaard-Larsen, 1993:234).

- A dubbed production is never able to suppress visual source culture elements and pass as an original (Ivarsson, 1992:19; Goris, 1993:170; Nedergaard-Larsen, 1993:234; Delabastita, 1990:99). Counter-argument: the same applies to subtitling. In either case, the aim of an audiovisual language transfer is not to increase credibility and try to disguise a foreign production as local, but to increase the comprehensibility and the appreciation of the original production in the best way possible. Dubbing can achieve this better than subtitling because, on the one hand, it is enriched with crucial paralinguistic and phonetic features that the target recipients can recognise and immediately understand, and on the other, it frees the viewers' attention and allows them to make the best out of the visual details.
- Dubbing deprives the audience of the opportunity to appreciate the voices and the verbal acting of certain famous actors or cartoon/puppet-characters (Zabalbeascoa, 1994:92; Vitkus, 1995:319). Counter-argument: voice-simulating technology can adapt the pitch and intonation of a dubbing actor's voice to match that of the original actor's. At any rate, dubbing actors are approved by the original film-production companies to the extent that they can imitate the original actor's oral performance and in terms of their ability to present an equivalent aesthetic result (Whitman-Linsen, 1992:93).
- Subtitles interferes with the viewers' appreciation of the visual image by monopolising attention (Moskowitz, 1979:1; Grillo & Kawin, 1981:26; Krogstad, 1998:61). Counter-argument: the reading of subtitles has been proven not to require any conscious cognitive effort on the part of an audience already accustomed to this specific language transfer method (Delabastita, 1990:98; Challier & Mueller, 1998:100). It becomes an automatic process (d'Ydewalle et al., 1991:650; cf. Gunter, 1982:8).
- Dubbing ruins the artistic intentions of the original film director by imposing an external foreign voice on the body of the original actors (Sadoux, 1982:56; Turner, 1974:382). Counter-argument: in

most audiovisual productions - especially for cinema - dialogues and various other sound effects are imposed on the image at a later stage, in a process also called 'dubbing', because of background noise during shooting (Armes, 1988, 122). In this respect, sound is not imposed on the image but subordinated to it, as it is used to 'fix' the meaning of the image rather than to motivate the image itself (Turner, 1988:56). The time consuming reading of subtitles is a process executed by the left brain hemisphere (Grillo & Kawin, 1981:31). What the original film director intends by inserting aural verbal or non-verbal elements in the first place is to increase a right-hemisphere - namely more artistic - response to his/her work, which the reading of subtitles diminishes to a considerable extent (ibid:32).

Cineastes - the advocates and defenders of audiovisual aesthetics and quality - seem to prefer subtitling as the 'optimum' language transfer method even in countries where the norm is to revoice (*KINO*, May 1994:28). Commissioners, however, although in theory defenders of audiovisual aesthetics as well, do not seem to share the 'romantic' attitudes of cinephile viewers. Although supposed to do whatever best to guard and preserve the audiovisual merits of the original product, commissioners' motivations and decisions are guided in reality by the pursuit of more profit. A great number of European producers, for example, oppose the United States' decision to release most non-Anglophone films subtitled, because they believe they are losing part of the American audience that they could easily access through dubbing (*Screen International*, December 17 1993:8; *Moving Pictures International*, September 2 1993:5). The subordination of audiovisual aesthetics to the more powerful financial laws of the global market is particularly visible in the case of children's products. At one time, much merchandise aimed at children was a by-product of cartoon-movies or series (think of the Warner Bros and Walt Disney stores worldwide, promoting goods that are based on cartoon heroes of audiovisual products). Today, the opposite is also available: cartoon series or movies can be by-products of the toy industry. The production of *Thundercats* in the US is one case where a cartoon series was created in order to promote the launching of 'Thundercats' doll figurines (Davies, 1989:35). In Greece, the *Power Rangers* live-action children's TV series provides a similar example: it was broadcast in order to support the promotion of 'Power Rangers' products in the local toy market. The film production and distribution company, affiliated to the toy manufacturing company, sponsored a high quality dubbing of the series. In addition, it invested a lot of money in advertising both the toys and the series. The more the toys sold, the more children watched the series. Similarly, the more children watched the series, the more toys were sold. This phenomenon indicates the complex nature of the audiovisual industry. The choice to release the specific cartoon series dubbed was not based on any considerations related to the individual merits of the one or the other language transfer method as listed above but was dictated from outside the audiovisual industry in order to support the toy industry.

CONCLUSIONS

Audiovisual translation has not received much attention in translation studies, especially at the theoretical level. A study such as this, therefore, finds itself faced with an almost virgin territory, which makes the task of validating results by comparing them with previous findings rather difficult. The situation is made more difficult by the lack of any studies in the Greek context specifically.

A number of weaknesses must then inevitably restrict the validity of the empirical results reported in this study. First of all, there is the question of limited bibliographical information on Greek audiovisual reality and the outdated status of most existing studies. In certain cases, I have tried to borrow and cautiously apply findings of investigations conducted in other countries, namely in different socio-cultural frameworks. In terms of the empirical research of the present study, it is based on data and information from a set of factors geographically situated within the greater Athens area only. This is because there is no consistent audiovisual translation activity (i.e. audiovisual translation agencies or in-house audiovisual translation departments) outside the Greek capital, with the exception of some video products (e.g. industrial/commercial companies' promotional clips or B-rated erotic movies) translated under unorthodox situations. No cinema-film or video distribution agencies are based outside Athens and, as far as TV is concerned, the only non-Athens based TV stations that achieve national coverage have their foreign audiovisual products translated by agencies in the capital. Even for the greater Athens area, however, it would be very difficult to account for the total number of broadcasting TV stations or the total number of operating cinema and video distribution agencies. As a result, the representative samples come from a range of stations and companies that claim to cover around 85% - rather than 100% - of the Greek market (for TV stations in terms of their appeal to the public, i.e. their viewing rates, and for cinema and video distribution agencies in terms of their percentage share in the total volume of cinema and video products released in the country).

The lack of an existing consistent corpus of audiovisual products meant that a personal corpus based on daily programme flows (for TV programmes) and yearly releases (for cinema and video products) had to be compiled. Such a corpus, however, is unofficial and of relevance only to the present research. Although aiming to cover the time period between 1994 and 1996, data on TV programmes had to be restricted to the manageable size of two indicative months per TV-year (March 1995 and March 1996). As a result, certain types of programmes that are not widely broadcast on Greek TV were inevitably underrepresented (e.g. children's puppet movies). The notion of 'time period' also proved problematic for the synchronic evaluation of the results since the notion of TV-years does not coincide with the notion of cinema-years, which in turn does not coincide with the notion of video years. Furthermore, the latest available data on local written literary productions came from 1993, i.e. a time period that covers a socio-cultural situation slightly prior to the one under study.

As far as the study of recipients is concerned, no data (in terms of viewing rates or market shares) was available for children under the age of six, who still constitute part of the overall category of children viewers and are a potential target group in their own right. There was even no data on the reception of the private cable TV channel (FILMNET). Furthermore, the lack of official figures on the reception of cinema and video products led to the inevitable use of quoted comparative percentages whose validity and status can be questioned. But even the viewing rates that were eventually collected for TV have to be treated carefully since they do not account for phenomena such as repeat viewing, audience duplication or the recording of particular programmes for later viewing.

As far as the study of human agents is concerned, the large number of individuals involved in the choice of language transfer method and the multiplicity of their roles led quite often to the use of collective descriptions (e.g. 'the x TV station personnel' or 'the y cinema distribution agency staff') instead of attributing particular views to specific members of the industry. This is often due to the fact that in a number of cases individuals from the same station/agency answered the questionnaires in a collective fashion, claiming that their views represented the same general policy. Furthermore, the questionnaire could only provide access to post-production retrospective attitudes of human agents reflecting upon the motivations that made them choose the one or the other language transfer method. Given the gap between the time they filled in the questionnaire (summer 1997) and the actual time period under study, transcripts or recordings of the proceedings of the actual meetings / conversations where the issue was discussed might have proven more useful. Such data was not available however. In order to counter-balance this weakness, a series of unofficial interviews/chats with the same human agents had to be conducted. But unofficial verbal data of this type (acquired through phone calls, friendly confidential talks etc.) is not retrievable for further consultation and cross-examination, since none of these conversations were taped.

Summary of findings

The first conclusion that seems to emerge from the thesis is that it *is* feasible to study audiovisual translation within the scope of translation studies. The polysystem approach to translation allows us to regard audiovisual translation products as 'literary facts' that can be studied in a systematic fashion.

Within the framework of polysystem theory, norms in audiovisual translation, as in written translation, are regarded as recurrent patterns of behaviour guided and motivated by a number of choices and constraints. Due to the inter-relatedness of these choices and constraints it seems impossible to fully restructure the exact logical sequence of a norm in terms of a series of probabilistic variables (e.g.. if x had happened then, y would not have happened but z would be very likely to have happened). What seems to be possible though is to study and account for – a number of - the subjective or objective factors involved in the production and operation of a specific norm in a systematic rather than random fashion.

Norms and systems in audiovisual translation, just as in written translation, presuppose and overlap with each other. A system is the coherent grid of the norms that operate in it; similarly, a norm is a constellation of factors (a minute sub-system) that leads to the emergence of a specific behavioural pattern. Deviation from or conformity to (audiovisual) translation norms is a matter of what the target system is willing to accept, modify or reject. In this respect, the role of the source system, as well as that of the 'equivalence' established between the source and target poles (language/ text /culture/ system) is considerably restricted, since it can serve only as a reference point that one has taken for granted before proceeding with the actual investigation into the function of target products within the target system.

Deviation from or conformity to the norms of the target system might involve decisions instigated by human agents alone; nevertheless, these decisions are taken on the basis of a series of considerations and numerous factors involved in the target system. In the case of norms in audiovisual translation, these factors include - apart from the human agents - the audiovisual target products themselves, the recipients of these products and the audiovisual mode which distinguishes the particular activity of audiovisual translation from other literary activities within the broader target system. In this respect, a) human agents are seen as involved in a variety of decisions taken within the target system (from commissioning the translation to actually suggesting the linguistic signs of the target product), b) target products are seen as consisting of the totality of the (new target) verbal and the (retained source) non-verbal elements, i.e. in the form released in the target system, c) recipients are seen as consisting of that part of the general public that has consciously consumed the target product and towards which the product itself is addressed, and d) the audiovisual mode is seen as the particular linguistic and social framework/background within which the specific product operates.

The four factors are seen as interdependent, and it is the interaction between them that generates a specific norm. Each *set* of (relations between) these factors, though, can be seen as constituting smaller sub-systems and sub-sub-systems, placed the one within the other in a kind of hierarchy which can dictate the breadth and applicability of the norm in question. Smaller sub-systems start at the concrete level of a limited set of (or individual) audiovisual products, examined within their particular audiovisual film type and genre as created by a specific group of human agents and targeted at a specific group of recipients/ viewers (lower level). Broader sub-systems cover audiovisual products from other audiovisual modes, film types and genres as well, created by various other human agents and targeted at various other groups of recipients/ viewers (middle level); even broader sub-systems cover literary products outside the audiovisual framework, created by human agents involved in other kinds of literary production, and targeted at a wider range of recipients (upper level). If the same norm which is found to operate at the lower level is seen to operate at the middle or even upper level, then it can be claimed as having a broader applicability and higher status. The investigation is guided by a series of discovery-and-justification procedures and the results are based on size and frequency. Quantitative results, however, will have to be accompanied by a number of qualitative results which reinforce the reliability and the validity of the conclusions. In the attempt to investigate norms in audiovisual translation, a number of data-analysis techniques can be applicable; for the purposes of the present case study, observation, official questionnaires and unofficial interviews were used.

This study chose to test the proposed model for investigating norms in audiovisual translation by focusing on the choice between subtitling and revoicing children's TV programmes in Greece between 1994-1996, because there were certain indications that the norm and the motivations behind it are guided by factors operating at both the middle and upper levels. The findings have supported this initial hypothesis.

Although Greece is described as a predominantly subtitling country, most children's TV programmes are broadcast dubbed. The percentage, however, is not so high in favour of dubbing (around 55%) and is by no means close to what the majority of audiovisual scholars, suggesting that all children's products should be dubbed irrespective of the overall tradition of the country, would rather expect. All children's TV movies (100%), for example, as well as most live-action children's TV series (around 75%) are broadcast subtitled because of the influence of the relevant adult film types. It is mostly cartoon TV series - which nevertheless account for the majority of children's broadcasts - that are dubbed (around 70%). Walt Disney's and Warner Bros' classic cartoon productions remain subtitled since their high status in the Greek community requires retaining the original voices of the characters as well as the original music soundtrack. Most cartoon TV series which are broadcast subtitled have a more adult theme and humour and are, therefore, likely to be targeted at older rather than younger children. In any case, the use of both subtitling and dubbing for children's TV programmes entails that Greek children nowadays are accustomed to and familiarised with both language transfer methods early on.

Children are more vulnerable to linguistic phenomena around them, so from an educational point of view subtitling might prove better than dubbing not only because it promotes reading abilities but also because it accommodates fewer idiomatic expressions and anglicisms. Since, however, children watch TV mostly for fun and less for information/education purposes and dubbing can allow an audience with limited reading abilities to access a product it is natural for children to favour dubbed material precisely because it involves less cognitive effort. The much acclaimed use of subtitling for educational purposes of promoting second language learning through the presence of the spoken language on screen has been proven false, since it is actually reverse subtitling (spoken native language with second language subtitles) that has this beneficial effect. Other technical constraints related to the need for multiple language broadcasts, however, might dictate the choice of subtitling - available via teletext - even when it comes to children's programmes (e.g. the broadcasts of the European satellite Children's channel). In addition, children are better lip-readers than adults, so they are more liable to spot bad lip-sync and be disappointed by a hastily dubbed production.

The lower the children's family class, the more they are likely to stay at home, the more they watch TV, the more they regard it as a means of entertainment and, therefore, the more they favour dubbing. On the other hand, the higher the children's family class and education, the less they watch TV, the more they regard it as a source of information and not just entertainment and, therefore, the less they favour dubbing. As children grow older, they watch more adult TV material and, consequently, they are expected to be more conditioned by it. On the other hand, children's programmes themselves are not viewed by children alone; a large sector of the adult audience watch them too. In this respect, we cannot claim that children's TV programme commissioners can clearly idealise a potential homogeneous 'children's audience'; they rather cater for the needs of adult viewers too. Considering, then, that the viewing rates for adults as far as children's programmes are concerned are high whereas the viewing rates for children are relatively low, it is reasonable for the language transfer commissioners to think that a potential investment in dubbing in order to satisfy the children's audience will not be justified (dubbing is approximately 10-15 times more expensive than subtitling and three times as expensive as revoicing). This hypothesis seems to be reinforced by the fact that the general move towards more dubbed children's TV programmes - as experienced in 1996 - was not found to be accompanied by higher viewing rates. The higher response of the audience towards some dubbed productions seems to be more the result of the promotion and individual quality of the specific programmes than an outcome of the choice of language transfer method. The astonishing viewing rates achieved by a dubbed live-action series proves that there is nothing in the film genre (cartoon or other) which is inherently related to the appreciation of either language transfer method.

An increase or decrease in the amount of time allocated to children's TV programmes by various TV stations does not seem to result in a respective tendency in favour of the one or the other language transfer method. All Greek TV programme commissioners claim that they prefer dubbing as the optimum language transfer method for children's TV programmes; some, however, differentiate between programmes targeted at older children, for which they explicitly recommend subtitling. In most cases, it is the TV station's administrative board (plus staff from the marketing department) who will decide on the language transfer of all programmes, including children's programmes, unless there is an in-house translation department which is sometimes also consulted. The commissioning of children's programmes in particular is only occasionally supported financially by international TV programme distributors, in which case dubbing is more likely to be used.

Figures indicate that Greece *is* a predominantly subtitling country after all. On TV, 91.4% of the total volume of foreign programmes is broadcast subtitled, 5.7% dubbed, 1.9% in free-commentary and 1% in narration+subtitling; all non-children's TV programmes are broadcast subtitled except for some documentaries and news/ information programmes which are broadcast in narration+subtitling, and some sports programmes which are broadcast in free-commentary (it is only lately that some soap operas have started to be dubbed). In cinema, 94.3% of the total volume of foreign products is released subtitled and 5.7% dubbed; all non-children's cinema movies are released subtitled. As for video, 69% of the total volume of foreign products is released subtitled, 18% dubbed and 13% in narration; all non-children's video products are released subtitled except for most of the documentaries and sports programmes which are released in narration. The above findings indicate that the subtitling norm is strong enough to influence children's TV programmes.

The general norm for children's cinema movies is to release them subtitled, unless their theme and humour are clearly targeted at younger children, in which case they are released dubbed. This justifies the established norm to subtitle children's TV movies. On the other hand, the general norm for children's video products is to release them dubbed, unless their theme and humour are clearly targeted at older children, in which case they are released subtitled. It is only live-action children's video movies that are mostly released subtitled, following the trend set by both TV and cinema. This overall tendency of video towards dubbing children's products, however, counterbalances the norms applicable in cinema and influence TV in the direction of more dubbing, therefore justifying the norm established for children's TV programmes in general. Such closer interaction between TV and video rather than TV and cinema is justified and motivated by the wider overlap of product types available on both TV and video.

Significant differences between subtitling and revoicing for TV, cinema or video due to technical, financial or socio-cultural constraints result in the need to investigate each of the language transfer methods within the scope of the respective audiovisual mode. The watching habits for TV, a more 'live' and 'unmediated' medium, are in theory served better by the more 'realistic' method of dubbing. The watching habits for cinema, viewed as an escape from reality, are in theory served better by the more 'foreignising' method of subtitling. The watching habits for video lie somewhere between the two modes, slightly closer to the mode of TV. This justifies the fact that in other countries different methods are used for each of the three audiovisual modes. Intertextuality which dictates that a product first released in a specific mode (i.e. a cinema premiere) should have a similar treatment in other modes does not seem to be respected in the Greek context and each release/broadcast seems to receive an individual treatment, even as far as the choice of language transfer method is concerned. The distinction, largely taken for granted, between dialogues- or action-oriented film genres as well as between 'informative' or 'expressive' film types does not seem to affect the choice of language transfer method at all.

As seen in other countries, quite often it is the lack of technical equipment that determines the choice of either method. A deeper fear of unemployment in case the dominant method is rejected in favour of another also seems to support the continued dominance of that method. Time and cost constraints favour subtitling. The existence of many predominantly dubbing countries, however, proves that audience accustoming overrides the cost factor. The overall accustoming of the audience with the method that dominates a country seems to disfavour tolerance for other methods. However, cinephiles in particular seem to favour subtitling irrespective of the country's dominant norm. This bias against dubbing in particular seems to derive from broader and more abstract reasons to do with general artistic appreciation. Furthermore, dubbing seems to be more suitable from the point of view of women's domestic social role (taking care of house activities while watching TV), whereas subtitling seems to be more suitable for the social role associated with men (the need to satisfy their desire to be able to feel that they can cross-check whatever they are watching).

The profile of the Greek TV, video and cinema audiences does not seem to differ from that of other predominantly subtitling Western European countries. In general, it is more difficult to pinpoint and cater for TV audiences (because of their random nature), whereas cinema and video audiences seem to be more predictable. On TV, younger, more educated audiences of higher socio-economic status claim to favour subtitling; older, less educated audiences of lower socio-economic status claim to favour dubbing. In this respect, the overall norm of subtitling which was found to dominate the mode of TV is only partly justified. This happens because some language transfer commissioners do not seem to be in tune with the Greek TV audience, whereas others who are aware of the above findings choose to disregard them and opt for the cheaper method of subtitling. The core of the Greek cinema and video audience seems to consist predominantly of male, urban, upper-middle class viewers who tend to favour subtitling. In this respect, the overall norm of subtitling which was found to dominate the mode of cinema (and to a lesser extent the mode of video) is fully justified. Since, however, young audiences seem to favour subtitling invariably, the neighbouring - in terms of age - children's audiences (especially the older group of children) are bound to be influenced by those tendencies too. The choice to subtitle children's products aimed at older rather than younger children, then, seems perfectly justified.

In the Greek audiovisual context, the role of the audiovisual translator is considerably limited and subject to constant control by the commissioners. Major decisions such as the choice of language transfer method are very often taken in the absence of the audiovisual translator per se. As with TV, in cinema and video too it is the administrative board (plus some staff from the marketing department) who decide on the language transfer method to be used. Unlike TV, however, when it comes to children's products, cinema (in particular) and video distribution agencies consult directly with the original production companies abroad: if these companies are willing to invest extra money, the product will be released not only in a subtitled version but in a dubbed version too. This explains the double release of a number of Walt Disney's cartoon movies for both cinema and video products. The double release of such cartoon movies, however, inevitably influences and confuses even more the already fuzzy picture of cartoon TV series. If it is the economics of the media that should dictate the influence of one or the other mode, TV should influence both cinema and video. When it comes to children's products in particular, however, the economics of language transfer for cinema are higher than the economics of TV or video and, as a result, can be seen to influence the choices amongst the other two audiovisual modes more than the choices for cinema is influenced by them.

Unlike TV personnel who voted for dubbing as the optimum language transfer method for children's products, cinema and video staff seem to have rather mixed attitudes. This overall mixed tendency in the broader audiovisual industry, however, can be seen to influence the attitudes of TV personnel who prefer to disregard their own personal pro-dubbing preferences because they believe that audiovisual commissioners from the other two media would not approve of their choice. Apart from technical and financial considerations, TV staff stressed the following parameters as possible motivations/constraints for a possible deviation from the overall norm of subtitling: a) the potential recipients of the programme, b) the time of the product's broadcast, c) its specific film type and genre, and d) the language of the original production (if other than English). The first parameter reflects the way in which children's and adult products are treated and is justified by the relevant findings. The second parameter refers to early-morning or late-night broadcasts but its influence is not borne out by the findings in this study, since a number of dubbed children's programmes were found to be broadcast during the early morning hours too. The third parameter seems to be only partly relevant in practice, since there is no consistent approach to the treatment of various programmes in terms of either their film type (only documentaries, news/information and children's cartoon series seem to receive special treatment) or their film genre (a degree of consistency was found only amongst certain 'genres' within cartoon series, e.g. 'classic' cartoons). The fourth parameter again seems to be only partly relevant in practice, since the decision to revoice some non-English programmes is limited to children's products. Similarly, apart from technical and financial considerations, cinema and video staff stressed the following parameters as possible motivations/constraints for a possible deviation from the overall norm of subtitling: a) the target audience, and b) support from the film production company in the language transfer budget. Both these parameters are supported by the relevant findings. We see, therefore, that the basic motivations/constraints expressed by commissioners from various audiovisual modes are not in conflict; on the contrary, whenever they do not overlap they seem to be complementary. Subtitling seems to be firmly established as an overall norm not just because of its broad applicability across the whole spectrum of audiovisual modes but also because of the complementary motivations that lie behind it. Its influence on children's TV programmes, then, can be seen to derive from and be rooted in the overall audiovisual environment and not just in the environment of TV alone.

As a result of the global expansion of anglophone products and the fact that Greece is by definition a nation of travelling people open to innovative elements and interaction with foreign cultures, foreign literary products have a considerable influence and a high status in Greek culture. As a result, the phenomena of 'xenomania' or rather 'Anglo-mania' were bound to appear. The comparative figures between local and foreign audiovisual productions released for cinema and video are indicative of the above phenomenon: only 4.5% of total cinema releases are Greek products, whereas 74.4% of the foreign productions have English as the original language on screen; on video, Greek productions account for only 1.6% of total releases, whereas 99.7% of foreign productions have English as the original language on screen. On TV, however, things appear to be different: since TV is seen as more 'live' and 'unmediated', the carrier of news, information and local affairs as well as entertainment, it is more intimately associated with the local culture than cinema and video. Only around 47.5% of overall TV airtime is dedicated to foreign productions. The same picture is reflected in the comparative figures between local productions and foreign imports for written literary material: in terms of newspapers and magazines, which are more intimately related to the local culture and events, Greek products account for 98.9% of total circulation. For fiction and scientific books, however, local productions account for only 56.5%; as far as foreign imports are concerned, 68% come from the UK and the US. One can safely say, then, that the figures obtained for the audiovisual industry do not constitute an isolated case but reflect a general trend in the Greek culture.

The balanced distribution of TV airtime between Greek and foreign programmes seems to explain the mismatch that we encountered between strong pro-dubbing feelings expressed by a certain section of the Greek audience and the actual overwhelming norm of subtitling. Some sectors of the population seem to react to the domination of cinema and video by Anglophone products and regard TV as the defender of their national identity and integrity. As a matter of fact, those who say they like dubbing mean that they would rather listen to Greek on TV. The distribution of overall market shares indicates that TV viewers do prefer to watch local rather than foreign productions (37% vs. 33.5%). Commissioners choose to opt for subtitling foreign products in order to satisfy those in favour of subtitling as a language transfer method, whereas in order to satisfy the pro-dubbing group, they prefer to increase the airtime of Greek original productions.

The situation is different however for children's programmes in particular, since only 10% of the total airtime devoted to such products is actually dedicated to Greek productions. This occurs because of a general reluctance and inability to produce children's programmes locally, because they require high standards of production. Given the lack of local children's TV productions, commissioners can only solve the problem of a large number of children's audience wanting to listen to Greek on TV by dubbing some of the foreign productions. This explains the norm of dubbing in the case of children's TV programmes. At the same time, however, it strengthens the norm of subtitling for adult programmes, since Greek viewers become accustomed to viewing subtitled foreign programmes at quite an early age and expect to watch such subtitled productions as they grow older as well.

Out of the case study as a whole, two conclusions can be drawn overall: a) the choice of language transfer method for children's TV programmes in the Greek audiovisual context is not as straightforward as some audiovisual translation scholars have indicated for other European countries, and b) the dominant national norm of subtitling which applies to all audiovisual modes and the motivations that lead to its continued strength have some influence on the choice of language transfer method for children's TV programmes. Today, the advent of digital TV technology seems to favour subtitling. In the non-distant future, however, the prospect of digital image processing is expected to enhance and promote dubbing for children's TV programmes, especially cartoons. We might then expect in the immediate future the overall norm of subtitling to persist for adult products, and the norm of dubbing to gain in strength for children's programmes. Nevertheless, the choice between subtitling and revoicing will not be based so much on the individual merits of each language transfer method, but it will continue to be motivated by the pursuit of higher profits.

Suggestions for further research

The present study points to a number of potential topics for further investigation:

- The methodology proposed here may be applied and tested in an investigation of linguistic or textual target norms operating within audiovisual products. This would mean focusing on specific 'operational' rather than 'preliminary' norms.
- The findings of the present case study could be investigated beyond the upper level in an attempt to account for even broader norms in a broader socio-cultural context. But this would require a strong sociological background.
- The same methodology with the same aims could be applied to other synchronic time-points in order to develop a diachronic view of the evolution of norms. However, the further back in time a study will go, the more difficulties it will encounter in terms of collecting data.
- The same methodology could be used to investigate the motivations behind the choice to subtitle or to revoice other film types and genres. In this respect, the findings established at the middle and upper level could be retained, but a different initial hypothesis would have to be set as a starting point at the lower level.
- In a more ambitious attempt, the present methodology could be taken as a starting point for developing a model for investigating norms in other fields of the target literary system (e.g. in the field of translated drama). Various adjustments would have to be made, the most obvious concerns accounting for a different mode (e.g. drama rather than the audiovisual mode).

APPENDIX 1.1
QUESTIONNAIRE FOR TV STATIONS (Greek Original)

ΕΡΕΥΝΑ ΓΙΑ ΤΗ ΜΕΤΑΦΡΑΣΗ ΤΑΙΝΙΩΝ ΣΤΗΝ ΕΛΛΑΔΑ
ΕΡΩΤΗΜΑΤΟΛΟΓΙΟ ΠΡΟΣ ΤΗΛΕΟΠΤΙΚΟΥΣ ΣΤΑΘΜΟΥΣ / ΚΑΝΑΛΙΑ

Τηλεοπτικός Σταθμός / Κανάλι:

Ημερομηνία:
Ώρα:
Τόπος:

1. Ποιοι αποφασίζουν στο κανάλι σας αν κάποιο <u>παιδικό</u> πρόγραμμα θα μεταδοθεί υποτιτλισμένο (subtitled), μεταγλωτισμένο (dubbed), ή με αφήγηση (voiced-over);

2. Είναι αυτοί οι ίδιοι που αποφασίζουν για την μετάφραση και των υπολοίπων προγραμμάτων που μεταδίδει το κανάλι σας;

3. Ποιος μεταφράζει τα ξένα προγράμματα στο κανάλι σας; Διαθέτει το κανάλι σας δικό του τμήμα μετάφρασης προγραμμάτων ή συνεργάζεται με ανεξάρτητες ιδιωτικές εταιρείες / γραφεία μετάφρασης προγραμμάτων;

4. Αν οι μεταφράσεις γίνονται από τμήμα μετάφρασης του καναλιού σας, διαθέτετε ξεχωριστό τμήμα υποτιτλισμού (subtitling) από αυτό του επιγλωτισμού (dubbing and voice-over);

5. Αν τα ξένα προγράμματά σας μεταφράζονται από ανεξάρτητες ιδιωτικές εταιρείες / γραφεία, υπάρχουν κάποια γραφεία / εταιρείες με τα οποία είστε συμβεβλημένοι ή με τα οποία συνεργαζεστε σε σταθερή βάση και ποια είναι αυτά;

6. Αν τα ξένα προγράμματά σας μεταφράζονται από ανεξάρτητες ιδιωτικές εταιρείες / γραφεία, έχετε αναθέσει ποτέ τον υποτιλτισμό *και* τον επιγλωτισμό κάποιου προγράμματος στο ίδιο γραφείο / εταιρεία και ποιο γραφείο ήταν αυτό;

7. Αν τα ξένα προγράμματά σας μεταφράζονται από ανεξάρτητες ιδιωτικές εταιρείες / γραφεία, έχετε επιλέξει ποτέ την εταιρεία / γραφείο στην οποία θα αναθέσετε τη μετάφραση κάποιου ξένου προγραμματος ανάλογα με το αν πρόκειται να υποτιτλίσετε ή να επιγλωτίσετε το πρόγραμμα αυτό;

8. Επιβάλετε ή επανασυζητάτε με τις ανεξάρτητες ιδιωτικές εταιρείες / γραφεία ή με το τμήμα μετάφρασης προγραμμάτων του καναλιού σας την επιλογή σας να μεταδώσετε ένα συγκεκριμένο πρόγραμμα υποτιτλισμένο, μεταγλωτισμένο ή με αφήγηση;

9. Με ποια κριτήρια αποφασίζετε αν κάποιο ξένο πρόγραμμα του καναλιού σας θα πρέπει να μεταδοθεί υποτιτλισμένο, μεταγλωτισμένο ή με αφήγηση;

10. Ποια είναι η προσωπική σας άποψη σχετικά με την ιδανικότερη μέθοδο μετάφρασης ξένων παιδικών τηλεοπτικών προγραμμάτων;

11. Ποια είναι η προσωπική σας άποψη σχετικά με την ιδανικότερη μέθοδο μετάφρασης ξένων τηλεοπτικών προγραμμάτων γενικότερα;

12. Είστε ικανοποιημένοι με τα ποσοστά τηλεθέασης των ξένων <u>παιδικών</u> προγραμμάτων σας;

13. Πιστεύετε ότι μια διαφορετική μέθοδος μετάφρασης κάποιων παιδικών προγραμμάτων σας θα ανέβαζε ή θα κατέβαζε τα ποσοστά τηλεθέασης τους;

Ονοματεπώνυμο ερωτηθέντος:
Ηλικία:
Φύλο:
Θέση / αρμοδιότητες στο κανάλι:

APPENDIX 1.2
QUESTIONNAIRE FOR TV STATIONS (English translation)

RESEARCH ON AUDIOVISUAL TRANSLATION IN GREECE
QUESTIONNAIRE FOR TV STATIONS / CHANNELS

TV station / channel:
Date:
Time:
Place:

1. Who in your station decides whether a children's programme will be broadcast subtitled, dubbed or narrated?
2. Do the same people decide on the translation of the other programmes that your station broadcasts?
3. Who translates the programmes you broadcast? Does your station have its own in-house audiovisual translation department or does it co-operate with private independent audiovisual translation offices?
4. If the translations are undertaken by the translation department of your station, do you have one administration for subtitling and a separate one for revoicing (narration and dubbing)?
5. If your foreign programmes are translated by private independent offices, are there any offices with which you are contracted or with which you co-operate on a regular basis?
6. If your foreign programmes are translated by private independent offices, have you ever entrusted both the subtitling and the revoicing of a programme to the same office, and if so which office?
7. If your foreign programmes are translated by private independent offices, have you ever chosen the office to which you will entrust the translation of a foreign programme according to whether this programme will be broadcast subtitled or revoiced?
8. Do you impose or negotiate with private independent offices your choice to subtitle or to revoice a particular programme?
9. What are your criteria for deciding whether a foreign programme should be subtitled or dubbed?
10. What is your personal opinion on the optimum language transfer method for foreign children's programmes?
11. What is your personal opinion on the optimum language transfer method for foreign programmes in general?
12. Are you satisfied with the viewing rates that the children's programmes you have broadcast managed to achieve?
13. Do you believe that a different language transfer method for some of your children's programmes would decrease or increase their viewing rates?

Name and surname of questionee:
Age:
Gender:
Position / Responsibilities in the station:

APPENDIX 2.1
QUESTIONNAIRE FOR CINEMA DISTRIBUTION AGENCIES (Greek Original)

ΕΡΕΥΝΑ ΓΙΑ ΤΗ ΜΕΤΑΦΡΑΣΗ ΤΑΙΝΙΩΝ ΣΤΗΝ ΕΛΛΑΔΑ
ΕΡΩΤΗΜΑΤΟΛΟΓΙΟ ΠΡΟΣ ΕΤΑΙΡΕΙΕΣ ΔΙΑΝΟΜΗΣ
ΚΙΝΗΜΑΤΟΓΡΑΦΙΚΩΝ ΤΑΙΝΙΩΝ

Εταιρεία διάνομής:

Ημερομηνία:
Ώρα:
Τόπος:

1. Ποιοι αποφασίζουν στην εταιρεία σας αν κάποια <u>παιδική</u> ταινία θα προβληθεί υποτιτλισμένη (subtitled) ή μεταγλωτισμένη (dubbed);

2. Είναι αυτοί οι ίδιοι που αποφασίζουν για τη μετάφραση και των υπολοίπων ταινιών που διανέμει η εταιρεία σας;

3. Ποιος μεταφράζει τις ταινίες που διανέμετε; Διαθέτει η εταιρεία σας δικό της τμήμα μετάφρασης ταινιών ή συνεργάζεται με ανεξάρτητα ιδιωτικά γραφεία μετάφρασης ταινιών;

4. Αν οι μεταφράσεις γίνονται από τμήμα μετάφρασης της εταιρείας σας, διαθέτετε ξεχωριστή υποδιεύθυνση υποτιτλισμού από αυτή του μεταγλωτισμού;

5. Αν οι ξένες ταινίες σας μεταφράζονται από ανεξάρτητα ιδιωτικά γραφεία, υπάρχουν κάποια με τα οποία είστε συμβεβλημένοι ή με τα οποία συνεργάζεστε σε σταθερή βάση και ποια είναι αυτά;

6. Αν οι ξένες ταινίες σας μεταφράζονται από ανεξάρτητα ιδιωτικά γραφεία, έχετε αναθέσει ποτέ τον υποτιτλισμό και το μεταγλωτισμό κάποιας ταινίας στο ίδιο γραφείο και ποιο ήταν αυτό;

7. Αν οι ξένες ταινιες σας μεταφράζονται από ανεξάρτητα ιδιωτικά γραφεία, έχετε επιλέξει ποτέ το γραφείο στο οποίο θα αναθέσετε τη μετάφραση κάποιας ξένης ταινίας ανάλογα με το αν πρόκειται να υποτιτλίσετε ή να μεταγλωτίσετε την ταινία αυτή;

8. Επιβάλετε ή επανασυζητάτε με τα ανεξάρτητα ιδιωτικά γραφεία την επιλογή σας να υποτιτλίσετε ή να μεταγλωτίσετε μια συγκεκριμένη ταινία;

9. Με ποια κριτήρια αποφασίζετε αν μια ξένη ταινια θα πρέπει να υποτιτλιστεί ή να μεταγλωτισθεί;

10. Ποια είναι η προσωπική σας άποψη σχετικά με την ιδανικότερη μέθοδο μετάφρασης ξένων παιδικών ταινιών;

11. Ποια είναι η προσωπική σας άποψη σχετικά με την ιδανικότερη μέθοδο μετάφρασης ξένων ταινιών γενικότερα;

12. Ειστε ικανοποιημένοι με τον αριθμό εισητηρίων που συγκέντρωσαν οι ξένες παιδικές ταινίες που διανείματε;

13. Πιστεύετε οτι μια διαφορετική μέθοδος μετάφρασης κάποιων παιδικών ταινιών σας θα μείωνε ή θα αύξανε τον αριθμό εισητηρίων που συγκέντρωσαν;

Ονοματεπώνυμο ερωτηθέντος:
Ηλικία:
Φύλο:
Θέση / αρμοδιότητες στην εταιρεία:

APPENDIX 2.2
QUESTIONNAIRE FOR CINEMA DISTRIBUTION AGENCIES (English translation)

RESEARCH ON AUDIOVISUAL TRANSLATION IN GREECE
QUESTIONNAIRE FOR CINEMA FILM DISTRIBUTION AGENCIES

Distribution agency:
Date:
Time:
Place:

1. Who in your agency decides whether a children's movie will be shown subtitled or dubbed?
2. Do the same people decide on the translation of the other movies that your agency distributes?
3. Who translates the movies you distribute? Does your agency have its own in-house audiovisual translation department or does it co-operate with private independent audiovisual translation offices?
4. If the translations are undertaken by the translation department of your agency, do you have one administration for subtitling and a separate one for dubbing?
5. If your foreign movies are translated by private independent offices, are there any offices with which you are contracted or with which you co-operate on a regular basis?
6. If your foreign movies are translated by private independent offices, have you ever entrusted both the subtitling and the dubbing of a movie to the same office, and if so which office?
7. If your foreign movies are translated by private independent offices, have you ever chosen the office to which you will entrust the translation of a foreign movie according to whether this movie will be shown subtitled or dubbed?
8. Do you impose or negotiate with private independent offices your choice to subtitle or to dub a particular movie?
9. What are your criteria for deciding whether a foreign movie should be subtitled or dubbed?
10. What is your personal opinion on the optimum language transfer method for foreign children's movies?
11. What is your personal opinion on the optimum language transfer method for foreign movies in general?
12. Are you satisfied with the ticket figures that the children's movies you distribute have managed to achieve?
13. Do you believe that a different language transfer method for some of your children's movies would decrease or increase their ticket figures?

Name and surname of questionee:
Age:
Gender:
Position / Responsibilities in the agency:

APPENDIX 3.1
QUESTIONNAIRE FOR VIDEO DISTRIBUTION AGENCIES (Greek Original)

ΕΡΕΥΝΑ ΓΙΑ ΤΗ ΜΕΤΑΦΡΑΣΗ ΤΑΙΝΙΩΝ ΣΤΗΝ ΕΛΛΑΔΑ
ΕΡΩΤΗΜΑΤΟΛΟΓΙΟ ΠΡΟΣ ΕΤΑΙΡΕΙΕΣ ΔΙΑΝΟΜΗΣ
ΠΡΟΓΡΑΜΜΑΤΩΝ ΒΙΝΤΕΟ

Εταιρεία διάνομής:

Ημερομηνία:
Ώρα:
Τόπος:

1. Ποιοι αποφασίζουν στην εταιρεία σας αν κάποιο <u>παιδικό</u> πρόγραμμα θα διανεμηθεί υποτιτλισμένο (subtitled), μεταγλωτισμένο (dubbed), ή με αφήγηση (voiced-over);

2. Είναι αυτοί οι ίδιοι που αποφασίζουν για τη μετάφραση και των υπολοίπων προγραμμάτων που διανέμει η εταιρεία σας;

3. Ποιος μεταφράζει τις ταινίες που διανέμετε; Διαθέτει η εταιρεία σας δικό της τμήμα μετάφρασης ή συνεργάζεται με ανεξάρτητα ιδιωτικά γραφεία μετάφρασης προγραμμάτων;

4. Αν οι μεταφράσεις γίνονται από τμήμα μετάφρασης της εταιρείας σας, διαθέτετε ξεχωριστή υποδιεύθυνση υποτιτλισμού (subtitling) από αυτή του επιγλωτισμού (dubbing and voice-over);

5. Αν τα ξένα προγράμματά σας μεταφράζονται από ανεξάρτητα ιδιωτικά γραφεία, υπάρχουν κάποια με τα οποία είστε συμβεβλημένοι ή με τα οποία συνεργάζεστε σε σταθερή βάση και ποια είναι αυτά;

6. Αν τα ξένα προγράμματά σας μεταφράζονται από ανεξάρτητα ιδιωτικά γραφεία, έχετε αναθέσει ποτέ τον υποτιτλισμό και τον επιγλωτισμό κάποιου προγράμματος στο ίδιο γραφείο και ποιο ήταν αυτό;

7. Αν τα ξένα προγράμματά σας μεταφράζονται από ανεξάρτητα ιδιωτικά γραφεία, έχετε επιλέξει ποτέ το γραφείο στο οποίο θα αναθέσετε τη μετάφραση κάποιου προγράμματος ανάλογα με το αν πρόκειται να το υποτιτλίσετε ή να το επιγλωτίσετε;

8. Επιβάλετε ή επανασυζητάτε με τα ανεξάρτητα ιδιωτικά γραφεία την επιλογή σας να υποτιτλίσετε ή να επιγλωτίσετε κάποιο συγκεκριμένο πρόγραμμα;

9. Με ποια κριτήρια αποφασίζετε αν κάποιο ξένο πρόγραμμα πρέπει να υποτιτλιστεί ή να επιγλωτισθεί;

10. Ποια είναι η προσωπικά σας άποψη σχετικά με την ιδανικότερη μέθοδο μετάφρασης ξένων παιδικών προγραμμάτων;

11. Ποια είναι η προσωπική σας άποψη σχετικά με την ιδανικότερη μέθοδο μετάφρασης ξένων προγραμμάτων γενικότερα;

12. Είστε ικανοποιημένοι από τις πωλήσεις και τις ενοικιάσεις των ξένων παιδικών προγραμμάτων που διανέμετε;

13. Πιστεύετε οτι μια διαφορετική μέθοδος μετάφρασης κάποιων παιδικών προγραμμάτων θα μείωνε ή θα αύξανε τις πωλήσεις και τις ενοικιάσεις τους;

Ονοματεπώνυμο ερωτηθέντος:
Ηλικία:
Φύλο:
Θέση / αρμοδιότητες στην εταιρεία:

APPENDIX 3.2
QUESTIONNAIRE FOR VIDEO DISTRIBUTION AGENCIES
(English translation)

RESEARCH ON AUDIOVISUAL TRANSLATION IN GREECE
QUESTIONNAIRE FOR VIDEO DISTRIBUTION AGENCIES

Distribution agency:
Date:
Time:
Place:

1. Who in your agency decides whether a children's product will be distributed subtitled, dubbed or narrated?
2. Do the same people decide on the translation of the other products that your agency distributes?
3. Who translates the products you distribute? Does your agency have its own in-house audiovisual translation department or does it co-operate with private independent audiovisual translation offices?
4. If the translations are undertaken by the translation department of your agency, do you have one administration for subtitling and a separate one for revoicing (narration and dubbing)?
5. If your foreign products are translated by private independent offices, are there any offices with which you are contracted or with which you co-operate on a regular basis?
6. If your foreign products are translated by private independent offices, have you ever entrusted both the subtitling and the revoicing of a product to the same office, and if so which office?
7. If your foreign products are translated by private independent offices, have you ever chosen the office to which you will entrust the translation of a foreign product according to whether this product will be distributed subtitled or revoiced?
8. Do you impose or negotiate with private independent offices your choice to subtitle or to revoice a particular product?
9. What are your criteria for deciding whether a foreign product should be subtitled or dubbed?
10. What is your personal opinion on the optimum language transfer method for foreign children's products?
11. What is your personal opinion on the optimum language transfer method for foreign products in general?
12. Are you satisfied with the sell-through and the rental figures that the children's products you distribute have managed to achieve?
13. Do you believe that a different language transfer method for some of your children's products would decrease or increase their sell-through and rental figures?

Name and surname of questionee: Age:
Gender: Position / Responsibilities in the agency:

APPENDIX 4
SAMPLE PAGE OF TV PROGRAMME FLOW (ANT1 TV)

ANT1 ΤΜΗΜΑ ΠΡΟΓΡΑΜΜΑΤΙΣΜΟΥ

Εβδομάδα 10/96 Πρόγραμμα 2/3-8/3

Ώρα	Σάββατο 2/3	Κυριακή 3/3	Δευτέρα 4/3	Τρίτη 5/3	Τετάρτη 6/3	Πέμπτη 7/3	Παρασκευή 8/3
5.30	05.30 Η ΠΟΛΗ ΠΟΤΕ ΔΕΝ ΚΟΙΜΑΤΑΙ (PICKET FENCES)	(συνέχεια)	(συνέχεια)	(συνέχεια)	(συνέχεια)	(συνέχεια)	05.30 ΟΙ ΥΠΟΠΤΟΙ
6.00				06.00 ΤΑ ΝΕΑ ΤΟΥ ANTENNA SATELLITE	ΤΑ ΝΕΑ ΤΟΥ ANTENNA SATELLITE	ΤΑ ΝΕΑ ΤΟΥ ANTENNA SATELLITE	ΤΑ ΝΕΑ ΤΟΥ ANTENNA SATELLITE
6.30	06.30		ΟΙ ΕΙΔΗΣΕΙΣ ΤΟΥ CBS	ΟΙ ΕΙΔΗΣΕΙΣ ΤΟΥ CBS	ΟΙ ΕΙΔΗΣΕΙΣ ΤΟΥ CBS	ΟΙ ΕΙΔΗΣΕΙΣ ΤΟΥ CBS	ΟΙ ΕΙΔΗΣΕΙΣ ΤΟΥ CBS
6.45	06.45		ΤΗΛΕ ΜΑΡΚΕΤΙΝΓΚ	ΤΗΛΕ ΜΑΡΚΕΤΙΝΓΚ	ΤΗΛΕ ΜΑΡΚΕΤΙΝΓΚ	ΤΗΛΕ ΜΑΡΚΕΤΙΝΓΚ	ΤΗΛΕ ΜΑΡΚΕΤΙΝΓΚ
7.00	07.00 ΣΚΥΛΑΚΙΑ ΕΝ ΔΡΑΣΕΙ	ΣΚΥΛΑΚΙΑ ΕΝ ΔΡΑΣΕΙ	07.00 ΚΑΛΗΜΕΡΑ ΕΛΛΑΔΑ	ΚΑΛΗΜΕΡΑ ΕΛΛΑΔΑ	ΚΑΛΗΜΕΡΑ ΕΛΛΑΔΑ	ΚΑΛΗΜΕΡΑ ΕΛΛΑΔΑ	ΚΑΛΗΜΕΡΑ ΕΛΛΑΔΑ
7.30	07.30 ΟΙ ΠΕΡΙΠΕΤΕΙΕΣ ΤΟΥ ΤΖΙΝ ΤΖΙΝ	ΟΙ ΠΕΡΙΠΕΤΕΙΕΣ ΤΟΥ ΤΖΙΝ ΤΖΙΝ					
8.00	08.00 Ο ΚΑΛΙΜΕΡΟ ΚΑΙ ΟΙ ΦΙΛΟΙ ΤΟΥ	Ο ΚΑΛΙΜΕΡΟ ΚΑΙ ΟΙ ΦΙΛΟΙ ΤΟΥ					
8.15	08.15 ΚΑΙΠΕΡ ΤΟ ΦΑΝΤΑΣΜΑΤΑΚΙ	ΚΑΙΠΕΡ ΤΟ ΦΑΝΤΑΣΜΑΤΑΚΙ					
8.30	08.30 DRAGONBALL	DRAGONBALL					
9.00	09.00 ΜΠΑΤΜΑΝ	ΜΠΑΤΜΑΝ					
9.30	09.30 SAILORMOON	SAILORMOON					
10.00	10.00 Ο ΜΠΑΓΚΣ ΜΠΑΝΝΥ ΚΑΙ Η ΠΑΡΕΑ ΤΟΥ	10.00 VR TROOPERS	10.00 ΠΡΩΙΝΟΣ ΚΑΦΕΣ	ΠΡΩΙΝΟΣ ΚΑΦΕΣ	ΠΡΩΙΝΟΣ ΚΑΦΕΣ	ΠΡΩΙΝΟΣ ΚΑΦΕΣ	ΠΡΩΙΝΟΣ ΚΑΦΕΣ
10.30		10.30 ΠΑΟΥΕΡ ΡΕΤΝΙΖΕΡΣ					
11.00	11.00 VR TROOPERS	11.00 ΑΠΟ ΤΗ ΘΕΣΗ ΤΟΥ ΟΔΗΓΟΥ					
11.30	11.30 ΠΑΟΥΕΡ ΡΕΤΝΙΖΕΡΣ						
12.00	12.00 BRAVO... ΧΑΣΑΤΕ	12.00 ΜΑΖΙ ΤΗΝ ΚΥΡΙΑΚΗ					
12.30	12.30 ΟΙΚΟΓΕΝΕΙΑ ΓΟΥΝΤΕΛΟΟΥ		12.30 ΚΕΝΤΡΙ	ΚΕΝΤΡΙ	ΚΕΝΤΡΙ	ΚΕΝΤΡΙ	ΚΕΝΤΡΙ
13.00	13.00 ΣΟΥΠΕΡ ΣΑΒΒΑΤΟ						
14.00	14.00	14.00	ΤΑ ΝΕΑ ΤΟΥ ΑΝΤ1	ΤΑ ΝΕΑ ΤΟΥ ΑΝΤ1	ΤΑ ΝΕΑ ΤΟΥ ΑΝΤ1	ΤΑ ΝΕΑ ΤΟΥ ΑΝΤ1	ΤΑ ΝΕΑ ΤΟΥ ΑΝΤ1
14.15	14.15 ΣΤΟ ΠΙ ΚΑΙ ΦΙ	14.15 Ο ΑΦΡΟΣ... ΠΟΥ ΣΚΟΤΩΝΕΙ (STRANGE BREW)					
14.40			14.40 ΜΠΕΤΓΟΥΟΤΣ	ΜΠΕΤΓΟΥΟΤΣ	ΜΠΕΤΓΟΥΟΤΣ	ΜΠΕΤΓΟΥΟΤΣ	ΜΠΕΤΓΟΥΟΤΣ
15.40 / 15.45	15.45 ΣΤΗ ΛΕΩΦΟΡΟ ΤΟΥ ΜΕΛΡΟΟΥΖ		15.45 ΑΤΙΘΑΣΑ ΝΙΑΤΑ	ΑΤΙΘΑΣΑ ΝΙΑΤΑ	ΑΤΙΘΑΣΑ ΝΙΑΤΑ	15.40 ΑΤΙΘΑΣΑ ΝΙΑΤΑ	15.45 ΑΤΙΘΑΣΑ ΝΙΑΤΑ
16.00		16.00 ΟΙ ΦΑΝΤΑΡΙΝΕΣ (Ελλ. ταινία)					
16.30 / 16.45	16.45 [illegible]		16.45 ΚΟΚΚΙΝΗ ΚΑΡΤΑ	ΚΟΚΚΙΝΗ ΚΑΡΤΑ	ΚΟΚΚΙΝΗ ΚΑΡΤΑ	16.30 ΚΟΚΚΙΝΗ ΚΑΡΤΑ	16.45 ΚΟΚΚΙΝΗ ΚΑΡΤΑ

APPENDIX 5
SAMPLE PAGE OF CINEMA RELEASES (Prooptiki)

PROOPTIKI 1995-1996

Π Ρ Ο Ο Π Τ Ι Κ Η Α.Ε.

ΚΙΝΗΜΑΤΟΓΡΑΦΙΚΕΣ ΚΑΙ ΕΜΠΟΡΙΚΕΣ ΕΠΙΧ/ΣΕΙΣ
ΚΩΛΕΤΤΗ 40-42, ΑΘΗΝΑ - 106 82
ΤΗΛ.: 3844541-5, FAX: 3813762, TLX: 216392 CDF GR 225806 CCT GR

ORION

ΤΙΤΛΟΣ	ΣΚΗΝΟΘΕΣΙΑ	ΠΡΩΤΑΓΩΝΙΣΤΕΣ	ΕΙΔΟΣ ΤΑΙΝΙΑΣ	ΧΑΡ/ΜΟΣ ΔΙΑΡΚΕΙΑ
ΤΑ ΚΑΚΑ ΠΑΙΔΙΑ BAD BOYS	ΜΑΙΚΛ ΜΠΕΗ	ΜΑΡΤΙΝ ΛΩΡΕΝΣ ΓΟΥΙΛ ΣΜΙΘ	ΑΣΤΥΝΟΜΙΚΗ ΠΕΡΙΠΕΤΕΙΑ	ΕΓΧΡ.Α-17 2.00'
ΜΠΛΕ ΟΥΡΑΝΟΣ BLUE SKY	TONY ΡΙΤΣΑΡΝΤΣΟΝ	ΤΖΕΣΙΚΑ ΛΑΝΓΚ ΤΟΜΥ ΛΗ ΤΖΟΟΥΝΣ	ΚΟΙΝΩΝΙΚΟ ΟΣΚΑΡ Α' ΓΥΝ. ΡΟΛΟΥ	ΕΓΧΡ. ΚΑΤ. 1.42'
ΝΤΕΣΠΕΡΑΝΤΟ DESPERADO	ΡΟΜΠΕΡΤ ΡΟΝΤΡΙΓΚΕΖ	ΑΝΤΟΝΙΟ ΜΠΑΝΤΕΡΑΣ ΣΑΛΜΑ ΧΑΗΕΚ	ΠΕΡΙΠΕΤΕΙΑ	ΕΓΧΡ. ΚΑΤ. 1.45'
Ο ΔΙΑΒΟΛΟΣ ΣΕ ΜΠΛΕ ΦΟΡΕΜΑ DEVIL IN A BLUE DRESS	ΚΑΡΛ ΦΡΑΝΚΛΙΝ	ΝΤΕΝΖΕΛ ΟΥΑΣΙΝΓΚΤΟΝ ΤΖΕΝΙΦΕΡ ΜΠΗΛΣ	ΦΙΛΜ ΝΟΥΑΡ	ΕΓΧΡ.Κ.13 1.42'
ΛΑΝΣΕΛΟΤ, Ο ΠΡΩΤΟΣ ΙΠΠΟΤΗΣ FIRST KNIGHT	ΤΖΕΡΥ ΖΟΥΚΕΡ	ΣΩΝ ΚΟΝΝΕΡΥ ΡΙΤΣΑΡΝΤ ΓΚΗΡ ΤΖΟΥΛΙΑ ΟΡΜΟΝΤ	ΕΠΙΚΗ ΠΕΡΙΠΕΤΕΙΑ	ΕΓΧΡ. ΚΑΤ. 2.15'
ΤΟ ΚΡΗΣΦΥΓΕΤΟ HIDEAWAY	ΜΠΡΕΤ ΛΕΟΝΑΡΝΤ	ΤΖΕΦ ΓΚΟΛΝΤΜΠΛΑΜ ΑΛΦΡΕΝΤ ΜΟΛΙΝΑ	ΘΡΙΛΕΡ	ΕΓΧΡ. Α. 17 ΣΚΟΠ. 1.45
ΤΖΟΥΜΑΝΤΖΙ JUMANJI	ΤΖΟ ΤΖΟΝΣΤΟΝ	ΡΟΜΠΙΝ ΓΟΥΙΛΛΙΑΜΣ ΜΠΟΝΙ ΧΑΝΤ	ΦΑΝΤΑΣΤΙΚΗ ΠΕΡΙΠΕΤΕΙΑ	ΕΓΧΡ. ΚΑΤ. 1.45'
ΜΙΚΡΕΣ ΚΥΡΙΕΣ LITTLE WOMEN	ΓΚΙΛΙΑΝ ΑΡΜΣΤΡΟΝΓΚ	ΓΟΥΙΝΟΝΑ ΡΑΙΝΤΕΡ ΣΟΥΖΑΝ ΣΑΡΑΝΤΟΝ	ΚΟΙΝΩΝΙΚΟ	ΕΓΧΡ. ΚΑΤ. 2.00'
ΜΑΙΡΗ ΡΑΙΛΥ MARY REILLY	ΣΤΗΒΕΝ ΦΡΗΑΡΣ	ΤΖΟΥΛΙΑ ΡΟΜΠΕΡΤΣ ΤΖΩΝ ΜΑΛΚΟΒΙΤΣ	ΔΡΑΜΑ ΕΠΟΧΗΣ	ΕΓΧΡ. Α-13 1.49'
ΛΟΓΙΚΗ & ΕΥΑΙΣΘΗΣΙΑ SENSE & SENSIBILITY	ΑΝΓΚ ΛΗ	ΕΜΑ ΤΟΜΣΟΝ ΧΙΟΥ ΓΚΡΑΝΤ	ΚΟΙΝΩΝΙΚΟ ΟΣΚΑΡ ΣΕΝΑΡΙΟΥ	ΕΓΧΡ. ΚΑΤ. 2.18'
ΠΑΓΙΔΕΥΜΕΝΗ ΣΤΟ ΔΙΚΤΥΟ THE NET	ΙΡΒΙΝ ΓΟΥΙΝΚΛΕΡ	ΣΑΝΤΡΑ ΜΠΟΥΛΟΚ ΝΤΕΝΙΣ ΜΙΛΕΡ ΤΖΕΡΕΜΙ ΝΟΡΘΑΜ	ΠΕΡΙΠΕΤΕΙΑ	ΕΓΧΡ.ΚΑΤ. 1.55'
ΓΡΗΓΟΡΗ & ΘΑΝΑΣΙΜΗ THE QUICK & THE DEAD	ΣΑΜ ΡΕΙΜΙ	ΣΑΡΟΝ ΣΤΟΟΥΝ ΤΖΗΝ ΧΑΚΜΑΝ	ΓΟΥΕΣΤΕΡΝ	ΕΓΧΡ. Α.17 1.49'

APPENDIX 6
SAMPLE PAGE OF VIDEO RELEASES (VIDEOSONIC)

VIDEOSONIC S.A

ΚΑΤΗΓΟΡΙΑ : ΠΑΙΔΙΚΑ

Α/Α	ΔΙΕΘΝΗΣ ΤΙΤΛΟΣ	ΕΛΛΗΝΙΚΟΣ ΤΙΤΛΟΣ	ΔΙΑΡΚΕΙΑ	SUBTITLED	DUBBED	NARRATION	CARTOON
1	BINGO	ΜΠΙΝΓΚΟ	86'	√			
2	LAST ACTION HERO	Ο ΤΕΛΕΥΤΑΙΟΣ ΜΕΓΑΛΟΣ ΗΡΩΑΣ	130'	√			
3	MY GIRL	ΤΟ ΚΟΡΙΤΣΙ ΜΟΥ	98'	√			
4	MY GIRL 2	ΤΟ ΚΟΡΙΤΣΙ ΜΟΥ No 2	110'	√			
5	HOOK	ΚΑΠΤΑΙΝ ΧΟΥΚ	135'	√			
6	ANNIE	ΑΝΝΥ	122'	√			
7	BARBIE	ΧΟΡΕΨΤΕ ΜΕ ΤΗΝ BARBIE	30'			√	
8	PIPPI LONGSTOCKING	ΟΙ ΠΕΡΙΠΕΤΕΙΕΣ ΤΗΣ ΠΙΠΗΣ ΦΑΚΙΔΟΜΥΤΗ	97'		√		
9	THE THIEF OF BAGHDAD	Ο ΚΛΕΦΤΗΣ ΤΗΣ ΒΑΓΔΑΤΗΣ	98'	√			
10	JASON & ARGONAUTS	ΙΑΣΩΝ & ΟΙ ΑΡΓΟΝΑΥΤΕΣ	100'	√			
11	LONG SHIPS	ΒΙΚΙΝΓΚΣ	122'	√			
12	SINBAD & EYE OF TIGER	Ο ΣΕΒΑΧ ΕΠΙΤΙΘΕΤΑΙ	110'	√			
13	THE 3 WORLDS OF GULLIVER	ΤΑ ΤΑΞΙΔΙΑ ΤΟΥ ΓΚΙΟΥΛΙΒΕΡ	95'	√			
14	MYSTERIOUS ISLAND	Η ΜΥΣΤΗΡΙΩΔΗΣ ΝΗΣΟΣ - ΙΟΥΛ ΒΕΡΝ	96'	√			
15	WILLOW	ΓΟΥΙΛΛΟΟΥ, Η ΟΡΓΗ ΤΩΝ ΘΡΥΛΩΝ	125'	√			
16	KRULL	ΚΡΟΥΛ	115'	√			
17	ADVENTURES MUNCHAUSEN	ΟΙ ΠΕΡΙΠ ΒΑΡΩΝΟΥ ΜΥΝΧΑΟΥΖΕΝ	121'	√			
18	THE SWAN PRINCESS	Η ΠΡΙΓΚΙΠΙΣΣΑ ΤΩΝ ΚΥΚΝΩΝ	90'		√		√
19	PRINCESS AND THE GOBLIN	Η ΒΑΣΙΛΟΠΟΥΛΑ & ΚΑΣΤΡΟ ΠΑΡΑΜΥΘΙΩΝ	85'		√		√
20	POWER RANGERS - GREEN MO MORE	ΕΠΙΧΕΙΡΗΣΗ ΔΙΑΣΩΣΗΣ	60'		√		
21	POWER RANGERS - WHITE LIGHT	ΣΤΗΝ ΠΑΓΙΔΑ ΤΟΥ ΖΕΝΤ	60'		√		
22	POWER RANGERS - THE POWER TRANSFER	ΔΙΠΛΗ ΕΝΕΡΓΕΙΑ	60'		√		
23	POWER RANGERS RANGERS BACK IN TIME	ΕΠΙΣΤΡΟΦΗ ΣΤΟ ΠΑΡΕΛΘΟΝ	60'		√		
24	POWER RANGERS - WILD WEST POWER RANGERS	ΠΕΡΙΠΕΤΕΙΑ ΣΤΗΝ ΑΓΡΙΑ ΔΥΣΗ	50'		√		
25	3 NINJAS KICK BACK	ΟΙ 3 ΝΙΝΤΖΑ ΞΑΝΑΧΤΥΠΟΥΝ	101'	√			
26	3 NINJAS KNUCKLE UP	3 ΓΕΝΝΑΙΟΙ ΜΑΧΗΤΕΣ	90'	√			
27	INSPECTOR GADGET SAVES CHRISTMAS	Ο ΑΣΤΥΝΟΜΟΣ ΣΑΙΝΗΣ / ΧΡΙΣΤ ΠΕΡΙΠ	30'		√		√
28	SANTA & THE MAGICIAN	Ο ΑΗ ΒΑΣΙΛΗΣ & Ο ΜΑΓΟΣ	30'		√		√
29	SANTA AND THE TOOTHFAIRIES	ΤΟ ΧΡΙΣΤΟΥΓΕΝΝΙΑΤΙΚΟ ΔΩΡΟ	30'		√		√
30	SANTA ' S FIRST CHRISTMAS	ΤΑ ΠΡΩΤΑ ΧΡΙΣΤΟΥΓΕΝΝΑ	30'		√		√
31	NICK & NOEL	ΝΙΚ & ΝΟΕΛ / ΜΙΑ ΧΡΙΣΤΟΥΓ ΕΥΧΗ	30'		√		√
32	THE BEARS WHO SAVED CHRISTMAS	ΤΑ ΑΡΚΟΥΔΑΚΙΑ ΣΩΖΟΥΝ / ΧΡΙΣΤΟΥΓ	30'		√		√
33	THE SECRET GARDEN	Ο ΜΥΣΤΙΚΟΣ ΚΗΠΟΣ	75'		√		√
34	PETER PAN	ΠΗΤΕΡ ΠΑΝ	60'		√		√
35	THE MAGIC FLUTE	Ο ΜΑΓΕΜΕΝΟΣ ΑΥΛΟΣ	60'		√		√
36	SKY SURFERS No1 - CITY OF TERROR & DEATH PAINT	Η ΠΟΛΗ ΤΟΥ ΤΡΟΜΟΥ	50'		√		√
37	STARLA No1 - JEWEL QUEST	ΤΟ ΜΑΓΙΚΟ ΔΙΑΜΑΝΤΙ	50'		√		√
38	ACTION MAN No1 - EXPLOSIVE SITUATION	ΕΚΡΗΚΤΙΚΗ ΚΑΤΑΣΤΑΣΗ	50'		√		√
39	ULTRA FORCE No1 - PRIME TIME & STUFF OF HEROES	ΑΤΣΑΛΙΝΟΙ ΗΡΩΕΣ	50'		√		√

APPENDIX 7.1
SAMPLE SHEET OF COLLECTIVE VIEWING RATES (AGB Hellas)

...RONO-TV : Printing GREECE -- (C) 1990 A 2 M [23-06-1997] [14:03:27] 84
Number of programmes found 476
01/03/96-31/03/96
[Weighted averages] (Filt'd)

CHN	WD	DATE	S.Tim	PROGRAMMES	DUR	TVRs ΣΥΝ	MktSh ΣΥΝ	TVRs ΠΑΙΔ	MktSh ΠΑΙΔ
			10.34	Unnamed request	27	0.8	8.3	3.3	23.0
ΜΕΓ	Sa	16/03/96	08.07	ΦΛΙΝΤΣΤΟΟΥΝΣ	26	0.5	13.2	4.2	28.6
ΜΕΓ	Sa	16/03/96	07.42	ΤΕΝ-ΤΕΝ	23	0.3	9.7	3.0	32.6
ΜΕΓ	Sa	16/03/96	07.14	ΣΤΡΟΥΜΦ	25	0.3	14.3	1.5	30.6
ΜΕΓ	Sa	16/03/96	09.00	ΝΤΙΣΝΕΪ ΚΛΑΜΠ (ΣΥΝ)	103	1.8	23.1	9.2	29.7
ΜΕΓ	Su	17/03/96	08.10	ΦΛΙΝΤΣΤΟΟΥΝΣ	25	0.4	11.8	2.2	22.0
ΜΕΓ	Su	17/03/96	07.04	ΝΤΡΟΥΠΙ Ο ΦΟΒΕΡΟΣ ΝΤΕΤΕΚΤΙΒ	22	0.2	15.4	0.1	7.7
ΜΕΓ	Su	17/03/96	07.44	ΤΕΝ-ΤΕΝ	23	0.3	13.0	1.0	17.2
ΜΕΓ	Su	17/03/96	08.38	ΝΤΑΡΚΓΟΥΙΝΓΚ ΝΤΑΚ	22	0.6	13.6	3.6	27.9
ΜΕΓ	Su	17/03/96	09.03	ΝΤΙΣΝΕΪ ΚΛΑΜΠ (ΣΥΝ)	55	1.3	18.6	6.4	32.3
ΜΕΓ	Su	17/03/96	07.29	ΣΤΡΟΥΜΦ	12	0.2	11.1	0.9	22.5
ΜΕΓ	Su	17/03/96	06.40	ΟΙ ΔΕΙΝΟΣΑΥΡΟΙ	22	0.1	9.1	0.1	12.5
ΜΕΓ	Su	17/03/96	10.04	ΜΙΚΡΟ ΜΟΥ ΠΟΝΥ	22	1.4	14.9	7.1	29.[illegible]
ΜΕΓ	Mo	18/03/96	06.05	ΟΙ ΔΕΙΝΟΣΑΥΡΟΙ (ΣΥΝ)	46	0.1	9.1	0.8	0.0
ΜΕΓ	Tu	19/03/96	06.06	ΟΙ ΔΕΙΝΟΣΑΥΡΟΙ (ΣΥΝ)	47	0.1	11.1	0.0	0.0
ΜΕΓ	We	20/03/96	06.04	ΟΙ ΔΕΙΝΟΣΑΥΡΟΙ	23	0.0	0.0	0.9	0.0
ΜΕΓ	Sa	23/03/96	08.58	ΝΤΙΣΝΕΪ ΚΛΑΜΠ (ΣΥΝ)	106	1.8	27.7	10.1	42.4
ΜΕΓ	Sa	23/03/96	08.05	ΦΛΙΝΤΣΤΟΟΥΝΣ	25	0.6	15.8	3.1	27.4
ΜΕΓ	Sa	23/03/96	08.34	ΜΑΪΤΙ ΜΑΞ	20	0.9	19.1	4.8	29.1
ΜΕΓ	Sa	23/03/96	06.45	Ο ΧΑΖΟΣ ΚΑΙ Ο ΧΑΖΟΥΛΗΣ,ΔΥΟ ΥΠΕΡΟΧΑ ΣΚΥΛΑ	23	0.2	16.7	0.6	27.3
ΜΕΓ	Sa	23/03/96	07.11	ΣΤΡΟΥΜΦ	24	0.2	13.3	1.3	38.2
ΜΕΓ	Sa	23/03/96	07.38	ΤΕΝ-ΤΕΝ	23	0.3	11.5	2.7	35.5
ΜΕΓ	Su	24/03/96	09.14	ΝΤΙΣΝΕΪ ΚΛΑΜΠ (ΣΥΝ)	56	1.5	18.8	6.4	37.2
ΜΕΓ	Su	24/03/96	10.16	ΜΙΚΡΟ ΜΟΥ ΠΟΝΥ	22	1.9	19.6	7.8	37.5
ΜΕΓ	Su	24/03/96	07.29	ΣΤΡΟΥΜΦ	23	0.3	17.6	1.3	33.3
ΜΕΓ	Su	24/03/96	08.20	ΦΛΙΝΤΣΤΟΟΥΝΣ	25	0.4	9.8	1.8	20.9
ΜΕΓ	Su	24/03/96	08.49	ΝΤΑΡΚΓΟΥΙΝΓΚ ΝΤΑΚ	22	0.8	14.5	2.9	26.0
ΜΕΓ	Su	24/03/96	07.55	ΤΕΝ-ΤΕΝ	23	0.2	7.1	0.9	16.7
ΜΕΓ	Su	24/03/96	07.05	ΝΤΡΟΥΠΙ Ο ΦΟΒΕΡΟΣ ΝΤΕΤΕΚΤΙΒ	21	0.2	16.7	1.3	48.1
ΜΕΓ	Mo	25/03/96	07.10	ΣΚΛΩΝΟΝΙΤΣΑΚΙΑ (ΣΥΝ)	49	0.3	17.6	0.9	64.3
ΜΕΓ	Mo	25/03/96	06.48	ΚΙΝΟΥΜΕΝΑ ΣΧΕΔΙΑ: THE TERRIBLE TWO	21	0.3	23.1	0.6	50.0
ΜΕΓ	Tu	26/03/96	06.10	ΚΙΝΟΥΜΕΝΑ ΣΧΕΔΙΑ: ΝΤΑΓΚ	25	0.2	14.3	0.0	0.0
ΜΕΓ	We	27/03/96	06.00	ΚΙΝΟΥΜΕΝΑ ΣΧΕΔΙΑ: ΝΤΑΓΚ (ΣΥΝ)	50	0.1	10.0	0.2	66.7
ΜΕΓ	Th	28/03/96	06.02	ΚΙΝΟΥΜΕΝΑ ΣΧΕΔΙΑ: ΝΤΑΓΚ (ΣΥΝ)	50	0.1	9.1	0.0	0.0
ΜΕΓ	Fr	29/03/96	06.04	ΚΙΝΟΥΜΕΝΑ ΣΧΕΔΙΑ: ΝΤΑΓΚ (ΣΥΝ)	48	0.0	0.0	0.0	0.0
ΜΕΓ	Sa	30/03/96	08.20	ΦΛΙΝΤΣΤΟΟΥΝΣ	25	1.1	22.9	6.8	35.9
ΜΕΓ	Sa	30/03/96	07.40	ΣΤΡΟΥΜΦ	13	0.2	8.0	0.8	12.3
ΜΕΓ	Sa	30/03/96	07.56	ΤΕΝ-ΤΕΝ	22	0.8	21.6	4.2	35.9
ΜΕΓ	Sa	30/03/96	09.11	ΝΤΙΣΝΕΪ ΚΛΑΜΠ (ΣΥΝ)	99	1.8	26.5	9.3	48.1
ΜΕΓ	Sa	30/03/96	06.25	ΚΙΝΟΥΜΕΝΑ ΣΧΕΔΙΑ: ΝΤΑΓΚ (ΣΥΝ)	48	0.1	10.0	0.3	30.8
ΜΕΓ	Sa	30/03/96	07.16	Ο ΧΑΖΟΣ ΚΑΙ Ο ΧΑΖΟΥΛΗΣ,ΔΥΟ ΥΠΕΡΟΧΑ ΣΚΥΛΑ	21	0.2	10.8	0.7	15.2
ΜΕΓ	Sa	30/03/96	10.50	ΠΑΙΔΙΚΗ ΤΑΙΝΙΑ: ΕΛΙΟΤ, Ο ΤΡΕΛΛΟΣ ΤΡΕΛΛΟΣ	126	0.8	10.5	3.4	19.9
ΜΕΓ	Sa	30/03/96	08.48	ΜΑΪΤΙ ΜΑΞ	20	1.2	21.8	7.7	37.7
ΜΕΓ	Su	31/03/96	08.04	ΦΛΙΝΤΣΤΟΟΥΝΣ	26	0.5	19.2	0.4	10.3
ΜΕΓ	Su	31/03/96	06.57	ΝΤΡΟΥΠΙ Ο ΦΟΒΕΡΟΣ ΝΤΕΤΕΚΤΙΒ	23	0.1	10.0	0.0	0.0
ΜΕΓ	Su	31/03/96	10.02	ΜΙΚΡΟ ΜΟΥ ΠΟΝΥ	22	2.8	25.0	9.3	45.7
ΜΕΓ	Su	31/03/96	08.59	ΝΤΙΣΝΕΪ ΚΛΑΜΠ (ΣΥΝ)	56	1.0	22.7	3.4	33.0
ΜΕΓ	Su	31/03/96	07.22	ΣΤΡΟΥΜΦ	13	0.1	11.1	0.2	66.7
ΜΕΓ	Su	31/03/96	07.41	ΤΕΝ-ΤΕΝ	20	0.3	18.6	0.0	0.0
ΜΕΓ	Su	31/03/96	08.34	ΝΤΑΡΚΓΟΥΙΝΓΚ ΝΤΑΚ	22	0.4	12.9	1.8	19.2
ΑΝΤ	Sa	02/03/96	11.02	VR TROOPERS (ΣΥΝ)	24	2.2	28.2	12.7	49.4
ΑΝΤ	Sa	02/03/96	09.54	Ο ΜΠΑΓΚΣ ΜΠΑΝΙ ΚΑΙ Η ΠΑΡΕΑ ΤΟΥ (ΣΥΝ)	65	1.6	20.8	8.6	30.7
ΑΝΤ	Sa	02/03/96	08.27	DRAGONBALL (ΣΥΝ)	26	1.8	36.7	8.6	54.8
ΑΝΤ	Sa	02/03/96	08.58	ΜΠΑΤΜΑΝ (ΣΥΝ)	26	1.7	27.9	8.7	62.6
ΑΝΤ	Sa	02/03/96	07.34	Ο ΚΑΛΙΜΕΡΟ ΚΑΙ ΟΙ ΦΙΛΟΙ ΤΟΥ	13	0.5	15.2	2.8	37.3
ΑΝΤ	Sa	02/03/96	07.27	ΟΙ ΠΕΡΙΠΕΤΕΙΕΣ ΤΟΥ ΤΣΙΝ-ΤΣΙΝ (ΣΥΝ)	22	0.3	11.5	1.6	36.4
ΑΝΤ	Sa	02/03/96	08.11	ΚΑΙΣΕΡ	13	1.1	28.2	6.6	63.4
ΑΝΤ	Sa	02/03/96	09.25	SAILORMOON (ΣΥΝ)	25	1.5	21.7	8.4	33.8
ΑΝΤ	Sa	02/03/96	07.00	ΣΚΥΛΑΚΙΑ ΣΕ ΔΡΑΣΗ (ΣΥΝ)	22	0.1	5.3	4.3	27.3
ΑΝΤ	Sa	02/03/96	11.31	ΠΑΟΥΕΡ ΡΕΪΝΤΖΕΡΣ (ΣΥΝ)	22	2.6	32.1	14.8	52.2
ΑΝΤ	Su	03/03/96	08.59	ΜΠΑΤΜΑΝ (ΣΥΝ)	23	1.5	20.8	7.6	50.0
ΑΝΤ	Su	03/03/96	09.58	VR TROOPERS (ΣΥΝ)	24	1.7	16.5	8.0	34.2
ΑΝΤ	Su	03/03/96	08.29	DRAGONBALL (ΣΥΝ)	26	1.1	19.3	6.6	54.1
ΑΝΤ	Su	03/03/96	10.28	ΠΑΟΥΕΡ ΡΕΪΝΤΖΕΡΣ (ΣΥΝ)	23	2.2	19.7	13.8	51.3
ΑΝΤ	Su	03/03/96	09.29	SAILORMOON (ΣΥΝ)	23	1.5	17.8	7.6	37.6
ΑΝΤ	Su	03/03/96	08.13	ΚΑΙΣΕΡ	13	0.8	21.1	5.3	62.4
ΑΝΤ	Su	03/03/96	07.58	Ο ΚΑΛΙΜΕΡΟ ΚΑΙ ΟΙ ΦΙΛΟΙ ΤΟΥ	13	0.4	15.4	2.7	46.6
ΑΝΤ	Su	03/03/96	07.28	ΟΙ ΠΕΡΙΠΕΤΕΙΕΣ ΤΟΥ ΤΣΙΝ-ΤΣΙΝ (ΣΥΝ)	22	0.3	17.6	1.8	48.4
ΑΝΤ	Su	03/03/96	07.02	ΣΚΥΛΑΚΙΑ ΣΕ ΔΡΑΣΗ (ΣΥΝ)	22	0.0	0.0	0.0	0.0
ΑΝΤ	Sa	09/03/96	11.20	ΠΑΟΥΕΡ ΡΕΪΝΤΖΕΡΣ (ΣΥΝ)	22	3.3	34.0	15.6	62.9
ΑΝΤ	Sa	09/03/96	07.08	ΣΚΥΛΑΚΙΑ ΣΕ ΔΡΑΣΗ (ΣΥΝ)	22	0.2	5.3	0.7	31.8
ΑΝΤ	Sa	09/03/96	08.31	DRAGONBALL (ΣΥΝ)	24	1.2	25.0	6.6	34.1

APPENDIX 7.2
SAMPLE SHEET OF ANALYTIC VIEWING RATES (AGB Hellas)

* P R O G R A M M I N G   G R I D *
ΤΕΤ 20/03/1996 - ΣΥΝΟΛΟ (ΠΛΗΘΥΣΜΟΣ: 5832925)
ΤΗΛ=ΤΗΛΕΘΕΑΣΗ ΜΕΣΟΥ ΛΕΠΤΟΥ ΜΡΔ=ΜΕΡΙΔΙΟ

	MEGA			ANT1			ΣΚΑΙ			STAR			TOTAL		
	ΤΙΤΛΟΣ ΕΚΠΟΜΠΗΣ	ΤΗΛ%	ΜΡΔ%	ΤΙΤΛΟΣ ΕΚΠΟΜΠΗΣ	ΤΗΛ%	ΜΡΔ%	ΤΙΤΛΟΣ ΕΚΠΟΜΠΗΣ	ΤΗΛ%	ΜΡΔ%	ΤΙΤΛΟΣ ΕΚΠΟΜΠΗΣ	ΤΗΛ%	ΜΡΔ%	ΤΗΛ%	ΜΡΔ%	
02.00-07:59	ΠΡΩΙΝΗ ΣΥΧΝΟΤΗΤΑ 06:59	0.5	21.2	ΚΑΛΗΜΕΡΑ ΕΛΛΑΔΑ 07:00	0.6	26.8	24 ΩΡΕΣ ΣΕ 90 ΛΕΠΤΑ 02.02	0.3	12.7	ΟΙ ΔΡΟΜΟΙ ΤΟΥ ΣΑΝ Φ 02:04	0.2	10.7	2.4	100.0	02.00-07:59
08.00-08:59		1.0	19.9		2.6	53.9	ΣΚΑΙ ΕΝΗΜΕΡΩΣΗ 07:30	0.3	5.2	ΩΛΑ ΓΙΑ ΤΟ ΓΕΛΙΟ 08.06	0.3	6.2	4.9	100.0	08.00-08:59
09.00-09:59		1.4	20.0		3.9	53.8		0.3	4.2	ΡΕΠΟΡΤΑΖ ΣΤΗΝ ΟΜΙΧΛΗ 09.12	0.5	6.6	7.2	100.0	09:00-09:59
10.00-10:59	ΜΕΤΑΞΥ ΜΑΣ 10.05	2.1	25.2	ΠΡΩΙΝΟΣ ΚΑΦΕΣ 10:13	3.6	42.1	ΧΩΡΙΣ ΑΝΑΙΣΘΗΤΙΚΟ: 10:02	0.1	4.8		1.4	16.1	8.5	100.0	10:00-10:59
11.00-11:59		2.8	28.5		3.4	33.8	ΑΛΗΘΙΝΕΣ ΙΣΤΟΡΙΕΣ: 11:14	0.7	6.7		1.5	14.6	10.0	100.0	11:00-11:59
12.00-12:29		2.7	26.6		3.6	35.5	24 ΩΡΕΣ ΣΕ 90 ΛΕΠΤΑ 11:59	0.8	7.9		0.9	3.0	10.0	100.0	12:00-12:29
12:30-12:59	ΤΟ ΡΕΤΙΡΕ ΕΠΑΝΑΛΗΨ 12:38	3.3	30.7	ΚΕΝΤΡΙ 12:3[illegible]	4.0	37.0		0.3	8.0	ΠΕΣΤΟ ΣΤΗ ΣΕΜΙΝΑ: Ε 12:21	0.5	[illegible]	10.9	100.0	12:30-12:59
13:00-13:29		[illegible]	29.9		5.1	15.1		0.8	6.1		0.4	2.9	13.4	100.0	13:00-13:29
13:30-13:59	ΡΟΥΚ ΤΣΙΚ 13:21	5.2	33.3		4.8	31.1	ΜΕΣΗΜΕΡΙΑΝΕΣ ΕΙΔΗΣΕ 13:31	1.8	11.3	ΜΕΣΗΜΕΡΙΑΝΕΣ ΕΙΔΗΣΕ 13:27	0.9	6.0	15.6	100.0	13:30-13:59
14:00-14:14	ΜΙΚΡΑ ΚΑΙ ΜΕΓΑΛΑ ΣΕ 13:59	6.7	37.4	ΕΙΔΗΣΕΙΣ ΑΝΤΕΝΝΑ ΣΤ 13:58	4.7	26.5		1.6	8.7		1.4	7.7	17.9	100.0	14:00-14:14
14:15-14:29		7.4	37.6		5.5	28.2	ΔΙΑΦΗΜΙΣΕΙΣ: 11 14:22	1.0	4.9	ΜΑΥΡΗ ΚΑΛΛΟΝΗ 14:10	2.3	12.0	19.6	100.0	14:15-14:29
14:30-14:44		7.2	34.8		4.9	23.4	ΕΛΛ.ΤΑΙΝΙΑ ΣΤΟ ΣΚΑΙ 14:27	1.6	7.9		3.7	17.7	20.9	100.0	14:30-14:44
14:45-14:59	ΧΑΜΟΓΕΛΑΣΤΕ ΕΙΝΑΙ ΜΕ 14:50	5.0	23.5	ΚΛΕΙΓΟΥΣΙ. ΕΠΑΝΑΛΗ 14:43	5.3	24.8		2.8	13.3	ΤΟ ΘΑΥΜΑ ΤΗΣ ΑΓΑΠΗΣ 14:38	4.5	21.1	21.5	100.0	14:45-14:59
15:00-15:14		4.3	18.0		6.5	27.1		3.1	13.0	ΔΙΑΦΗΜΙΣΕΙΣ: 12 15:06	4.7	19.8	23.9	100.0	15:00-15:14
15:15-15:29		3.4	13.7		5.8	23.4	ΔΙΑΦΗΜΙΣΕΙΣ-ΣΦΗΝΕΣ: 15:16	1.9	7.7	ΤΟΛΜΗ ΚΑΙ ΓΟΗΤΕΙΑ 15:11	8.5	33.9	24.9	100.0	15:15-15:29
15:30-15:44		4.5	18.7		4.6	18.4	ΕΛΛ.ΤΑΙΝΙΑ ΣΤΟ ΣΚΑΙ 14:27	1.9	7.7		8.4	34.3	24.7	100.0	15:30-15:44
15:45-15:59		5.6	24.6	ΑΤΙΘΑΣΑ ΝΙΑΤΑ 15:42	3.6	16.2	ΑΛΗΘΙΝΕΣ ΙΣΤΟΡΙΕΣ 15:49	2.0	9.1	ΔΙΑΦΗΜΙΣΕΙΣ-ΣΦΗΝΕΣ: 15:50	4.9	21.8	22.6	100.0	15:45-15:59
16:00-16:14		5.3	23.8		3.6	16.4		2.8	12.6	ΓΙΑ ΤΗΝ ΑΓΑΠΗ ΤΗΣ Ρ 15:48	4.7	21.4	22.2	100.0	16:00-16:14
16:15-16:29		5.7	26.0		4.3	19.6		3.0	13.6	ΔΙΑΦΗΜΙΣΕΙΣ-ΣΦΗΝΕΣ: 16.15	3.5	15.8	22.0	100.0	16:15-16:29
16:30-16:44		6.4	30.2	ΚΟΚΚΙΝΗ ΚΑΡΤΑ 16:35	3.8	18.2		2.1	9.9	ΠΕΣΤΟ ΣΤΗ ΣΕΜΙΝΑ 16:30	3.7	17.5	21.0	100.0	16:30-16:44
16:45-16:59		5.1	23.9		6.1	28.6	ΣΤΟ ΒΑΡΕΛΑΔΙΚΟ 16:41	1.0	4.8		3.8	18.0	21.3	100.0	16:45-16:59
17:00-17:14		4.6	22.7		6.7	33.2		1.1	5.5		2.8	13.8	20.2	100.0	17:00-17:14
17:15-17:29		4.3	21.7		7.0	35.4		1.5	7.4	ΕΛΛ.ΤΑΙΝΙΑ ΣΤΟ STAR 17:20	2.0	10.3	19.9	100.0	17:15-17:29
17:30-17:44		4.7	22.5		7.0	33.9	ΑΠΟΓΕΥΜΑΤΙΝΕΣ ΕΙΔΗΣ 17:25	2.0	9.9		2.8	13.8	20.7	100.0	17:30-17:44
17:45-17:59		3.6	17.1		6.8	33.0	ΧΩΡΙΣ ΑΝΑΙΣΘΗΤΙΚΟ 17:44	2.6	12.6		3.6	17.6	20.8	100.0	17:45-17:59
18:00-18:14	ΔΙΑΦΗΜΙΣΕΙΣ-ΣΦΗΝΕΣ 18:08	3.2	15.5	ΕΙΔΗΣΕΙΣ ΑΝΤΕΝΝΑ ΣΤ 18:03	7.5	35.1		2.5	11.6		3.5	16.4	21.5	100.0	18:00-18:14
18:15-18:29	ΟΙ ΑΝΑΡΑΒΕΚΙΟΙ ΕΠΑ 18.07	4.8	20.5	ΚΑΛΗΜΕΡΑ ΖΩΗ 18:10	9.4	40.0		2.3	9.7		2.9	12.5	23.4	100.0	18:15-18:29
18:30-18:44	ΗΡΑΚΛΕΙ Α'ΗΜΙΧ : ΗΡ 18:3[illegible]	4.0	16.6		12.0	49.4		2.3	9.4		2.6	10.6	24.3	100.0	18:30-18:44
18:45-18:59		6.4	26.3	ΔΙΑΦΗΜΙΣΕΙΣ-ΣΦΗΝΕΣ 18:53	7.6	31.0		2.5	10.1		3.8	15.7	24.5	100.0	18:45-18:59
19:00-19:14		[illegible]	32.4	Ο ΚΑΛΥΤΕΡΟΣ [illegible] 18:57	5.8	22.7	ΜΑΛΒΙΝΑ LIVE 19:02	2.8	10.7		4.2	16.4	25.7	100.0	19:00-19:14
19:15-19:29	ΔΙΑΦΗΜΙΣΕΙΣ-ΣΦΗΝΕΣ 19:18	5.8	22.0		7.8	29.7		4.5	17.3	ΠΟΙΝΤΜΑΝ 19.10	2.5	9.7	26.2	100.0	19:15-19:29
19:30-19:44	ΗΡΑΚΛΕΙ Β'ΗΜΙΧ : ΠΑ 19:27	8.4	29.7	Η ΛΑΜΨΗ 19:35	8.8	31.2		2.9	10.2		3.2	11.3	28.1	100.0	19:30-19:44
19:45-19:59		9.2	[illegible]		11.5	37.6	ΓΗ ΒΕΓΗ 19.41	2.0	6.6		2.6	8.6	30.5	100.0	19:45-19:59
20:00-20:14		[illegible]	31.2		12.9	40.5		2.6	8.1	ΒΡΑΔΥΝΕΣ ΕΙΔΗΣΕΙΣ S 19.59	1.7	5.5	31.6	100.0	20:00-20:14
20:15-20:29	ΒΡΑΔΥΝΕΣ ΕΙΔΗΣΕΙΣ Μ 20.23	8.6	27.6	ΒΡΑΔΥΝΕΣ ΕΙΔΗΣΕΙΣ Α 20.22	9.8	31.3	ΒΡΑΔΥΝΕΣ ΕΙΔΗΣΕΙΣ Σ 20:16	4.3	13.6		3.4	10.9	31.2	100.0	20:15-20:29
20:30-20:44		11.8	36.1		9.6	29.2		4.6	14.0		2.2	6.8	32.8	100.0	20:30-20:44
20:45-20:59		13.2	39.0		9.2	27.4		4.4	13.1	ΑΘΛΟΡΑΜΑ 20:54	2.2	6.6	33.8	100.0	20:45-20:59
21:00-21:14	ΑΘΛΗΤΙΚΗ ΕΚΠΟΜΠΗ Ο 21.08	11.3	31.2	ΕΛΛΗ ΚΑΙ ΑΝΝΑ 21:09	7.2	19.9		6.2	17.2	ΕΛΛ.ΤΑΙΝΙΑ ΣΤΟ STAR 21:03	4.4	12.2	36.2	100.0	21:00-21:14
21:15-21:29	ΔΙΑΦΗΜΙΣΕΙΣ: 15 21:18	11.0	27.7		10.9	27.5		4.8	12.1		7.2	18.0	39.8	100.0	21:15-21:29
21:30-21:44	ΠΟΔΟΣΦΑΙΡΟ Α'ΗΜΙΧ.. 21:25	18.6	42.6		8.1	19.7		3.8	8.8		8.1	18.5	43.6	100.0	21:30-21:44
21:45-21:59		20.3	44.5	ΕΛΛ. ΤΑΙΝΙΑ ΣΤΟΝ ΑΝ 21.42	9.0	19.7	ΕΛΛ ΤΑΙΝΙΑ ΣΤΟ ΣΚΑΙ 21.48	2.8	6.1	ΔΙΑΦΗΜΙΣΕΙΣ-ΣΦΗΝΕΣ: 21:44	7.3	16.0	45.5	100.0	21:45-21:59
22:00-22:14		20.5	44.4		9.2	20.1		2.3	5.0	ΕΛΛ.ΤΑΙΝΙΑ ΣΤΟ STAR 21:03	8.6	18.6	46.1	100.0	22:00-22:14
22:15-22:29	ΔΙΑΦΗΜΙΣΕΙΣ ΣΦΗΝΕΣ 22:16	11.6	25.0		11.2	24.0		3.2	6.9		12.0	25.7	46.7	100.0	22:15-22:29
22:30-22:44	ΠΟΔΟΣΦΑΙΡΟ Β'ΗΜΙΧ.: 22.30	18.0	38.3		10.7	22.8		3.0	6.5	ΔΙΑΦΗΜΙΣΕΙΣ-ΣΦΗΝΕΣ: 22:37	8.4	17.8	47.0	100.0	22:30-22:44
22:45-22:59		20.8	44.4		12.0	25.6		2.1	4.5	ΕΛΛ ΤΑΙΝΙΑ ΣΤΟ STAR 21:03	5.3	11.2	46.9	100.0	22:45-22:59
23:00-23:14		20.9	45.8		13.0	28.4		3.4	7.4	ΣΙΝΕ STAR: ΤΟ ΠΝΕΥΜ 22:59	3.4	7.5	45.7	100.0	23:00-23:14
23:15-23:29		14.4	34.1		14.5	34.3	ΑΚΟΥ ΝΑ ΔΕΙΣ 23:17	4.9	11.5	ΔΙΑΦΗΜΙΣΕΙΣ-ΣΦΗΝΕΣ: 23:19	3.2	7.5	42.3	100.0	23:15-23:29
23:30-23:44	ΠΟΔΟΣΦΑΙΡΟ Α'ΗΜΙΧ.. 23:32	10.0	27.2	Η ΩΡΑ ΤΗΣ ΑΛΗΘΕΙΑΣ 23:34	5.0	13.7	ΔΙΑΦΗΜΙΣΕΙΣ-ΣΦΗΝΕΣ: 23:31	6.3	17.2	ΣΙΝΕ STAR: ΤΟ ΠΝΕΥΜ 22:59	7.5	20.4	36.7	100.0	23:30-23:44
23:45-23:59		9.5	28.0		4.7	13.9	ΑΚΟΥ ΝΑ ΔΕΙΣ 23:17	6.6	19.3		5.9	17.3	33.9	100.0	23:45-23:59
24:00-24:29		6.5	22.2		4.4	14.8		5.3	18.0		5.8	19.7	29.5	100.0	24:00-24:29
24:30-24:59	ΕΙΔΗΣΕΙΣ MEGA ΣΤΙΣ 24:30	4.4	19.9		2.7	12.2	ΝΥΚΤΕΡΙΝΕΣ ΕΙΔΗΣΕΙΣ 24:27	3.1	14.1		4.8	21.8	21.9	100.0	24:30-24:59
25:00-25:29	ΠΟΔΟΣΦΑΙΡΟ Β'ΗΜΙΧ.: 24:51	5.1	28.5	ΝΥΧΤΕΡΙΝΕΣ ΕΙΔΗΣΕΙΣ 24:53	1.9	10.6		1.4	8.1	ΞΕΝΗ ΤΑΙΝΙΑ ΣΤΟ STA 25:07	2.9	16.0	17.9	100.0	25:00-25:29
25:30-25:59	ΑΘΛΗΤΙΚΗ ΕΚΠΟΜΠΗ: Η 25.43	3.2	24.6	ΓΚΟΛ ΚΑΙ ΑΛΛΑ 25:20	1.5	11.9	ΤΟ ΜΕΓΑΛΟ ΚΟΛΠΟ: ΕΠ 25.29	1.2	9.4		2.0	15.4	12.8	100.0	25:30-25:59

- 1 -

APPENDIX 8
SAMPLE PAGE WITH DATA ON LOCAL LITERARY PRODUCTS (National Statistics Bureau)

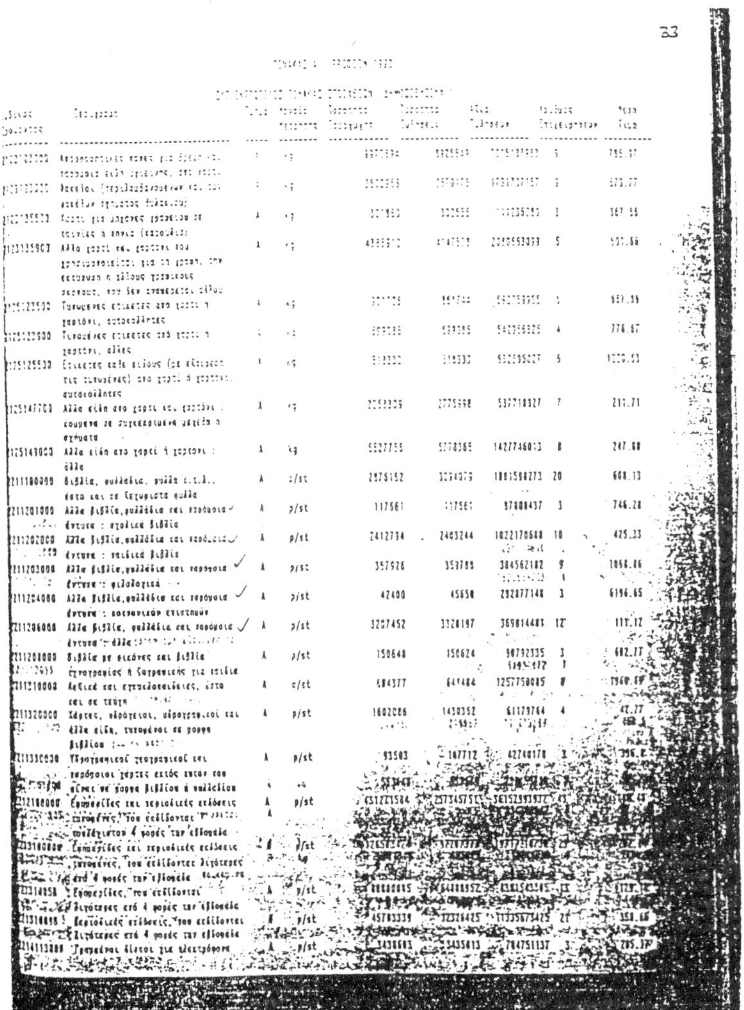

33

[illegible]	[illegible]	[illegible]	kg	[illegible]	[illegible]	[illegible]	5	785.37
[illegible]	[illegible]	[illegible]	kg	[illegible]	[illegible]	[illegible]	[illegible]	[illegible]
[illegible]	[illegible]	A	kg	[illegible]	[illegible]	[illegible]	3	367.56
[illegible]	Άλλο χαρτί και χαρτόνι του χρησιμοποιείται για τη γραφή, την εκτύπωση ή άλλους γραφικούς σκοπούς, που δεν αναφέρεται αλλού	A	kg	[illegible]	[illegible]	2080553099	5	501.66
[illegible]	Τυπωμένες ετικέτες από χαρτί ή χαρτόνι, αυτοκόλλητες	A	kg	[illegible]	[illegible]	[illegible]	[illegible]	657.35
[illegible]	Τυπωμένες ετικέτες από χαρτί ή χαρτόνι, άλλες	[illegible]	kg	[illegible]	[illegible]	542056325	4	776.67
1125125500	Ετικέτες κάθε είδους (μη εκτός τις τυπωμένες) από χαρτί ή χαρτόνι, αυτοκόλλητες	A	kg	[illegible]	[illegible]	532095027	5	[illegible]
1125147700	Άλλα είδη από χαρτί και χαρτόνι κομμένα σε συγκεκριμένα μεγέθη ή σχήματα	A	kg	2052309	2775598	537718327	7	211.71
1125143000	Άλλα είδη από χαρτί ή χαρτόνι : άλλα	A	kg	5527755	5778365	1427746013	8	247.08
2211100000	Βιβλία, φυλλάδια, φύλλα κ.τ.λ., έστω και σε ξεχωριστά φύλλα	A	p/st	2975152	3034079	1881598273	20	608.13
2211201000	Άλλα βιβλία, φυλλάδια και παρόμοια έντυπα : σχολικά βιβλία ✓	A	p/st	117561	117561	97800437	3	746.28
2211202000	Άλλα βιβλία, φυλλάδια και παρόμοια έντυπα : παιδικά βιβλία ✓	A	p/st	2412794	2403244	1022170688	10	425.33
2211203000	Άλλα βιβλία, φυλλάδια και παρόμοια έντυπα : φιλολογικά ✓	A	p/st	357926	353783	384562182	9	1068.16
2211204000	Άλλα βιβλία, φυλλάδια και παρόμοια έντυπα : κοινωνικών επιστημών ✓	A	p/st	42400	45650	282877148	3	6196.65
2211206000	Άλλα βιβλία, φυλλάδια και παρόμοια έντυπα : άλλα ✓	A	p/st	3207452	3320197	369814483	12	111.12
2211208000	Βιβλία με εικόνες και βιβλία ιχνογραφίας ή ζωγραφικής για παιδιά	A	p/st	150648	150624	90792335	3	602.77
2211210000	Λεξικά και εγκυκλοπαίδειες, έστω και σε τεύχη	A	c/st	684377	641484	1257758085	8	[illegible]
2211320000	Χάρτες, υδρόγειοι, υδρογραφικοί και άλλα είδη, τυπωμένοι σε μορφή βιβλίου	A	p/st	1602026	1430352	61173764	4	42.77
2211330000	Υδρογραφικοί γεωγραφικοί και παρόμοιοι χάρτες εκτός αυτών που είναι σε μορφή βιβλίου ή φυλλαδίου	A	p/st	93503	107712	42740178	3	[illegible]
2212100000	Εφημερίδες και περιοδικές εκδόσεις τυπωμένες, που εκδίδονται τουλάχιστον 4 φορές την εβδομάδα	A	p/st	[illegible]	[illegible]	[illegible]	43	[illegible]
2213100000	Εφημερίδες και περιοδικές εκδόσεις τυπωμένες, που εκδίδονται λιγότερες από 4 φορές την εβδομάδα	A	p/st	[illegible]	[illegible]	[illegible]	[illegible]	[illegible]
[illegible]	Εφημερίδες, που εκδίδονται λιγότερες από 4 φορές την εβδομάδα	A	p/st	[illegible]	[illegible]	[illegible]	[illegible]	[illegible]
[illegible]	Περιοδικές εκδόσεις, που εκδίδονται λιγότερες από 4 φορές την εβδομάδα	A	p/st	45783339	32326425	11335673425	21	358.66
[illegible]	Τυπωμένοι δίσκοι για ηλεκτρόφωνα	A	p/st	3438603	3435013	784751137	3	[illegible]

REFERENCES

- Aaltonen, Outi. 1995a. "The Role of the Free-Lance Translator in the Process of Programme Making at TV2, Finland". In *Translatio*. p.282-287.
- Aaltonen, Outi. 1995b. "Subtitling as Culture-Bound Meaning Production". In *Translatio*. p.384-387.
- Adler, Tim. 1995. "The Perfect Subtitle is the One you don't Notice". In *Moving Pictures International*, September. p. 21.
- AGB Hellas (eds.). 1995. *TV Yearbook 94-95*. Organopublica A.E. Athens.
- AGB Hellas (eds.). 1996. *TV Yearbook 95-96*. Organopublica A.E. Athens.
- Álvarez, Román & Vidal, M. Carmen-África (eds.). 1996. *Translation, Power, Subversion*. Multilingual Matters Ltd. Clevendon / Philadelphia / Adelaide.
- *American Film*, Vol 8, April 1983. "Dubs Flubbed". p. 6.
- Armes, Roy. 1988. *On Video*. Routledge. London & New York.
- Ascheid, Antje. 1997. "Speaking Tongues: Voice Dubbing in the Cinema as Cultural Ventriloquism". In *The Velvet Light Trap*, 40, Fall 1997. p. 32-41.
- Baker, Mona. 1995. "Corpora in Translation Studies: An Overview and Some Suggestions for Future Research". In *Target* 7:2. p.223-243.
- Baker, Mona. 1996. "Corpus-based Translation Studies: The Challenges that Lie Ahead". In Somers, Harold (ed.), *Terminology, LSP and Translation: Studies in Language Engineering in Honour of Juan C. Sager*. John Benjamins. Amsterdam / Philadelphia. p.175-186.
- Baker, Mona (ed.). 1998. *Encyclopedia of Translation Studies*. Routledge. London & New York.
- Baker, Robert et al. 1984. *Handbook for Television Subtitlers*. Engineering division. Independent Broadcasting Authority. London. England.

- Bakewell, Michael. 1987. "Factors Affecting the Cost of Dubbing". In *EBU Review. Programmes, Administration, Law*, XXXVIII/6, November. p. 16-17.
- Ballester, Ana. 1995. "The Politics of Dubbing. Spain: a Case Study". In Jansen, P. (ed.). p. 159-181.
- Baranitch, Vladimir. 1995. "Pratiques Nationales / National Practices: General Situation with Electronic Media in Belarus". In *Translatio*. p.308-311.
- Barbe, Katharine. 1996. "Dubbing in the Translation Classroom". In *Perspectives: Studies in Translatology* 4:2. p.255-274.
- Barwise, Patrick & Ehrenberg, Andrew. 1988. *Television and its Audience*. SAGE. London / Thousand Oaks / New Delhi.
- Bassols, Margarida et al. 1995. "Adapting Translation for Dubbing to the Customer's Requirements". In *Translatio*. p.410-417.
- Bicknell, Marcus. 1998. "Europe, Broadcasting in English and the Information Society". In Gambier (ed.). p.35-50.
- Blane, Sandra. 1996. "Interlingual Subtitling in the Languages Degree". In Sewell & Higgins (eds.) *Teaching Translation in Universities: Present and Future Perspecives*. CILT. London. p.183-207.
- Brown, Mary Ellen. 1994. *Soap Opera and Women's Talk: The Pleasure of Resistance*. SAGE. Thousand Oaks / London / New Delhi.
- Canós, Rosa Agost. 1995. "The Colloquial Register and Dubbing". In Jansen, P. (ed.). p. 183-196.
- Carr, John. 1991a. "American Fare Continues to Dominate Greek Market". In *The Hollywood Reporter Weekly International Edition,* May 21. p. I-5.
- Carr, John. 1991b. "Greeks bank on Sell-Through". In *The Hollywood Reporter Weekly International Edition*, May 21. p. I-5 & I-8.
- Cattrysse, Patrick, 1998. "Translation in the New Media Age: Implications for Research and Training". In Gambier (ed.). p.7-12.

- Cattrysse, Patrick. 1992. "Film (Adaptation) as Translation: Some Methodological Proposals". In *Target* 4:1. p.53-70.
- Chalier, Chantal & Mueller, Felicity. 1998. "Subtitling for Australian Television: The SBS Endeavour". In Gambier (ed.). p.97-101
- Chesterman, Andrew (ed.). 1989. *Readings in Translation Theory*. Lectura Ab: Oy Finn.
- Chesterman, Andrew. 1993. "From 'Is' to 'Ought': Laws, Norms and Strategies in Translation Studies. In *Target* 5:1. p.1-20.
- *Cinema*, June 1993. "Synentefxi me ton Dionyssi Martinego" [Interview with Dionyssis Martinegos]. p. 71-75.
- *The Cinema: News and Property Gazette*, Vol 68, Monday May 7 1947. "New Method for Sub-Titles?". p. 21.
- Coll, Clare Kelly. 1998. "Language, Film and Nationalism". In Gambier (ed.). p.201-205.
- Corner, John and Denise. 1987. "And then Video". In Simpson, Philip (ed.) *Parents Talking Television: Television in the Home*. Comedia Publishing Group. London. p. 19-25.
- Davies Messenger, Máire. 1989. *Television is Good for your Kids*. Hilary Shipman. London.
- Delabastita, Dirk. 1989. "Translation and Mass-Communication: Film and TV Translation as Evidence of Cultural Dynamics". In *Babel* 35:4. p.193-218.
- Delabastita, Dirk. 1990. "Translation and the Mass Media". In Bassnett & Lefevere *Translation History and Culture*. Pinter Publishers Ltd. London. p.97-109.
- Dollerup, G. & Lindegaard, A. (eds.). 1994. *Teaching Translation and Interpreting 2*. John Benjamins. Amsterdam / Philadelphia.
- Doulkeri, Tessa. 1992. *Elliniki Tileorasi: Empiriki Erevna* [*Greek Television: Empirical Research*]. Papazisi. Athens.
- Dries, Josephine. 1994-95. "Breaking Language Barriers Behind the Broken Wall (Voice-over, Dubbing or Subtitling?)". In *Intermedia* XXII/6, December-January. p. 35-37.

- Dries, Josephine. 1995a. *Dubbing and Subtitling: Guidelines for Production and Distribution.* The European Institute for the Media. Düsseldorf.
- Dries, Josephine. 1995b. "Language Transfer in Europe: What's the Problem". In *Translatio.* p.235-256.
- Drummond, Phillip & Paterson, Richard. 1988. "Introducing the Television Audience". In Drummond and Paterson (eds.). p.1-13.
- Drummond, Phillip & Paterson, Richard (eds.). 1988. *Television and its Audience: International Research Perspectives.* BFI Publishing. London.
- Du-Nour, Miryam. 1995. "Retranslation of Children's Books as Evidence of Changes of Norms". In *Target* 7:2. p.327-346.
- *EBU Review. Programmes, Administration, Law*, XXXVIII/6, November 1987. "Dubbers and Subtitlers Have a Prime Role in the International Distribution of Television Programmes". p. 8-13.
- El-Sakran, Tharwat M. 1997. "Subtitling versus dubbing: a Case Study of Egyptian TV programmes". In *Translatio, Nouvelles de la FIT - FIT Newsletter*. Nouvelle serie XVI, Nos 1-2. p. 95-104.
- Even-Zohar, Itamar. 1987. "The Position of Translated Literature within the Literary Polysystem". In Toury, Gideon (ed.). p.107-113.
- Even-Zohar, Itamar. 1990. "Polysystem Theory". In *Poetics Today* 11:1. p.9-94
- Even-Zohar, Itamar. 1994. "Culture Planning and the Market: Making and Maintaining Socio-Semiotic Entities". Paper delivered at the Darmouth Colloquium, "The Making of Culture", Darmouth College, 22-27 July 1994. (Printed from http://www.tau.ac.il/~itamarez/papers/plan_clt.html p.1-31).
- Even-Zohar, Itamar. 1996a. "The Making of Culture Repertoire and the Role of Transfer". Paper presented to the International Conference "Translations: (Re)shaping of Literature and Culture", Bogaziçi University, Istanbul, 24-25 October 1996. (Printed from http://www.tau.ac.il/~itamarez/papers/rep_trns.htm p.1-10).
- Even-Zohar, Itamar. 1996b. "The Role of Literature in the Making of the Nations of Europe: A Socio-Semiotic Examination". In *Applied Semiotics / Sémiotique Appliquée* (A refereed periodical

on the World Wide Web) http://www.epas.utoronto.ca:8080/french /as-sa/ASSA-No1/index.html p.20-30

- Even-Zohar, Itamar. 1997. "Factors and Dependencies in Culture: A Revised Draft for Polysystem Culture Research". In *Canadian Review of Comparative Literature* 24:1. p. 15-34 (Printed from http://www.tau.ac.il/~itamarez/papers/fac&dep.htm p.1-26).
- Even-Zohar, Itamar & Toury, Gideon (eds.). 1981. "Translation Theory and Intercultural Relations: Introduction". In *Poetics Today* 2:4. p.v-xi.
- Fawcett, Peter. 1996. "Translating Film". In Harris, Geoffrey (ed.), *On Translating French Literature and Film.* Rodopi. Amsterdam - Atlanta. p.65-88.
- *Film Weekly*, September 24 1938. "Glyn Roberts Goes Dubbing". p. 14.
- Fodor, István. 1976. *Film Dubbing: Phonetic, Semiotic, Esthetic and Psychological Aspects*. Helmut Buske Verlag. Hamburg.
- Gambier, Yves. 1994. "Audiovisual Communication: Typological Detour". In Dollerup & Lindegaard (eds.). p.275-283.
- Gambier, Yves (ed.). 1998. *Translating for the Media: Papers from the International Conference Languages & the Media.* University of Turku. Centre for Translation and Interpreting.
- Ganz-Blättler, Ursula. 1995. "Language Transfer as Cultural Transfer: Some Perspectives on National Practices of Synchronisation". In *Translatio*. p.247-255.
- Gentzler, Edwin. 1993. *Contemporary Translation Theories*. Routledge. London and New York.
- Giles, Jean. 1997. "Joined-up Reading: The Problem of Subtitles". In *Vertigo*, 40, Autumn 1997. p. 47-49.
- Goodhart, G.J. et al. 1975. *The Television Audience: Patterns of Viewing*. SAXON House. Westmead / Farnborough / Hants. England.
- Goris, Olivier. 1993. "The Question of French Dubbing: Towards a Frame of Systematic Investigation". In *Target* 5:2. p. 169-190.
- Gottlieb, Henrik. 1994a. "Subtitling: Diagonal Translation". In *Perspectives: Studies in Translatology* 2:1. p.101-121

- Gottlieb, Henrik. 1994b. "Subtitling: People Translating People". In Dollerup & Lindegaard (ed.). p.261-274.
- Gottlieb, Henrik. 1995. "Establishing a Framework for a Typology of Subtitle Reading Strategies: Viewer Reactions to Deviations from Subtitling Standards". In *Translatio.* p.388-409.
- Gotttlieb, Henrik. 1997. "You Got the Picture? On The Polysemiotics of Subtitling Wordplay". In Delabastita (ed.), *Traductio: Essays on Punning and Translation.* St. Jerome Publishing. Manchester. p. 207-232.
- Gottlieb, Henrik. 1998. "Subtitling". In Baker (ed.). p. 244-248.
- Grillo, V. & Kawin, B. 1981. "Reading at the Movies: Subtitles, Silence, and the Structure of the Brain". In *Post Script* I/1, Autumn. p.25-32.
- Gunter, Barrie. 1982. *The Effects of Subtitles on the Appreciation of TV Programmes Among the Hearing Audience.* Audience Research Department. Independent Broadcasting Authority. London.
- Gunter, Barrie & McAleer, Jill. 1990. *Children and Television: The One Eyed Monster?* Routledge. London & New York.
- Gunter, Barrie & Svennevig, Michael. 1987. *Behind and in Front of the Screen: Television's Involvement with Family Life.* John Libbey. London / Paris.
- Harris, Brian. 1990. "Norms in Interpretation". In *Target* 2:1. p.115-119.
- Hartley, John. 1989. "Invisible Fictions: Television Audiences, Paedocracy, Pleasure". In Burns, Gary & Thompson, Robert J. (eds.) *Television Studies: Textual Analysis.* Praeger. New York / Westport, Connecticut / London. p. 223-243.
- Harvey, Sylvia. 1996. "What is cinema?: The Sensuous, the Abstract and the Political". In Williams, Christopher (ed.) *Cinema: The Beginnings and the Future.* University of Westminster Press. London. p. 228-251.
- Hatim, Basil & Mason, Ian. 1997. *The Translator as Communicator*. Routledge. London & New York.

- Hay, Josiane. 1998. "Subtitling and Surtitling". In Gambier (ed.). p.131-137.
- Hellenic Republic, Ministry of Press and Mass Media (eds.). 1995. *N.2328/1995: Nomiko Kathestos tis Idiotikis Tileorasis kai tis Topikis Radiofonias, Rythmisi Thematon tis Radiotileoptikis Agoras kai Alles Diataxis* [*Legal Status of Private Television and Local Radio, Regulation of Issues on Radio-television Market and Other Statements*]. Ethniko Typografio. Athens.
- Hempen, Frans. 1998. "Introducing the VVFT, the Dutch Union of Translators for the Media". In Gambier (ed.). p.51-56.
- Herbst, Thomas. 1995. "People do not Talk in Sentences: Dubbing and the Idiom Principle". In *Translatio*. p.257-271.
- Hermans, Theo (ed.). 1985. *The Manipulation of Literature: Studies in Literary Translation*. Croom Helm. London & Sydney.
- Hermans, Theo. 1995. "Revisiting the Classics. Toury's Empiricism Version One". In *The Translator* 1:2. p.215-223.
- Hermans, Theo. 1996. "Norms and the Determination of Translation: A Theoretical Framework". In Álvarez & Vidal (eds.). p.25-51.
- Hochel, Brano. 1985. "Communicative Aspects of Translation for TV". In *Rocnik* 20:4. p.1-4.
- *The Hollywood Reporter, Tuesday March 15 1983*. "Italian Dubbers' Strike Hurts Both Film and TV Industries". p. 12.
- Holmes, J.S., Lambert, J. & van der Broek, R. (eds.). 1978. *Literature and Translation*. ACCO. Leuven.
- Hood, Stuart. 1967. *A Survey of Television*. Heineman. London.
- House, J. & Blum-Kulka, S. (eds.). 1986. *Interlingual and Intercultural Communication. Discourse and Cognition in Translation and Second Language Acquisition Studies*. Gunter Narr. Tübingen.
- ITC (Independent Television Commission) (eds.). 1997. *ITC Guidance on Standards for Subtitling*. ITC. London. England.
- ITC (Independent Television Commission) (eds.). 1996. *Television: Ethnic Minorities' Views*. ITC. London. England.

- Ivarsson, Jan. 1992. *Subtitling for the Media.* Ljunglöfs Offset AB. Stockholm.
- Ivarsson, Jan. 1995a. "The History of Subtitles". In *Translatio.* p.294-302.
- Ivarsson, Jan. 1995b. "Digital Subtitling". In *Translatio.* p.422-424.
- James, Heulwen. 1998. "Screen Translation Training and European Co-Operation". In Gambier (ed.). p.243-258.
- James, Heulwen. 1995. "Training in Screen Translation: From Lampeter to a European Association". In *Translatio.* p.446-450.
- Jansen, Peter (ed.). 1995. *Translation and the Manipulation of Discourse: Selected Papers of the CETRA Research Seminars in Translation Studies 1992-1993.* CETRA - The Leuven Research Centre for Translation, Communication and Cultures.
- Kanavakis, Emmanuel. 1977. *I Thesi tis Tileoraseos stin Elliniki Ikogenia* [*The Place of Greek Television in Greek Family*] (PhD Thesis). Iatriki Sholi. Athens.
- Karamitroglou, Fotios. 1996. *Translation Theory and Screen/Film Translation: An Evaluative Overview.* MSc Dissertation submitted to the University of Manchester Institute of Science and Technology, Dept. of Language Engineering.
- Kilborn, Richard. 1993. " 'Speak my Language': Current Attitudes to Television Subtitling and Dubbing". In *Media Culture and Society,* XV/4 October 1993. p.641-660.
- *KINO (German Film), May 1994.* "Interview with Mary Carroll, Titel-Bild Berlin". p. 28.
- Klaudy, Kinga et al. (eds.). 1993. *Transferre Necesse Est...: Current Issues of Translation Theory. Aktuelle Fragen der Übersetzung.*Dániel Berzsenyi College Printing Press. Szombathely.
- Koronaiou, Alexandra. 1992. *Neoi kai Mesa Mazikis Enimerosis.* [*Youth and Mass Media*]. Odysseas. Athens.
- Kovacic, Irena. 1998. "Language in the Media – A New Challenge for Translator Trainers". In Gambier (ed.). p.123-129.

- Kovacic, Irena. 1994. "Relevance as a Factor in Subtitling Reductions". In Dollerup & Lindegaard (eds.). p.245-251.
- Kovacic, Irena. 1995. "Compréhension et Réception du Sous-Titrage et du Doublage / Comprehension and Reception of Subtilting and Dubbing: Reception of Subtitles - The Non-Existent Ideal Viewer". In *Translatio*. p.376-383.
- Krogstad, Morten. 1998. "Subtitling for Cinema Films and Video/Television". In Gambier (ed.). p.57-64.
- Kurz, I. & Pöchhacker, F. 1995. "Quality in TV Interpreting". In *Translatio*. p.350-358.
- Lambert, José. 1998. "Language and Social Challenges for Tomorrow: Questions, Strategies, Programs". In Gambier (ed.). p.13-33.
- Lambert, José & van Gorp, Hendrik. 1985. "On Describing Translations". In Hermans, Theo (ed.). p.42-53.
- Li, Jian. 1998. "Intonation Unit as Unit of Translation of Film Dialogue: FIT to Keep". In Gambier (ed.). p.151-181.
- de Linde, Zoe. 1995. " 'Read my Lips': Subtitling Principles, Practices and Problems". In *Perspectives: Studies in Translatology* 3:1. p.9-20.
- de Linde, Zoe Clare. 1997. *Linguistic and Visual Complexity of Television Subtitles*. PhD Thesis submitted to the University of Bristol.
- Lörscher, Wolfgang. 1991. *Translation Performance, Translation Process and Translation Strategies: A Psycholinguistic Investigation*. Gunter Narr Verlag. Tübingen.
- Luyken, Georg-Michael et al. 1991. *Overcoming Language Barriers in Television: Dubbing and Subtitling for the European Audience*. The European Institute for the Media. Düsseldorf.
- MacDougall, David. 1995. "Subtitling Ethnographic Films: Archetypes Into Individualities". In *Visual Anthropology Review* 11:1, Spring. p. 83-90.
- Mailhac, Jean-Pierre. 1998. "Optimising the Linguistic Transfer in the Case of Commercial Videos". In Gambier (ed.). p.207-223.

- Marks, John. 1983. "One Picture's Words are Worth Thousands". In *The Independent,* Vol 6, October. p. 18-19.
- Metz, Christian. 1974. *Film Language: A Semiotics of the Cinema.* Oxford University Press. New York.
- Minchinton, John. 1963a. "Subtitles". In *Film (Federation of Film Societies)* No 37, Autumn. p. 42-43.
- Minchinton, John. 1963b. "What the Eye Does Not Hear". In *Film (Federation of Societies)* No 35, Spring. p. 39-40.
- Minchinton, John. 1987. "Fitting Titles". In *Sight & Sound* 56. p. 279-282.
- Minchinton, John. 1993. *Sub-titling.* Minchinton J. Hertfordshire, England
- Morley, David. 1986. *Family Television: Cultural Power and Domestic Leisure.* Comedia Publishing Group. London.
- Moskowitz, Ken. 1979. "Subtitles vs. Dubbing: Debate Goes On". In *Take One* 7:5, April 15. p. 1.
- *Motion Picture Herald,* February 22 1947. "Egypt". p. 43.
- *Motion Picture Herald,* April 19 1947. "Spain". p. 42.
- *Moving Pictures International,* September 2 1993. "First Shots Fired in Dubbing War". p. 5.
- Myers, Lora. 1973. "The Art of Dubbing". In *Filmmakers Newsletter* 6:6. p. 56-58.
- Nedergaard-Larsen, Birgit. 1993. "Culture-bound Problems in Subtitling". In *Perspectives: Studies in Translatology* 1:2. p.207-241.
- Nord, Christiane.1991a. "Scopos, Loyalty, and Translational Conventions". In *Target* 3:1. p.91-109.
- Nord, Christiane. 1991b. *Text Analysis in Translation: Theory, Methodology and Didactic Applications of a Model for Translation-Oriented Text Analysis.* Rodopi. Amsterdam - Atlanta.
- O'Connell, Eithne. 1998. "Choices and Constraints in Film Translation". In Lynne Bowker, Michael Cronin, Dorothy Kenny & Jennifer Pearson (eds.) *Unity in Diversity: Current Trends in Translation Studies.* St. Jerome Publishing. Manchester. p.61-67.

- O'Shea, Billy. 1996. "Equivalence in Danish News Subtitling from Northern Ireland". In *Perspectives: Studies in Translatology* 4:2. p.235-254.
- Palmer, Patricia. 1988. "The Social Nature of Children's Television Viewing". In Drummond and Paterson (eds.). p.139-153.
- Panourgia, Eumorfia. 1998. "Television and Video in English for Science and Technology". In *ELT Review* 6. p.4-5.
- Papadakis, Ioannis. 1998. "Greece, a Subtitling Country". In Gambier (ed.). p.65-70.
- Papadakis, Ioannis. 1997. "Ypotitlismos: Metafrasi i Parafrasi" [Subtitling: Translation or Paraphrase]. Featuring on the World Wide Web at http://book.culture.gr/7/72/721/13_gr.html. p.1-6.
- Papageorgiou, Ioannis. 1981. *Tileorasi kai Paidi* [*Television and the Child*]. Epitheorisi Horofylakis. Athens.
- *The Picturegoer*, Vol 1, May 1921. "The Art of the Sub-Title". p. 21.
- Poyatos, Fernando (ed.). 1997. *Nonverbal Communication and Translation: New Perspectives and Challenges in Literature, Interpretation and the Media.* John Benjamins. Amsterdam / Philadelphia.
- Puurtinen, Tina. 1989. "Assessing Acceptability in Translated Children's Books". In *Target* 1:2. p. 210-213.
- Rath, Claus-Dieter. 1988. "Live/Life: Television as a Generator of Events in Everyday Life". In Drummond and Paterson (eds.). p.32-37.
- Reeve, Barry. 1995. "Outils Technologiques et Conversion Linguistique / Technological Tools for Language Transfer". In *Translatio*. p.418-421.
- Remael, Aline. 1995. "Film Adaptation as Translation and the Case of the Screenplay". In Jansen, P. (ed.). p. 125-132.
- Reynoso, Monica & Cárdenas, Miguel. 1998. "An International Videoconference Model for Distance Instruction Programs". In Gambier (ed.). p.231-242

- Robyns, Clem. 1990. "The Normative Model of Twentieth Century Belles Infidèles: Detective Novels in French Translation". In *Target* 2:1. p.23-42.
- Roffe, I. & Thorne, D. 1994. "Transcultural Language Transfer: Subtitling from a Minority Language". In Dollerup & Lindegaard (eds.). p.253-259.
- Ross, Alf. 1968. *Directives and Norms*. Routledge & Kegan Paul: London. Humanities Press. New York.
- Ross, Nigel. 1995. "Dubbing American in Italy". In *English Today* 41, 11:1. p.45-48.
- Russo, Mariachiara. 1995. "Media Interpreting: Variables and Strategies". In *Translatio*. p.343-349.
- Sadoux, Jean-Jacques. 1982. "On Dubbing Not Considered One of the Fine Arts". In *Classic Images* No 79, January. p. 56.
- *Screen Digest*, July 1992. "Watching Your Language: Foreign Version Issues". p. 153-160
- *Screen International*, Friday December 17 1993. "Hearing is Believing". p. 8.
- Shlesinger, Miriam. 1989. "Extending the Theory of Translation to Interpretation: Norms as a Case in Point". In *Target* 1:1. p.111-115.
- Siefert, Marsha. 1995. "Image/Music/Voice: Song Dubbing in Hollywood Musicals". In *Journal of Communication* XLV/2, Spring. p. 44-64.
- Silverman, David. 1993. *Interpreting Qualitative Data: Methods for Analysing Talk, Text and Interaction*. SAGE Publications. London / Thousand Oaks / New Delhi.
- Solholm, Rolleiv. 1990. "Subtitling". In *Intermedia* 18:4-5, August-September. p. 38.
- Stipp, Horst. 1993. "The Challenge to Improve Television for Children: A New Perspective". In Berry, Gordon & Asamen, Joy Keiko (eds.) *Children & Television: Images in a Changing Sociocultural World*. SAGE. Newbury Park / London / New Delhi. p. 296-302.

- Tirkkonen-Condit, Sonja & Laffling, John (eds.). 1993. *Recent Trends in Empirical Translation Research.* University of Joensuu, Faculty of Arts.
- Toury, Gideon. 1978. "The Nature and Role of Norms in Literary Translation". In Holmes et al. (eds.). p.83-100.
- Toury, Gideon. 1980. *In Search of a Theory of Translation.* The Porter Institute for Poetics and Semiotics. Tel Aviv.
- Toury, Gideon. 1985. "A Rationale for Descriptive Translation". In Hermans. p.16-41.
- Toury, Gideon. 1986. "Monitoring Discourse Transfer: A Test-Case for a Developmental Model of Translation". In House & Blum-Kulka (eds.). p.79-94.
- Toury, Gideon. (ed.). 1987. *Translation Across Cultures.* Bahri Publications Private Limited. New Delhi.
- Toury, Gideon. 1993a. "'Translation of Literary Texts' vs 'Literary Translation': A Distinction Reconsidered". In Tirkkonen-Condit & Laffling (eds.). p.10-23.
- Toury, Gideon. 1993b. "Still in Search of Laws of Translational Behaviour: Closing in on Discourse Interference". In Klaudy et al. (eds.). 1993. p.21-38.
- Toury, Gideon. 1995. *Descriptive Translation Studies and Beyond.* John Benjamins Publishing Company. Amsterdam / Philadelphia.
- *Translatio.* 1995. *Nouvelles de la FIT - FIT Newsletter.* Communication Audiovisuelle et Transferts Linguistiques / Audiovisual Communication and Language Transfer. Nouvelle serie XIV:3-4. International Forum. Strasbourg.
- Turner, Adrian. 1974. "Dubbed and Snubbed". In *Films Illustrated*, Vol 34, June. p. 382-383.
- Turner, Graeme. 1988. *Film As Social Practice.* Routledge. London & New York.
- *TV World* X/5 June-July 1987. "The Subs and Dubs Divide". p.38-39.

- Vanderauwera, Ria. 1985. *Dutch Novels Translated into English: The Transformation of a 'Minority' Literature.* Rodopi. Amsterdam.
- Van der Weel, Adriaan. 1990. "Subtitling and the SBS Audience". In *Media Information Australia* No 56, May. p.22-26.
- Varela, Chaume Frederic. 1997. "Translating Non-Verbal Information in Dubbing". In Poyatos (ed.). p.315-326.
- Vaughan, Paul. 1990. "BBC, BSB Blast Dubbing Critics". In *Broadcast*, July 20. p. 4.
- Venuti, Lawrence. 1995. *The Translator's Invisibility: A History of Translation.* Routledge. London and New York.
- Venuti, Lawrence. 1997. "Unequal Developments: Current Trends in Translation Studies". In *Comparative Literature* 49:4. p. 360-368.
- Vermeer, Hans. 1987. "What does it Mean to Translate?". In Toury (ed.). p.25-33.
- Vermeer, Hans. 1989. "Skopos and Commission in Translational Action". In Chesterman (ed.). p.173-187.
- Vitkus, Inesse. 1995. "Film and Programme Translation Policy and Techniques in Latvia: Latvian Television, Cinemas and Private TV Stations". In *Translatio*. p.316-320.
- Vöge, Hans. 1977. "The Translation of Films: Sub-Titling Versus Dubbing". In *Babel* 23:5. p.120-125.
- Volmar, Victor. 1950. "Foreign Versions". In *Journal of the Society of Motion Picture*, Vol 55, November. p. 536-546.
- Whitman-Linsen, Candace. 1992. *Through the Dubbing Glass: The Synchronisation of American Motion Pictures into German, French and Spanish.* Peter Lang. Frankfurt am Main.
- d'Ydewalle, Géry et al. 1991. "Watching Subtitled Television: Automatic Reading Behaviour". In *Communication Research* 18:5, October 1991. p.650-666.
- Zabalbeascoa, Patrick. 1994. "Factors in Dubbing Television Comedy". In *Perspectives: Studies in Translatology* 2:1. p.89-99.
- Zabalbeascoa, Patrick. 1996. "Translating Jokes for Dubbed Television Situation Comedies". In *The Translator* 2:2. p.235-257.

- Zabalbeascoa, Patrick. 1997. "Dubbing and the Nonverbal Dimension of Translation". In Poyatos (ed.). p.327-342.
- Zucker, Ralph. 1966. "In Defense of Dubbing". In *Motion Picture Herald*, July 6. p. 5.